THE PLACES WE'VE BEEN:

Field Reports from Travelers Under 35

Edited by Asha Veal Brisebois

THE PLACES WE'VE BEEN BOOKS

Chicago

To Maya –
In excitement for all of the places you'll go

To Doris Marie –
In respect for all of the places you've been

CONTENTS

EDITOR'S NOTE XI

MONDAY MORNING – *Cameroon*
by Lindsey Laveaux 3

THE MUSIC AND GIFTS OF MY COUNTRY – *Dar es Salaam, Tanzania*
an interview with Vanessa Mdee, MTV VJ / Choice FM DJ / HIV/AIDS activist . . . 16

SURFING THE SAHARA – *Western Sahara*
by Nathan Myers 21

SPRING – *Jordan*
by Craig Smith 25

RUNNING IN PLACE – *Lebanon, Qatar, and Dubai*
by Sophie Chamas 28

THE LAND OF A THOUSAND HILLS – *Rwanda*
an interview with Derek Helwig, television producer 34

THE HUMAN ARROW – *Tangier, Morocco*
by Christian Lewis 42

KABILA: THE FIRST FAMILY OF THE DEMOCRATIC REPUBLIC
OF THE CONGO – *Kinshasa, DRC*
by Edward C. Davis IV 52

THE SLAVE ROUTE – *Ghana*
by Kim Coleman Foote 59

WHO NEEDS A FLASHLIGHT WHEN YOU HAVE
A MZUNGU? – *Msambweni, Kenya*
by Mike Madej 74

THE IMPACT OF OIL – *Niger Delta, Nigeria*
an interview with Laine Strutton, researcher and academic 78

RUNNING – *South Sudan*
by S. Imran Ali 85

AGATO – *Tokyo, Japan*
by Yuki Aizawa 89

A HAIRCUT – *Australia, Indonesia, Cambodia, and Taiwan*
by Lisa Dazols 103

LIVING ON THE EDGE OF CHANGE – *China*
by Sierra Ross Gladfelter 106

SABAH – *Malaysian Borneo*
by Adam Karlin 115

ANYTHING IS POSSIBLE IN INDIA – *India*
by Cecilia Haynes 130

A MEMORY OF SEOUL – *Seoul, Korea*
by Sara Cooper. 137

WHEN COCONUTS ATTACK – *Hyderabad, India*
by Sarah Khan 139

BUNKING WITH THE ENEMY – *China and the North Korea Border*
by Kaitlin Solimine 142

ELEVEN MONTHS, ONE WEEK, FOUR DAYS: JAPAN IN
FRAGMENTS – *Japan*
by Brenna Fitzgerald 156

FANDOM INTERNATIONAL – *United States and Spain*
an interview with Daniel Ketchum, editor at Marvel Comics 171

NYCLOPEDIA – *New York City*
by Ian Bardenstein. 178

NO REGRETS – *New York City and Israel*
by Doc Halliday Golden 183

SCOT'S STORY – *San Francisco*
by Mark Bessen 189

ALLAH AND THE LOS ANGELES LAKERS – *United States – the coasts*
by Haroon Moghul 194

PREPARING FOR A LESSER-KNOWN JOURNEY – *Drumheller, Alberta*
by Carys Cragg. 199

"AIR GUITAR IS A MEDIUM THAT ALLOWS ME TO HAVE
A VOICE" – *United States and Finland*
an interview with Justin "Nordic Thunder" Howard 211

CLIMBING IN VENEZUELA – *Venezuela*
by Andrew Bisharat. 221

ASSAULT RIFLES IN THE RUINS – *Ciudad Perdida, Colombia*
by Frank Izaguirre. 239

NOTEBOOK – *Isla Providencia, Colombia*
by Pria Anand 244

WHEN NOWHERE ELSE WILL HAVE YOU – *Paraguay*
by Nick Dall 251

IT STARTED WITH A BANG – *Rio de Janeiro, Brazil*
by Alison Medina 258

BIRTH IN PACHAJ – *Pachaj, Guatemala*
by Liz Quinn 261

ANTARCTICA AND OUTER SPACE – *United States, Canada, and Antarctica*
an interview with Laura Drudi, aspiring aerospace physician 280

ANTARCTICA AND THE SOUTHERN OCEAN,
THE OLD-FASHIONED WAY – *Antarctica and the Southern Ocean*
by Colin Souness 286

FADING MEMORIES – *Athens, Greece*
by Theopi Skarlatos 301

BORN IN THE WRONG TIME – *France*
by Mari Amend 305

SIX MONTHS WITHOUT A MAP – *Canada, Scotland, Iceland, and Turkey*
by Lisa Hsia 317

DYING ABROAD – *Budapest, Hungary*
by Rachael Levitt 329

A NEW TONGUE – *Paris, France*
by Molly Headley-Benkaci 331

MAIKO – *Tbilisi, Georgia*
by Rhonda Gibson 333

RUGBY WORLD CUP – *France and New Zealand*
an interview with Louis Stanfill, American rugby player 336

RUSSIAN FACE – *St. Petersburg, Russia*
by E. B. Bartels 341

"I WAS IN COLLEGE, AND BY THE TIME I WENT TO STUDY IN ITALY
WE WERE IN THIS ALL-OUT WAR" – *Florence, Italy*
an interview with Joey Cavise, law student 347

HOW TO BE A RUSSIAN SLEEPER FOR U.S. – *Classified*
by Laura Madeline Wiseman 353

CAREFREE – *Usedom, Germany and Poland*
by Chaney Kwak 365

BRAVERY IN THE FACE OF CHANGE – *Cork, Ireland*
by Jessica Reff 369

CONTRIBUTORS 372

ACKNOWLEDGEMENTS 385

Editor's Note

FOR YOUNG, MODERN travelers, access and options have clearly expanded. That's why my college housemate and I set off to Vietnam, voluntarily, two days after graduation, as part of a small, amateur film crew researching the emotional effects of war. This friend, characterized by a short striking haircut and magenta shawl, became a star of the documentary. She was well spoken and emotional in describing the country's connection to her immigrant community in Houston, and the sadness of her father's history as a pilot in the South Vietnamese army. I, on the other hand, had no personal connection to our story, but for many reasons, also experienced a connection to a place that I will never forget.

Flash forward several years, to *The Places We've Been: Field Reports from Travelers Under 35*. The goal here is reminiscent and simple: to check in and see where else on the map our wide peer group has gone to explore, and the experiences of life and travel that continue to shape us.

As Colin Souness, one of our Antarctica writers, says, every new place a person spends time in "…changes you, and those changed parts never go away… but when we leave we sometimes miss living out the parts of ourselves that came alive while we were there."

This is a book about places and passions. This is also, often, a book about the desire to be part of all sorts of communities that have no geographic walls.

The journeys in this book leap from country to country. The stories in this book explore issues of identity, determination, history, politics, fear, joy, hate, home, humanity, and love.

By the end, readers will have traveled from the peak of Mt. Bisoke in Rwanda, to an enclave on the Tibetan Plateau, to the Southern Seas at the bottom of the world, and more.

"Is this project journalism or a travel guide?" a friend once asked me over coffee.

"Neither," I told her. "It's a collection of original work, all creative nonfiction."

"What's that?"

As the writer Lee Gutkind describes this wide genre: *true stories, well told.*

It is my own belief that one of a writer's most important tasks is to provide his or her readers with insider, alternate ways of looking at what they may or may not already know about different pockets of the world.

Each of the following narratives and interviews comes from a unique perspective. The stories are organized into sections, by wide region.

Most all of the book's contributors are still under the thirty-five mark. A few have recently had their just-over birthdays.

A great feeling about working on this collection is that by the end, I wanted to do (almost) everything and go everywhere that the stories show.

So I hope that these stories make you feel like I did.

The Places We've Been. Here we go.

– Asha Veal Brisebois

(HINT: For the especially curious, who may want to learn more about your reporters before reading their stories, a bio list is included in the back.)

Monday Morning

CAMEROON

Lindsey Laveaux

AS THEY CAME running down the hillside, I recognized them. Jean-Claude, one of the local moto-taxi men who many mornings would laugh lightheartedly and ask, "What about me and my head?" right after I'd strap on my bright-red safety helmet and climb onto the back of his motorcycle.

That Monday I also saw Bienvenue, another moto-taxi driver. He often rushed to pick me up by the side of the road whenever he saw me in town. Flashing a handsome smile, Bienvenue liked to confidently promise that I'd be totally safe since I was on *his* motorcycle and that he was, of course, the best driver in town.

Descending from the hill, I also saw Alphonse, running closely alongside Patrick. Seeing these two men usually provided a sense of comfort. Upon my return from long trips, the pair, like stone-carved lions, proudly and majestically placed at the main roundabout at the entrance of town, signaled that I had arrived safely back in my village. After passing by them on a few of my returns, Alphonse and Patrick began to wave at me, welcoming me back into town. I'd never had a full conversation with either of them, but I'd come to recognize them as friendly and warm faces in our village.

I also recognized the other men on the hill. With one, I had spent hours at his shop, negotiating cheap prices to buy my furniture. The other faces I had seen daily, when I went out walking through the market, through the outskirts of town, and past their homes. With each meeting, I had been welcomed with broad smiles that accompanied their *"Bonjour!"* These small gestures of kindness signaled my acceptance into the community.

But on that Monday, while teaching, I took a small step outside of my classroom and saw these men running down the hillside. I instantly recognized them. Blades that seemed like an illusion of gleaming lights circled around the group like a lightning ring, forcing my eyes into a squint with each of their movements. As my heart responded to what my eyes were attempting to decipher, it began to beat faster and faster like a drum. Running full force toward me with sticks and machetes in hand, were Jean-Claude, Bienvenue, Alphonse, Patrick, and more than fifty other men, who like a storm on an otherwise clear day, appeared determined to destroy anything in their path.

The night before, I had attended a small dinner party held by my friend Jacques. A local businessman, he owned one of the major stores in town and was the child of a neighboring village's king and queen. Jacques' solid academic abilities were recognized by many important people and organizations, including the government of France. He had been offered an academic scholarship to study abroad and at the age of eighteen left for Paris. There, he met his future wife, a French Caribbean woman named Nina, who was also studying in Paris. Together, Nina and Jacques returned to West Africa and established several lucrative business ventures including gas stations, travel agencies, and car dealerships. The running joke in town was that I was the family's niece, because so many people thought I closely resembled Nina, and like her, I have ethnic origins from the French-speaking Caribbean.

The night of the party, I arrived at the house via a chauffeured car sent by the family. In true African and Caribbean style, I was welcomed by a plump and robust woman with extended arms ready to envelop me. Many kisses, hugs, and introductions later, family and guests settled down and we began to talk about the state of affairs locally and abroad: the current conditions in Haiti, the various crises plaguing West and Central Africa, France's malevolence, and even the implications of the U.S. possibly electing its first black president. We discussed it all, while aromas from roasted meats seasoned with traditional spices, fried fish, and sautéed green legumes, filled the air.

At the end of the night, exhausted and ready to return home, I overheard one of the other guests make mention of a transit workers' strike. Planned for the next day, this strike was in response to unemployment, food shortages, and rising gases prices throughout the country. I didn't pay much attention to this comment since I was thinking about how late it was, and that I needed to get home.

We said our farewells and the driver took me home. From inside the car, I looked out at the broken and unpaved road made clear by the car's headlights. The ground's deep depressions and fractures made it difficult for the car to move at a steady pace. And like the various governments we'd discussed earlier—some fractured by corruption and others ravaged by political violence—I was reminded that the road to stability was going to be a bumpy one.

Despite this, I thought of Cameroon as quiet and peaceful. Many things may have needed fixing, but there was a sense of tranquility despite surprising obstacles. For instance, the modestly built home I'd previously lived in had proved to be very accessible to thieves; the year before, the home was burglarized while I was visiting a friend in a neighboring village. Even so, I had grown accustomed to not expect direct danger or violence here. This sense was fully solidified while leaving Jacques' home. For the first night in a very long time, I felt an affirmed sense of comfort. I thought, *Everything is fine here. We are OK, and we are safe here.*

That Monday morning seemed like any other Monday morning in town. I woke up early to eat my usual breakfast of oatmeal and fruit. After watching the news for a bit, it was time to get started on my walk to school.

Many roads ran throughout the village, but over time one particular road had become my favorite path. Running parallel to the main road, this side road was located deeper into the village. Separating both roads were homes, bushes, and oil palm trees. From this side road, the rest of the village was beautifully displayed as it sat in a deep and rounded crater. This picturesque path was much safer than the heavily trafficked two-lane main road. Each morning, the main road became congested with taxis, motorcycles, and private cars. On the side road however, there was no traffic and it was relatively quiet, except for the sounds and smells of morning: chatter as mothers prepared their children for school, and freshly fried beignets.

As usual on this morning, I took this side road. While I was walking, I quickly noticed how quiet the road was; I did not hear the usual hum of traffic in the distance or clusters of small children walking in the opposite direction to the primary school.

Oddly, upon approaching the first major intersection, I saw a huge oil palm tree lying in the road. It would have been very difficult for a vehicle or motorcycle to pass by, as the tree's thick base ran lengthwise across the road, connecting one side to the other. *Surely,* I thought, *the heavy rains from the night before have brought the tree crashing down, blocking the road.*

Taking note of the usual cluster of people at the crossroad, I began to strategically perch one foot on the side of the tree, ready to climb over. Just as I began to move, a motorcycle taxi and his passenger drove right up to the fallen tree. As the driver was struggling to circumvent one end of the tree, a man came running from the small group of people. He stood in the moto-taxi's path, thrust his finger in front of the driver, and yelled, "You cannot cross! This is a strike and everyone must follow!"

Culturally believing it as a curse for the day if a moto-driver does not successfully transport his first passenger, the driver pleaded with the angry man. Like negotiating prices at the market, the two men went back and forth.

"Please, let me transport her to school."

"*No!* I told you!"

"But please, brother, let us pass. She is my first passenger!"

Finally the angry man won his bid and the passenger got off the bike and continued her journey on foot. The driver, visibly frustrated, turned around and rode away.

While I climbed over the tree, putting one leg and then the other over, it finally occurred to me that someone deliberately put the palm down to block the street. But true to the ways of an optimist who ignores warning signs, I continued down the strikingly silent road with an uneasy feeling in my heart.

Arriving at school on time, I headed straight to my classroom. Tightly packed in the classroom like sardines in a can were my 101 students, all teenagers and young adults. Their eyes met mine and their mouths slowed to silence as I entered the classroom. Almost instantly, each student in his or her freshly pressed uniform—charcoal gray for the boys and a light turquoise for the girls—stood up and proclaimed in beautiful unison, "Good morning, Ms. Lindsey!"

As they sat down, I glanced at the usual offenders in the back, Christophe and Bernard. Every day, these two boys managed to disrupt themselves or someone around them. Thick as thieves, the friends would play and then fight, all in the span of a quick twenty minutes. Bernard might have taken Christophe's pen. In retaliation, Christophe would then take Bernard's backpack hostage while threatening to rub it into the classroom's dusty earthen floor. The other children liked to watch these arguments, and I would then look up to see a huddle of heads, arms, and shoulders of children watching them fight. Luckily my respite lay in knowing that beyond these occasional distractions, most of the students were focused and attentive.

On a bench close to the front of the classroom, sat The Girls. Syntiche, Collette, Kevine, and Juliette. I'd taught them the previous year and developed a particular interest in their personal lives. Syntiche, often the first in the room to raise her hand, loved school and especially English. The rest of the girls' antics would leave her uncontrollably laughing, gasping for air and bobbing her shoulders. She came from a strict and religious household and was not permitted to participate in after-school activities. Collette was quieter than Syntiche and more observant. Highly involved, she was part of my after-school club, the Girls' Circle, and was also on the soccer team. Kevine was a reformed troublemaker whose last classroom offense landed her in the office of the discipline master, who ordered her to kneel down for ten minutes and write a letter of apology. After that day of punishment, she voluntarily moved to the front of the room and addressed me as "Madame." Kevine now held my classroom's coveted position as board cleaner.

Juliette, the fourth, was a teenager growing before my eyes. In September, newly arrived from a neighboring village, Juliette was a lithe and soft-spoken fifteen-year-old. Much like Syntiche and Collette, she was quiet, shy, and reserved. Juliette showed a strong interest in her studies and often attended our Girls' Club meetings. By November, I saw her transform into a gregarious and lively girl with many friends from different class levels. However, by December and after many careful observations, I finally approached her, concerned.

"Juliette, are you pregnant?" I asked, in French. Her eyes fell to the floor and her toothy smile dropped. "Juliette, are you pregnant?" I repeated after a moment. Suddenly, like a child admitting her guilt, she meekly answered, "Yes." Her once lithe and slim figure had grown plump, with a slight bump in her midsection. Juliette explained the father-to-be was a fellow student several grades ahead of her. I remained stunned by her confirmation of her pregnancy. I did not want to believe it. From that point forward, she greeted me as usual but eventually stopped coming to our Girls' Club meetings. Week by week, I watched as her face became fuller as she began to wear sweaters in our hot classroom.

On this particular Monday morning, The Girls were all present and seated at their usual bench.

The first hour of instruction went by with few distractions. Having been satisfied with our progress, twenty minutes of the second hour was devoted to silent reading. Relieved that the students were finally quiet, I sat down at the edge of a bench located in the very front of the room at around 9 a.m.

The school building was a large square structure, resting on a plot of land. Constructed with a roof but no ceiling, the classrooms were separated by thin wooden walls that students pounded on when neighboring classes became too noisy. In the front of the building, makeshift stairs led up to the second floor. On the second level, there were additional, balcony-style classrooms that were built along the perimeter. Barriers prevented students and teachers alike from falling below into the first-floor classrooms. This set-up was ideal for the discipline master. Each hour, with both arms folded behind his back, he patrolled the second-floor walkways while looking down into the grid-like pattern of the classrooms down below. Often the discipline master could see what the teachers could not. A slight slip of a note between friends in the back of a classroom, or a student soundly asleep and shrouded by his classmates densely packed in the benches in front of him.

For the teachers, this two-story classroom building, with endless noise, caused piercing headaches, lost voices, increased classroom-management issues, and a common sensation of intensity upon walking through the door frame.

Although teaching was no easy task, this Monday morning seemed like a good day, since the school building was especially quiet and calm. On the first floor, where my classroom was located, there were only two other classes (out of the usual ten) in session, and only one class on the second floor was in session.

While writing in my lesson book, I sat on a long bench located in the front of the classroom and against a wall. Right next to where I sat was the door, our classroom's only exit to the outdoor walkway that lined the school grounds.

Settled and ready to update the lesson book, I began:

Lesson 14, completed. Reviewed pronouns and —

Out of the corner of my eye, I saw Christophe shoot up from his seat while holding his gaze at the window. He seemed to be looking at something in the distance, something beyond the schoolyard.

"Christophe! Sit down, please!" I casually called from my seat. Like a fragile widower seeing his wife in her casket for the first time, Christophe let out a deep and sorrowful moan, all the while maintaining his gaze. In confusion, I stood and repeated *"Christophe!"* as I positioned my back in the doorway. I took a step back out of the classroom, and turned around. In the distance, on the main road, I saw a throng of men coming out of the horizon and dragging something along the road that reflected against the sun. As I looked out, I saw these men scattered throughout the road. My eyes met another group of men rapidly descending down the hillside, right in front of school grounds and clutching what appeared to be long objects.

In what seemed like an instant, I struggled to shut the makeshift door. But when they saw the first man running and then suddenly standing in front of me, his machete held high, all 101 of my students began screaming and threw themselves in the doorway in an effort to escape the classroom. As quickly as he appeared, the man vanished. Several of the children gripped my body and we became stuck in the doorway. When we were finally able to push out to the walkway, we saw the man with the machete, along with several other armed men. I looked farther out into the schoolyard and saw a mob of armed men.

Running a few paces with the children, I tripped and fell down onto my knees while they scattered away. Crouching down, I screamed out as I felt a machete slice into my back.

Stunned and still screaming, I waited for the pain. Instead, I found myself able to stand back up. *The blow was from a stick,* I thought. There was no blood. I ran toward the end of the walkway with a small group of frightened children. At the end of the walkway, the children jumped down into the yard with ease. I abruptly stopped at the edge of this eight-foot drop, fearing that I would break my leg. I turned to look back, and running all around, wielding sticks, axes, and machetes, were local men from town. Incoherent, they raised their weapons as if they were going to strike. With eyes closed and a loud sob, I jumped down and landed on all fours.

By this time, over fifty men had surrounded the school grounds, moving from classroom to classroom to destroy its interiors. Stunned, but no longer silent, and now also clutching my heart, I screamed and pleaded with each attacker who approached me, asking him not to strike.

I recognized Patrick, my village greeter. He ran toward me, but quickly put his ax down when our eyes met. I attempted to hold his attention but was pushed to the side by another machete-wielding man. Like a domino effect, the group of children around me fell down one by one as we desperately tried to scramble away.

Bodies ran in all directions. Pulling the gray and turquoise uniforms close to me as they darted by, we all clung to each other in an instant of relief, only to be met again quickly by another mobber running towards us, screaming and lifting his weapon.

The pandemonium became more and more profound and it seemed like the mob grew larger. I saw many of the students, including Syntiche and Kevine, screaming in horror as they were being chased down in circles. There was nowhere to escape to. As each child managed to lose their attackers, the aggressor would swiftly target another child running by.

By this time in my stay abroad, I'd survived malaria, typhoid fever, mumps, and driving in unsafe cars. However, for the first time, the thought quickly flashed—*I might die in a place thousands of miles away from my family, and in a violent way.* Falling once more and now crouched into the earth, I looked up into the blue and white sky. I focused on the beautifully, brightly shining sun, and then, shifting my eyes slightly down and to the left, I saw into the horizon. The landscape stood peaceful and calm, its tall trees reaching to meet the sky. The leaves stood still as I suddenly kneeled. I hung my head down and tightly closed my eyes.

As I waited, the chaos around me began to grow quiet. Almost as quickly as the melee had begun, the mob began to disperse. The men ran from the school grounds, yelling for the children to go home. They said that they destroyed the school because we should not have come to class during a transit strike.

Scattered all across the schoolyard were frightened, shaken, and beaten children. Stunned and confused, I began weeping. Students surrounded me and helped me to my feet. Syntiche and Kevine came to my side and pleaded with me to stop crying. Juliette and several other students emerged from behind a large tree farther away from the school. Christophe and Bernard, the usual rabble-rousers, were markedly silent.

Without saying a word, the children stayed with me as I staggered around looking for others who might have been hurt. One would occasionally whisper, "Madame, it's OK," each time I started crying again. After finding only students, I began looking for other teachers but saw none.

Not knowing what lay in the front of the school, the students and I quickly went to hide behind the latrines located at the back of the school. My bouts of uncontrollable crying made the children think I was injured. They began moving my arms and touching my back and legs for any injuries.

After a few minutes, we began to hear faint shouting that sounded like the voice of the discipline master. Frightened, but confident it was him, I peeked out from behind the latrine and saw him running toward us.

"Several teachers were in the staff room and saw these men running past the window," he explained. He told us that the teachers had locked the door and stayed in the staff room. Through the windows barred with metal railings, the men then shouted insults and threatened the teachers with violence.

"One of them even tried to axe down the railing!"

The discipline master explained that he, the bursar, and the principal had also locked themselves in their respective offices after hearing the commotion and seeing the angry men stalk their windows.

In the second-floor classrooms, students had trampled each other as they attempted to run down the stairs all at once. In his confusion and fright, one teacher actually tried to jump from the second floor but was pulled back by a student.

No one could have predicted an ambush of this sort at the school.

Thirty minutes later and more composed, a group of teachers walked into town and we were met by hundreds of people out in the street. Burning tires and overturned garbage cans lay every hundred feet along the road. Motorcycles and taxis were nowhere in sight, as it had been declared that any man with his vehicle, private or commercial, was to be attacked. Unsure of how safe the side roads were, I took the main road home.

The following morning, I made my way to the market along the main road. The evening before, my neighbors warned of the possibility of a food shortage since all roads entering and exiting the village were blocked. With my chest beating at a quick pace, I tried to appear unaffected by the tense atmosphere. Large groups of people I recognized as motorcycle and taxi drivers assembled at different points along the road for more than a mile. Businesses were boarded up and more makeshift barricades blocked the road. For what felt like a mile, I practically held my breath until I reached the interior of the outdoor market. Frenzied, I bought pounds and pounds of food, some of which I had never eaten before and did not know how to prepare. My anxiety increased with each step on the return home, yet my pace was considerably slowed by the heavy shopping bags. I did not leave my home for another three days. Jacques and his family, concerned for my safety, called a few times to ask about the village and my wellbeing. The family was in another part of the country that too was wracked by the strike, but they stayed safe throughout the crisis.

The mobs looted and destroyed businesses in this once quiet village. Transportation was prohibited so food ran scarce in the market. The second day—right after a presidential speech that served only to anger citizens—a major political-party headquarters in the village was burned to the ground. That night, I stood in my enclosed courtyard and watched the flames color the sky and the smoke melt into the clouds above.

"Things will burn tonight," I heard one neighbor say.

By the fourth day, tensions in the village slightly subsided after one road blockade was removed. For safety measures and against my will, I was forced to leave the village for a few days.

Upon my return, passing the roundabout, I saw Patrick. Our eyes met, but he quickly looked away. I would often see Bienvenue or Jean-Claude, but we never talked about that day.

Perhaps they thought I hadn't recognized them, or maybe they thought it wise to act as if nothing happened.

The Music and Gifts of My Country

Dar es Salaam, Tanzania

An interview with
Vanessa Mdee, MTV VJ / Choice FM DJ / HIV/AIDS activist

TANZANIA 101:

So everywhere I've been outside of the African continent, no matter at what age, here's a response I get whenever I say that I live in Tanzania: *Where is that?* First of all, the Kilimanjaro is in Tanzania. The Kilimanjaro and the Serengeti. I have to keep reminding people, because everyone thinks that the mountain is in Kenya. I tell them, "No, honey. That's actually Tanzania." We have more than one hundred and twenty tribes in my country. Each tribe brings their elements to what makes us such a beautiful nation—this United Republic of Tanzania. In my own family, my father is Ethiopian and Tanzanian. My mother is Iraqi and Tanzanian, and she's Cushitic. I have such a plethora of different types and shades in my family, and they live here and also in different parts of the world. I love my nation. We're growing and we're developing. The margin between the rich and the poor is so great, but there is so much hope and so much love and passion.

One other kind of weird question I get is, "You're African?" Yes. "You live in Africa?" Yes. "Why do you speak English?" I reply, "Well, I learned English like you might have learned English. In a school." Yes, these are the first questions I get asked. People forget that we've had people speaking English throughout Africa for ages. At first it felt as if it was a system that we had to adhere to, but now we incorporate it in our everyday lives. I'm not just Vanessa from Africa who speaks Swahili. I'm Vanessa from Africa who speaks Swahili, who speaks English, who speaks French, who speaks other dialects as well. It enhances the many shades of me. So every time I get a chance to put a new color, a new flavor, into my understanding of our societies, I do that. I really am open every time I meet somebody new. I love to see what people do for fun, what they do for praise, what they cook, what they wear. For me it's always been, "Hey, I'm curious to know what you think." Everywhere I go is a new experience.

THE COSBY KIDS:

My parents left my hometown in Tanzania when I was nine months old. We moved around a bit, to New York and Paris, and then came back to Africa while I was still in my high school years. I went to university in Kenya, and then came back to Tanzania again. These days, I'm living out of my suitcase. I was actually in Atlanta the other day, and I got a chance to meet Keisha Knight Pulliam—who I love and grew up watching. No lie: My mother actually gave me my name based on *The Cosby Show*. She broke her water while watching an episode and said that the Cosby daughter Vanessa made her "laugh into labor." I told Keisha the whole story and she was dying of laughter. Also, my sister actually auditioned for her role of Rudy, back in the '80s, because we were living in New York at the time.

DREAM JOB:

I'm taping a new show—well, it's actually not a new show, but it's the first time that I get to host it. It's a Tanzanian version of *American Idol*. I was taping the show, and learned that my producer happens to be a young lady who has a master's degree in engineering. I thought, that's a big transition, from being an engineer to now producing television. She said to me, "You know, the thing about growing up African is that you have to pursue something professional." Now, "professional" to our parents means to be a doctor or lawyer. I'm sure this happens everywhere, but maybe more so in Africa, because of our past and where we're going and what we choose to achieve. What we want to achieve. But my producer said to me, "My dream always was to work in television. I did engineering for my mother and I completed that. Now I'm doing what I'm passionate about." There's a lot of compromise, and you have to compromise certain things here on the continent. My own parents said to me, "You have to go to law school," and I hated it. I remember being in every lecture and wanting to say, "When I'm done with this, I am going to do so many other things." My lectures were based on me dreaming about being done, but for all the wrong reasons.

A BIZ WITHOUT BORDERS:

So yes, I'm in a very interesting field because you can work from Africa and reach various parts of the continent and the world, all via the entertainment industry. Dar es Salaam has become a port of such popularity for urban artists, well American urban artists. We have found the means to bring them over. One of the media groups that I work for produces an annual party called Fiesta. It's a nationwide tour that goes to maybe eight cities in the country. It's a huge concert and everyone goes. The finale is in Dar es Salaam and we bring in a *huge* artist. We've become *that* city for East Africa. A lot of Kenyans and Ugandans, and Ethiopians and Rwandans, all come to Dar es Salaam for that weekend.

ON STAYING POSITIVE:

I'd never done radio before now. The opportunity just came to me. My radio program controller found out that I moved back into the city from South Africa, which is where I was posted doing television for a while, and he said, "We just launched the station and we'd love for you to join." I told him I'd never done radio, and he said, "It will be a great chance for you to learn. I promise you, within a year, your TV work will become so much better." What he said was no lie, and my TV work has become so much better. It's because radio is cutthroat. It's live and there are a million people listening and you have to deliver. Every day is so different. You have to be eloquent and mindful of your audience. Every day there's a new current topic that you need to address and put in your charm and your personality while trying to convey a message, and still be positive. I have a very young audience. Some of the people who tune in are thirteen, fourteen, and fifteen years old. At thirteen you're completely impressionable, and I don't want to ever be negative or plant a negative thought in their heads. So it's all these things to consider when you're on radio that kind of challenge you every day. The maturity that has come with radio, I couldn't get anywhere else. So I'm really proud that I did it the way that I did.

COOL AFRICAN ARTISTS:

I'm loving a lot of new, local artists. A dear friend of mine from Kenya, her name is Muthoni the Drummer Queen, she plays the African drums. That is her style. She has managed to tap into many different markets and she resonates. I'm really proud of her and I'm proud that she has refused to change her style. She's not yet as popular in our region as she is in other parts of the continent, yet it gives me hope to see that so many people are curious and listening to her, and also intrigued by other parts of the continent and the various cultures that we have. There's another new artist that I absolutely love. She's actually from Kenya as well and her name is Fena Gitu. I remember first hearing her music and saying, "She's a very diverse type. Southern African, Angolan, and Mozambique influences in her sound." She's doing some cool stuff about Africa and about our roots.

A GLOBAL LANGUAGE:

A lot of the people I work with are interested in other cultures and especially interested in what's going on across the different regions of Africa. As this applies to music, you want your sound to be able to fit in a club in Nigeria, or for someone from Nigeria to sit in a club in Tanzania and say, "OK, I really like that record. I don't understand one word they're saying, but I connect to it." When people say that it's possible to relate to music, it's very true. You don't necessarily have to speak the language that's being used in the song.

I remember being in Mozambique and going to a club. I was really impressed by the fact that they had all local music playing throughout the night, and young people my age, dancing to all *zouk* and *kuduru* genres. It was so nice. We all just had a good time.

Surfing the Sahara

Western Sahara

Nathan Myers

THERE'S SAND IN every crack. Tiny deserts in my shoes, my cameras, my earlobes, and fingernails. Last week, "Sahara" was just a word from the movies. Now I can't get it out of my eyes.

I remember a local news reporter asking us why we'd come here. It's a good question. I'm thinking: why is there a news crew here?

I remember driving into a town I'd seen from space. An abandoned jigsaw of cinder-block huts in this forgotten nowhere cove. Staring down from Google Earth before, I'd thought: why is this town abandoned? Later, actually standing there, I am no less confused.

Sahara is a place without answers. A shifting riddle of endless sand.

An old man crawls from the ruins. He is covered in mud. He yells when he speaks, telling us the government chased everyone away from this town years ago. They don't want people to know about it. He blames the octopus for everything. We nod and smile: the octopus is definitely to blame.

As he tells us this history, clean point waves reel across the water behind him. It's a hundred degrees out and we are putting on wetsuits.

There are military checkpoints every fifty kilometers out here. Why so many stops? What are they checking for? There's only one road for a thousand miles. What's changed since the last stop?

Some checkpoints are military. Some are police. Some are military police. They all want to see our passports. They all want to know what we're doing out here. They all want to make us tea.

No one is ever in a hurry here. But we are running late.

We left in a rush to arrive in Sahara in the first place—late already. Balinese pro surfers Marlon Gerber and Mikala Jones were ready to go within the hour. Filmmaker Taylor Steele and I were already at the airport. No sleep. Overpriced tickets. We lost half our camera gear to Moroccan customs and just kept moving.

And then we had to sip tea with strangers in the desert. And the strangers had guns. If not for our guide, we'd probably still be down there. Sipping tea.

Sahara is a no man's land. "A non-self-governing territory" is the official term. Morocco ran off the Mauritanians and the Algerians by 1991, but the United Nations won't fully recognize the claim. Much of Africa says the land belongs to the native Sahrawis, but these traditionally nomadic tribes don't control it.

A tension simmers in the dusty nowhere. A riddle of hospitable hostility in a place that makes no sense. Ask a question of the desert. The desert will ask one back.

Everything looks the same out here. Hour after hour. Dirt. Rocks. Dirt. Sometimes we stop hiking across the flat plains to stare at the Atlantic. There are land mines. And there are point breaks.

We locate the break we've come here for and make our approach on foot. Massive dunes and high cliffs separate us from the Atlantic. Sometimes we pause for Taylor to film some iconic "walking across the dunes" shots.

During one of these stops, two men appear from behind the dunes and begin screaming. "Get away from here!" they cry. "No pictures!"

Really? Localism? Here?

They are surfers, wearing pink boardies and familiar logos. And they are angry.

"Go home now!" they scream. "We will kill you."

There is pushing and shoving. Screaming and threats. The only surfers for a hundred thousand miles are fighting over an empty wave.

It's too strange to comprehend. We turn around and hike away. Confused. Stunned. Full of questions. Like, did that just happen?

Now it's New Year's Eve in the Sahara. Not exactly what we'd been dreaming of, but we're dealing with it.

We spent our day surfing the point break near that abandoned village. Talking with the crazy man from the ruins. The water was cold and the sets inconsistent, but Marlon and Mikala rode enough bombs to make the effort worthwhile.

Now it's celebration time and we're three million miles from a power outlet. How did this happen? There is sand in my nose.

We drive to the remote town of Dakhla, with its small, *Beyond Thunderdome* kitesurfing scene. In a dark, back alley, we locate a restaurant that serves beer. We order two each. And then they are gone. The Sahara is out of beer.

We drink tea and eat kabobs. We fall asleep without counting down the new year. Sand in my hair. Sand in my dreams. Sand in the final seconds of 2009.

In the morning, fierce sirocco wind is sending sand out to sea. Great for kitesurfers. Bad for us. Wind ripples the sand like a carpet of snakes. Agitated sands.

The Saharan news crew finds us staring at their tattered seas. "Why did you come to the Sahara?" she reads off a dusty cue card. Their cameras and microphones are riddled with sand. They want to know. Surfers in the Sahara? A good question.

The plump reporter winks at Marlon. He stops taking off his wetsuit. Mikala answers questions like he's between heats on the world tour. She continues to read questions from the card. She nods and smiles. Everybody nods and smiles.

If Sahara were a question, sand would be the answer.

We drive the long straight road back the way we came. We stop for the checkpoints. We share long slow cups of tea. Like a dream on rewind. Like this never happened. I don't remember a thing.

I remember conversations that made no sense. I remember flies crawling in my cup. I remember sand. I remember wind. I remember Sahara. And I blame the octopus for everything.

SPRING

JORDAN

CRAIG SMITH

THERE WAS A time this year when the prevailing wind announced that spring had arrived to Jordan. The desert had bloomed into swaths of green emerging from previously lifeless soil. Flowers appeared on olive trees. Kids could be seen and heard playing outside.

For three consecutive days I did not turn on my heater, a first for me in Jordan since my arrival from Northern California, in October of last year.

To take advantage of the warm days, I developed the habit of bringing a mattress out onto my front porch in the afternoons. I sat in the sun and listened to music, ate lunch and studied Arabic. I also liked to receive guests this way. By putting myself outside and more visible, neighbors and others passing by often took the opportunity to stop in and visit.

On one such warm day when I was walking to my home from school, I met my neighbor, a man from Syria, coming down the hill toward the bus stop. We spent a couple minutes going through the standard greetings and inquiries of health and happiness before I asked him where he was heading. He told me he was going to the city to look for a new house. I asked why and he merely said that he did not like living in our small and quiet village. I was sad to hear that he might be leaving but wished him luck in his search for a new house.

That was the second to last time I ever talked to him.

Later that afternoon I brought my lunch and a mattress outside to relax and enjoy the weather. The neighbor's six (of eight) children were outside running around. The kids saw me and waved hello. Soon a couple of the younger girls, ages two and four, walked over to sit with me, though they were too shy to speak. This was the first instance of a female being on my front porch since I moved in.

Next, the boys and the oldest daughter joined us on the porch. Comfortable, the children began to talk at once. They told me, and I could see the evidence on their faces, that their house was infested with mosquitoes and they couldn't sleep at night. In the same tone, the six-year-old boy explained, in more complicated Arabic than I am able to understand, all the reasons why his nation's President Bashar is bad. The two-year-old girl liked to walk up to me, giggle, and run back to her four-year-old sister. The nine-year-old boy demonstrated, by mock shooting, how Bashar's soldiers attack and kill civilians and families in Syria. The ten-year-old boy asked if I wanted to take a group picture.

Eventually their father arrived and shooed all his children home. I asked him if he found any houses and he responded that he couldn't find one. He reiterated the fact that he did not want to live in our village anymore. He then told me that he possibly planned to get his gun and go back home to Syria to fight.

Despite the fact that I am living in a highly militarized country that is surrounded on all sides by countries currently or recently going through conflict and war (Iraq, Syria, Lebanon, Palestine, Israel, Egypt), peace is still a fundamental ideal for which I stand. For basically my entire adult life, my home country, the U.S., has spent endless dollars engaging in two wars in which many lives have been lost. I do not know what our world would be like now if neither of those wars had happened. I cannot, however, imagine how the United States, Iraq, or Afghanistan would be worse off if those wars had not happened.

I do not understand, and I probably never can understand, how humanity has reached a point of constant and sustained violence. Again, I stand for peace.

But that day I didn't say all this to my neighbor. All I said was, "No, that's not good." He had no response and changed the subject.

The next day, when I got home from school, the neighbors' house was emptied and the only sign of their former presence was three bags of trash sitting in the street.

Now many months later, winter has returned to Jordan. I'm wearing six layers again. I'm careful to close all my doors to keep the heat in. The wind is howling. The rain is coming down. No trace of children can be seen or heard.

Running in Place

Lebanon, Qatar, and Dubai

Sophie Chamas

"WHAT'S QATAR?" I asked, when my father told me we were going to move there. It was 2001, I was thirteen, and I had never known a home other than the two-bedroom apartment we owned in Mar Elias—our neighborhood of Beirut, Lebanon, then famous for its abundant shoe stores. "It's in the Gulf," he responded. "You'll like it. Our compound has a tennis court."

I had never played tennis before.

When I think of my early years in Lebanon, I remember our neighbor across the street who shamelessly sat on the balcony in his underwear every day, casually reading a newspaper while smoking a cigarette. I recall clotheslines stretching across railings all over the city, allowing the colorful laundry of strangers to dance above our heads; the voices and laughter of domestic helpers bouncing off the walls of buildings as they exchanged gossip up, down, and across the layers of the neighborhood; and the street peddlers rhythmically chanting their calls to purchase, as if prophets of the holy food pyramid reminding me to always eat my vegetables.

After we moved away, I spent four years in Qatar, but it always felt like a non-place to me. We lived, like most privileged expatriates, in a gated compound of identical houses distinguishable only by number. I attended an American school, where I socialized primarily with young Texans whose parents worked in oil. We spent weekends at each other's compounds. We ate at Applebee's and Chili's, went to the movies to view the latest American blockbusters, and fearlessly skateboarded outside. But there was nothing I could ascribe the adjective "Qatari" to. Without the people, the backyards, the pool houses, and the school I had come of age knowing, it was an unfamiliar place.

Soon after graduating from high school, however, I grew to look forward to my visits to Qatar—visits that always expired just in time. I'd step into my mother's kitchen and be welcomed by the smell of deep-fried cauliflower, quesadillas, and garlic. Mornings would be spent in my pool, a cheek against the warm tiles, and in the afternoons I would sink into the folds of my comfy reclining chair. When evening came, I would cozy up next to my father, placing an ear on his belly. As he listened to the news, I would listen to the symphonic digestion emanating from his insides, the noises making me laugh just as they did when I was a child. And every morning I would wake to find my mother by my bedside, ready to usher in my day with that distinct high-pitched laugh of hers, always punctuated by the signature silly snort that is so contagious.

When I left Qatar to go back to Lebanon for college, I believed I had ended the chapter of my life set in the Gulf. But my mother cautioned me against making assertions about my future. Like many other Lebanese, she lived in constant fear of being jinxed, or worse, jinxing herself by "challenging fate." She warned me that at the snap of heavenly fingers, my intricate plans could collapse. "Don't try and bump heads with God. He'll knock you unconscious," she said. "Don't challenge fate. Or you'll find yourself back in the Gulf with your tail between your legs." But I believed that for the most part, we build our own futures; that there was enough that I could control to give my life a sense of purpose and direction.

Sometimes, however, fate deals you a slap in the face.

After the Israel-Lebanon war of 2006, my parents yanked me out of my studies at the American University of Beirut, and, for lack of a better option, dropped me in Dubai. I enrolled in the American University of Sharjah, which I had never heard of before, and that was that. I was back in the Gulf.

My life in Dubai felt dull and uninspiring. I spent three years plotting my next move. Everyone I met seemed to work in advertising or a field of that sort. They all defined a job as a means to an end, and judged it by what it reaped in terms of personal gain and prestige.

Retreating into fiction and literature, I drooled over beatific adventures on the open American road, brought to me by the golden tongues of Kerouac and Ginsberg, Snyder and Burroughs. My nose picked up the scent of New York. It was my promised land, and I was determined to make the pilgrimage across the ocean to sit where the poet-prophets I loved had sat; to write where they had written; to kiss the face of greasy pizza slices and bathe in American beer; to protest anything and everything, tearing off the muzzle of self-censorship I had been forced to wear for so long.

That's how I found myself at NYU, two months after receiving my BA, smack dab in the middle of the city of my dreams.

If you try hard enough, you can live ten lifetimes in New York in a short two years. There, I found myself in a constant state of stimulation. My peers and I would leave three-hour seminars and skip to the corner bar for happy-hour beers. I would sit on the grass in Prospect Park during the summer, reveling in the fact that this big, bustling metropolis shoves buildings and roads out of the way to map nature onto its torso. Everything I read and discussed felt important. My thesis felt significant. My chest ballooned with pride when professors praised my work, and I delighted in the thought that I had contributed new knowledge to the universe. I floated out into the world after graduation on the arms of an imaginary crowd, ready for it to receive me and everything I thought I had to offer.

I returned to Qatar triumphant—gripping my perfect GPA, departmental essay prize, and internship experience—for what I thought would be just another short pit stop on a smooth ride into the job market.

Back at home, my days began at noon. I would transfer my weight from bed to couch and, face tattooed to my laptop, would pop news articles like Prozac until my father came home for lunch. Then I'd try to spend afternoons in my backyard, for a change of pace. In the evenings I'd reluctantly change out of pajamas into tights to practice yoga in a hotel basement; saluting a sun I couldn't see, inhaling AC, and fixing my gaze on the hardwood floors as I tried to keep my balance. I would come home and sink into my reclining chair, leaving my body—rotting in its flannel—temporarily behind.

For months I lived what felt like a time loop. Rolling out of bed, a little less enthusiastically every morning, to an empty inbox. Spending hours reworking cover letters, desperately trying to make myself sound wittier and more unique. Rereading job descriptions like riddles, attempting to unlock the secrets hidden between the lines. Trying to spot the contours of that perfect candidate so I could sketch her face onto my applications.

My social parents often threw dinner parties that I was forced to attend. I would sit like a trophy child, smiling, listening as my father proudly recounted my achievements; stuttering as I explained the difficulties of the job hunt. I spoke in pre-recorded messages, rewinding and replaying my answers for the conveyor belt of people that moved in and out of our house. "It's a tough market," I told their nodding heads. "I am only suitable for very specialized work. I really haven't been looking for that long. I am freelancing." They smiled, I smiled, my parents smiled, and then a few weeks later we would do it all over again.

The world, I believed, was ravenous for knowledge about the Middle East, and I was itching to serve it up. So I turned to journalism, where I thought I would be a natural fit. Yet the "knowledge" I boasted of so proudly in my applications to bureaus in Beirut, Dubai, and Cairo sparked little interest. What I needed, instead, was to be fluent in newswire tongue; to be capable of masking—with surgical precision—any subjectivity, and creating the illusion of a detached observer who regurgitates information untainted by personal perspective.

I had never been taught this foreign speak and wasn't particularly interested in unlearning my entire approach to writing to make room for a language I didn't actually like. I found a place for my voice in the Middle East-focused *Jadaliyya* and *Kalimat Magazine*—mostly run not by journalists, but by people like me. Such publications, however, run on voluntary labor and couldn't get me out of my parents' house, out of my pajamas, out of the Qatar that had monstrously transformed from a family rest house into a purgatory.

As the weeks crawled past, I started to consider new exit paths. Remembering Dubai, I used to scoff at people who had "turned their backs" on their educations and entered the corporate world. Unlike so many before me, I'd planned on being faithful to my degree. I didn't realize at the time that what I took as my superior convictions were born out of privilege; out of the comfort of never having had to worry about feeding myself, paying my rent, affording transportation, or supporting a family.

Tucked within the insulated walls of my parents' home in Qatar, I had failed to grasp the connection between myself and the millions of youth protesting all over the world. I felt blanketed by shame as I watched them brave snowstorms and police batons while I sat curled up in my parents' lap, moaning my tale of woe, wondering why my dream job hadn't manifested itself yet. What I once immaturely dismissed as selling out, I began to understand as a coming to terms with reality. I realized it was braver to thrust myself into the world, trying to make the most of what it could offer, than to hide out in my pajamas, waiting for the Godot of jobs that was simply never going to come.

Perhaps fate is indeed a cruel mistress, or perhaps I stepped out of the academic bubble into a world in crisis. The reality of things is, the Gulf—with its abundance of well-paying jobs and tempting work packages—is seeing a steady stream of white-collar traffic. With a passport ranked among the world's most useless, work experience consisting of a few measly internships, and a nontechnical degree, I found myself yet again face-to-face with a Gulf not of my own choosing. I began peeking under the lids of research, education, and NGO work in search of vacancies, and even started perusing postings in advertising. In what I once perceived as a nauseating and soulless profession, I now saw potential. I saw a chance to write professionally, even if it meant writing jingles.

It is a strange feeling, to have run so far only to be yanked back into the world I'd worked so hard to escape from—as if I had been wearing an invisible bungee cord this whole time that would only let me stretch out so far, before pulling me back in and giving me whiplash. It is like the world has failed my generation; like it can't make room for all of us. We are forced to run in place, waiting for the world to either fix itself or implode; waiting for it to find a use for us.

Until then, we are putting our overeducated minds into storage and busying our hands for now. We are focusing on our day-to-day survival, and hoping that the sense of purpose that oiled our wheels in school will find its way back into our lives.

The Land of a
Thousand Hills

Rwanda

An interview with
Derek Helwig, television producer

OFF TO RWANDA:

After spending time in Kenya's Rift Valley for my girlfriend Deanna's dissertation research, we headed across Lake Victoria to Rwanda where I could do mine. I wanted to study the media's role in the Rwandan genocide. We were invited to go to a film festival that they started there called the Rwanda Film Festival. It's also called "Hillywood," because Rwanda is known as the land of a thousand hills. It's African films, but primarily Rwandan films. The stories are mostly told in Kinyarwanda, a language most people outside of Rwanda don't understand because it's only spoken there, in one of the tiniest countries in the world.

THE PURPOSE BEHIND HILLYWOOD:

Local Rwandan and other African filmmakers make the movies. They have these inflatable screens and they go around the entire country showing films to people as a way of reconciliation. That's part of the whole idea: reconciliation from the genocide. The people from an entire village, and all of the other villages surrounding, come to see the films. They're together, former Hutus and former Tutsis. In Rwanda, the rule now is that no one is allowed to say which tribe he or she is from. The new idea is that "We are all Rwandans." It's such a great testament to see all the people gathered together, after so many years of such hatred that obviously had to take place in order for people to commit to the killings. The hatred went back so far, with families hating each other and having resentment. Sure, that's still there for some of the people. But to see people work together and come together was really an amazing thing. It's like there's this bandage, and I think these films help make that bandage stronger. The films try and bring the country together. For many people a Hillywood film is the only movie they're going to see all year.

RECONCILIATION:

We went down to see the notorious church in the small town of Nyamata. When we walked in, we instantly noticed the light shining inside from bullet holes in the tin roof. It's just got that dusty haze inside where your eye can really see the light coming through. The bullet holes are everywhere. On the ground there are clothes. Bloodstained clothes. Even after fourteen years, the bloodstained clothes remain from all the victims who were killed inside this church. Back when everything happened, what the *génocidaires* did was, they told people, "Hey, go to the church and you'll be safe there. You'll be OK there." It was a trap. Once they got everyone in there, they hacked all the people to death with machetes. So now, when you see the blood, it's more vivid than any museum or memorial. The church in Nyamata is a hard reminder of the violence that humans can do to each other.

In the cellar below the church, the vivid reminders become even more real. Racks of bones and skulls of the victims are laid out. There are thousands. One skull that immediately caught my attention was that of a young child. The skull was not much bigger than a softball with a large chunk missing from the side. Even walking out of the church, you see hundreds and hundreds of skulls.

Across the road, I saw men wearing pink uniforms. I've never seen that. It was weird to see that. They were doing construction and I asked, "Why are construction workers wearing pink? That's kind of odd." The answer was that the workers were the former *génociduires*, people from the Gacaca courts. "Gacaca" is a type of court that occurs throughout the country of Rwanda. It's like a town-hall style of courtroom. So all the people that killed other people, or tried to, or stole from people while they were being killed and other things like that, they faced community trials to decide their punishment. But there wasn't a death penalty. So these people for years had been prisoners. Some of them eventually go home, some don't, depending on the level of the crime. They wear the pink outfits. You could see them all over the countryside, doing work projects right next to the place where they killed people. That's why right next to the church these guys were building a road or fixing infrastructure for a school. It's a bold, in-your-face reminder of why your punishment is happening and what you did back inside that church.

TRUE STORIES:

Long before I went on the Rwanda trip, even before I got into the film industry, I had a job at the Holocaust center at my undergraduate university. One of the speakers we hosted was hotel manager and humanitarian Paul Rusesabagina, the real-life character Don Cheadle played in *Hotel Rwanda*. There was also another Rwandan man who came to the school to tell his own story. He was able to get out of the country before all of the mass violence started happening. He then lived in Seattle for a long time and ended up working for Starbucks. At our center, he came to talk about small communities of coffee growers that he was trying to organize back in Rwanda, to sell to Starbucks, Costco, and other companies. His focus was on the high-end specialty coffee that Rwanda is able to grow. It intrigued me, how this guy wanted to go back and create jobs for people in his community who were basically killing his family. He wanted to hire them and employ them. Again, reconciliation was part of the driving idea. This guy's story always stuck with me. In the city where I lived and the campus where I worked, no one was really talking about the Rwandan genocide, although at the time it had only happened thirteen years before. It was still so fresh in the survivors' minds. So I decided that Rwanda was where I eventually wanted to go.

WHAT WE IMAGINE:

Since the genocide, Rwanda has become a place of investment. A lot of it is guilt money from the West for not doing anything to stop all that happened. Before my visit, I had this image in my head. But when we got there, the reality was completely different. The city center of Rwanda's capital, Kigali, has been rebuilt so much. The town has modern glass buildings, shopping centers, and even a fancy coffee shop where you will find just about every Westerner in town kicking back a latte. The hotel we stayed in was modern with tiled floors and new appliances. There's one area of town where there's a well-stocked grocery store you wouldn't expect to see. This was not the Rwanda I had imagined, but it is the Rwanda of today. And it's the Rwanda that their government is pressing hard to showcase.

FIRST TIME HITCHHIKING:

In Rwanda, I'd say that at every mile there's a policeman standing at a corner. It's very much a police state. Because of what happened, it has to be. One day we went down to see Butare, a museum and university town. We wanted to go to its big museum. We'd gotten our ticket to go there on the bus, but then later, after we were already in Butare, all the tickets to travel back were booked. So I asked around for a ride and met a guy. He was Rhodesian. I say Rhodesian and not Zimbabwean because he'd been kicked out when he was young, by current Zimbabwe President Robert Mugabe. We got in the car with this guy to get a ride back to Kigali. He had a driver. A Congolese driver. They'd been driving in from the Democratic Republic of the Congo, where they apparently lived. I'd never hitchhiked in my life, but there my girlfriend and I were, in the car with a driver and a Rhodesian oil worker. So we're going along the road, and the Rhodesian is telling us his story and his philosophies on life. He's got a complete hatred of all police and every sort of authority that you could imagine. He yells out at every policeman that we pass. He keeps on talking. He keeps yelling at all of the police. In my mind, I'm concerned that this guy is going to get us pulled over. But nothing happens, and we keep driving along. Eventually he invites us to stay in the DRC with him, because we'd mentioned visiting an area that's near the border and also near his house. At first, we say, "You know, this could be an adventure. This could be a fun time." Then he goes on to tell us more about the Congo. He says, "It gets a bad name. But it's fine. It's good. I live in a great place." He continues, "Well, yeah, there are body parts I was formerly attached to, but it's not a big deal." He pulls up his pants and there's a titanium leg. So we said, "OK, we're not going there with you."

A VIEW OF THIS COUNTRY:

We did make it out to a national park that is very close to the border between Rwanda and the DRC. To look around and see all the hills and the mountains and the vegetation, it all felt peaceful. Most people go there to see the gorillas. It's huge income for tourism and costs well over $500 per person. But as students, we weren't doing that. Instead of the gorillas, we decided to go hiking. So the next morning, almost everyone else at the hotel left to go see the gorillas. Only three of us left to go on this "nice little nature hike." It was me, my girlfriend, and a young woman from Montana we'd met that day. As we started hiking, I realized there were three soldiers walking right near us. I made the joke that we had our own personal escorts. Little did I realize. The hike guide replied, "Well, actually, these guys are coming with us the whole way. They're here for our protection. Don't take any pictures of them. They're not allowed to take any pictures." By that point, I'm thinking to myself about why the hell we might need guys with AK-47s on a nature hike. So there we are hiking up Mount Bisoke, which is actually an inactive volcano in the Virunga Mountains. We were actually pretty near the area where Dian Fossey, the zoologist, did most of her research. At first, I'd said, "Nature hike? No problem." It turns out, what this trail is, is the path where the rain comes down the mountain. It's a super-skinny, almost seventy-degree incline all the way up. Also, since it's where the rain comes down, the path is all mud. It had just been raining that morning, so we had to walk through about a foot and a half of solid mud at every step we took up this mountain. It was a five-hour trek to the top. At one point I started wondering why we'd even decided to do this. We kept falling down in the mud. That, along with armed guards around us to make sure that we didn't get caught by rebels from the DRC.

But then we got to the top of the mountain. We saw its crater with the lake inside. From that point we could see all of Rwanda. It was this moment, when all of the clouds and the mist start coming up the mountain and moving toward us. It's this feeling that you get like you're almost flying. It's such a great and unexpected thing after you've gone through the awful trek of getting up to the top. Then you're standing there and can literally see into the Congo as well, and you still have all of the mist and all the clouds just flying past you. We could hear the gorillas in the background.

AFTER HIKING THE MOUNTAIN:

Both of us were way too sore to keep moving on with our trip. We ended up staying an extra day in Virunga to rest. On a short walk down the road from our guest house, we came across a group of boys playing soccer in a field. Their ball looked rather odd to me as they kicked it around. Once the ball stopped, I could see that it was made of plastic bags bound together with old shoelaces. The boys invited me to run in and play for awhile. Just ten minutes of playing soccer with those kids made me feel like I was totally at peace with my surroundings. After we finished playing, all the boys wanted to exchange emails. All the kids had an email, even though many people in Rwanda don't, and they wanted pen pals.

One of the boys, Olivier, invited us back to his house to meet his family. After walking about a mile down the road (with about half the boys from the soccer game now in our entourage), we arrived at Olivier's house and met his mother. She was busy working in the yard sorting potatoes, the family's livelihood, that would be picked up by a truck the next day. This day was her busiest day of the year and yet she took the time to welcome us. Olivier was a great kid. Like many of the kids in the area, he was in school and he loved to learn and valued education. He and the rest of the kids were passionate about learning.

LOOKING BACK:

To stand on that mountain in Virunga, with the valleys of this amazing country sprawling out into the distance, really captured what this trip was all about. To visit a distant land that is known only for bloodshed and have that image completely reversed was truly a special trip. This country has turned around enormously in the past two decades and is a place that really means a lot to me now.

The Human Arrow

Tangier, Morocco

Christian Lewis

THE WORST PART of my job from 2000 to 2002 was an over-starched red plaid shirt.

I wore the shirt in hotel lobbies, while directing clients to strategy meetings, training seminars, breakfast buffets, and the nearest bathrooms. I wore it while shepherding them onto boats and buses, into cars and out of airports. I wore it escorting them to celebrated tourist sites, company-funded leisure activities, and expensive parties with celebrity guests. Following a man in red plaid made it less likely that the clients would get lost.

I called this part of the job "the human arrow."

My clients were Big Pharma, Big Auto, and Big Oil executives. These were confident, purposeful people, well informed and smartly dressed. Most were men, mostly white, and most were on the latter half of the median age. They talked often and with apparent authority on subjects such as the Dow, corporate mergers, partisan politics, industry trends, and golf.

At age twenty-five, I knew little about those things. My three years of work experience since finishing school included stints as a farmhand, a ski-lift operator, a waiter, and a bicycle-taxi driver. I had no desire to do those jobs again, nor to continue as a human arrow, but I also had no aspiration to be anything like the people who now employed me. I wanted to be the places we went.

To be them.

I wished to assume their identity, to constitute them and to be comprised of them, to equal them in meaning. Make me Vancouver harbor during the annual fireworks celebration, the boats drifting through explosions of color like motes in a kaleidoscope. Make me the cavernous hangar at Miramar with the latest incarnation of Kool & the Gang bouncing funk off hundred-million-dollar fighter jets. Make me the emerald tongue of a desert golf course licking arid beiges and browns—golfers cursing by day and coyotes yapping by night, my sprinklers skittering to life without warning. Why shouldn't I be the silhouette of Cabo's rocks at sunset, the shadows of the Sydney Opera House at dawn, or the walls of Montserrat when the choir starts to sing? Why couldn't I be the vineyards and lagoons, the racetracks and ski slopes, the revolving restaurants atop celebrated spires and the posh nightclubs dripping with attitude? Let me be every airport tarmac that ever rippled into the distance with evaporating jet fuel.

But to be these places, for now, I had to also be a human arrow.

The upside of "seasonal" employment—paid by the day without benefits or contract—was that I could take off work as much as I liked and extend my stay wherever the company brought me as soon as the job was done. This is how I came to be staring at the destinations board in Barcelona's Estación del Norte one June evening with a month of freedom in front of me.

And a guy had just spit on my boot.

My Spanish was a one-winged bird at best, so I didn't fully understand his reasoning—something about Americans and money. But his action alone rightly summed up my current sense of self-worth. There had been more clients on this trip than usual, with less patience and a greater sense of entitlement. The tourist attractions, from La Rambla to La Sagrada Familia to Tibidabo Hill, had felt more claustrophobic than any I could remember in two years with the company. And the guidebooks I'd studied, the landmarks I'd memorized, the routes I'd plotted...no one seemed to care where they were, let alone where they were going. It all added up to a feeling of useless exhaustion. No wonder my red plaid shirts had lost their starchy posture. But to realize that even worse than being an arrow in life was being an arrow that no one followed—well, it gave me an overwhelming urge to walk blindfolded.

Big sun, bald sky, the sea salted with white caps. I could see the soft slopes of the shore materializing and soon it looked like any other small hillside Mediterranean city. Mottled white boxes rose in haphazard stacks, occasional towers broke the skyline, and scattered clumps of greenery punctuated the drabness. When we docked, I waited for the ferry to empty and the crowd on the pier to thin out. I was determined to avoid the vultures—tour guides circling any non-native-looking arrivals. After the last one disappeared, I walked off the boat, excited to be alone.

"Hello, my name is Isam," he said from out of nowhere. "Where would you like to go?"

The best response to his illogical presence, I felt, was to pretend he wasn't there. Which I did, past boats and buoys and fishermen and two masons working with weathered trowels on a low sea wall, all the way up the hot dusty hill into the medina.

"I don't need a guide," I finally said, sweating in the dry heat.

"I know a hotel, very affordable."

"I'm not staying."

He was surprised. "Then we must see everything quickly!"

"I told you already."

"I will show you the bazaar."

"No."

"The new city."

"No."

"Tanger," as he pronounced it, "is dangerous—many strangers."

I stopped and looked at him and pointed out the obvious.

"But I am not a stranger," Isam said. "I am a professional tour guide. And you are very American."

He had a hard face with probing eyes, squint lines, and a Groucho moustache. His thick black hair was flecked white as if he'd been painting a ceiling.

"You are hungry," he said. "I know a restaurant, very affordable."

The plan, ever since the bum's spittle had shined my shoe, had been to proceed without a plan—without information or expectation. So far this non-strategy had achieved a thirteen-hour bus ride to Andalusia, stale croquettes at a midnight pit stop, a hot morning lost in Granada, a hotter afternoon wandering the Alhambra palace, salty chicken in a crowded plaza during a wedding procession, another bus ride, an evening lost in Algeciras, five beers in a hostel smelling of ammonia, and a groggy morning exchanging money before crossing the Strait of Gibraltar. On the whole, there was no argument to be made that traveling this way was intelligent, let alone efficient, but it was certainly more dramatic. In my mind, I was Christopher Columbus. But suddenly, faced with the medina, its baking walls, shadowed alleys, staring eyes, and dusty poverty, Columbus turned the boat around. I had no map, no guidebook, little cash. And if my Spanish was a lopsided bird, my Arabic had broken its neck flying into a windowpane. I could probably find some other tourists to trail around town, but that seemed like a cop-out. Maybe a little help here from a local was forgivable.

"You will not get sick," Isam assured me.

"Where?"

"Just here," he said, gesturing up the road. "Very affordable."

We were the only customers in a large dim room, illuminated by only the sunlight beaming through the open door. Fringed square pillows lined the benches where we sat and silverware lay embalmed in cloth napkins along clean wooden tables. A TV in the corner aired World Cup soccer: Brazil vs. Belgium, tied at zero. Our waiter, scrawny and eager, recited the menu in a single breath of English and I was so transfixed by his pace that I didn't listen to what he said. When I asked for clarification of the third course, he repeated it all, unabridged.

We slurped vegetable broth as Isam talked. He said he was fluent in five languages and enough of a sixth, Japanese, to be relevant. "Tanger" was his home, his father's home, and his father's father's home. Isam's father was seventy-six, his mother fifteen years younger. He made me play the guessing game with his own age, so I went low. He was in his forties. When I asked him to guess mine, he said twenty-six without hesitation. I'd be there in three months.

Over chicken and couscous, Isam described the old city and the new, the poor and the rich, the government.

"This new king," he whispered, looking around the empty room. "He is not so good. He is in Europe, he is in the Middle East, he is in America—he is never here! If he eats breakfast in Tanger he must be eating lunch in España."

He looked around again before hissing: "He is like Yasser Arafat."

I braced for the secret police to swarm the restaurant. Plates would spill from tables. The TV would crash to the floor in a fit of sparks. Our waiter, having fled out the back, would try to relay it all to his friends but his dialogue, even more frenzied with adrenaline, would be impossible to understand. Maybe after six months of questioning in a dank underground cell, I would emerge at three-quarters my body weight vowing never again to leave U.S. soil. Isam would have vanished completely. There would be a book deal, of course; and the talk-show circuit, parties, women. Alas, the cops never came.

Continuing to skirt danger, Isam criticized the government's practice of charging its national tour guides thirty thousand euros for "official" certification. The claim seemed questionable, but I let it go. I didn't want to ruin whatever rapport we were building.

"So you're not really official?" I asked.

"I'm not crazy."

I told him that I was something of a tour guide too. I explained my recent job in Barcelona, the wealthy corporate types and tourist traps and Med-gazing terraces with cocktail parties and expensive pillow gifts. I told him I thought it was a shame our clients traveled so far only to see so little.

"They spend more time taking pictures of each other than looking around," I said. I slapped the table for emphasis, rattling a teacup. "In such amazing places!"

Isam nodded politely. He'd never left Morocco but said he had a brother in the hash trade who'd been to Spain seven times. He would stock up in Tangier, cross the Mediterranean at night on a fishing boat, and travel inland through a network of poor families for the payoff in Madrid.

"He is very clever," Isam said bitterly.

Many people also traded heroin, he added, which made its way back into the shaking arms of Moroccan children. "Just here," he said, indicating the height maybe of an eight-year-old. "Many addictions, many people in jail."

Lunch continued this way, less a conversation than a view through the window of Isam. Or at least, the window he was showing me.

"The time of the hippies was good," he said. "People were not afraid. They would come to us. Tourists would sleep in the streets with their bags and their money out." Now the city had drawn jobseekers from all over the country. But the well was dry. Tourism was down. There was only September 11—"the fear everywhere," he said, shaking his head.

Tea arrived and with it the bill. The price was higher than I expected.

"No euros," the waiter said as I tried to hand him some money.

"Credit card?"

He apologized. "Dirham only."

I was sorry too. My groggy and uninformed attempt at currency exchange had left me dirham-poor. Isam offered to exchange my euros for me. The waiter nodded.

"I'll do it," I said.

The waiter stepped back politely. Isam leaned across the table with a furrowed brow. "You are the one buying," he said.

In my bag I had *Tales of the Alhambra*, by Washington Irving, two pens, and a notebook full of scattered notes and bad prose—nothing for collateral. I could offer my passport, but that would be completely stupid. Isam was my only other option. In disbelief, I watched myself hand over the only other cash I had, a fifty-euro bill. He vanished into the dusty sunlight.

I waited. The waiter waited. On the static-laden TV, Brazil was beating Belgium, one to zero. I sipped the last of my tea and drank the refill, grew antsy and slowly sick—not from the food, as Isam had promised. Why would someone incriminate himself and his brother in front of an absolute stranger? Why would I trust such a man, especially when he made a living convincing people to follow him? He hadn't expected me to be so ill-prepared, but he'd seen his chance and taken it. I couldn't even blame him; if I were in his shoes I'd do the same. I cursed and stood and tried not to look surprised when he reappeared in the doorway. I settled the bill and we walked outside.

"Your pockets are too big," he said, lighting a cigarette. "Put the money back in your money belt."

"*Shukran,*" I said. He'd taught me a few words over lunch but this was the one I remembered.

Isam suggested we see the rest of the medina, a bit of the new city, the bazaar, and some other sights of storied Tangier.

"I just want to walk around," I said.

"We can do that."

"What's your fee?"

He mustered the gravity of our drug-trade conversation. "I think of the long, not the short. What is in your heart to give, I am happy to receive."

It sounded like Zen meets Hallmark. Also like an open-ended invoice for people with big pockets. But what did it matter? He'd gained my trust and he knew it.

We walked through the heat, side by side, Isam smoking and talking and pointing. He nodded to people and stopped to ruffle the hair of kids playing soccer in the street. We climbed a crumbling stairway, passed under an arch stenciled in Arabic, and crossed a wide courtyard. At the far end, a shattered wall opened on the downward slope of the old city, exposing beige and white rooftops, TV antennas scratching the hot sky, the sea washing away distance. It was a stunning view, the juxtaposition of beauty and humble dwellings making it more authentic—it seemed to me—than any "scenic overlook."

Winding again through the medina, we heard shouts from a doorway as Brazil scored another goal on Belgium. Why they favored a country farther away, I couldn't guess. Then again I knew even less about soccer than I did about Morocco. In another door stood a man with one leg; in the next, a woman on a stool stuck her tongue out at me. The last door was orange, a neon rectangle on a plane of muted pastels, followed by a trash heap patrolled by cats. The dogs, beaten by the heat, lay dozing in the shade.

We eventually hit pavement with cars and buses and heavy diesel exhaust. The stores had glass doors and windows, and more people were dressed in business attire. We lingered awhile in a large square with a massive white marble fountain surrounded by gleaming white buildings and a few palm trees. Later, we turned down a side street, passing a cluster of pristine four-story apartment buildings with garages and balconies. Isam said it was the work of the drug trade and promptly unzipped his fly and urinated on one of the walls.

Back on the blemished streets of the medina, men sat on stoops riffling cards or playing backgammon at lightning speed or passing cigarettes and lighters—everyone either smoking or about to.

"Nothing else to do," Isam said, lighting another when I mentioned it.

The smell of his cigarette was quickly overpowered by the smell of fish. We rounded a corner and entered a roofless courtyard where the floor was filled with buckets of metallic silver bodies. Chickens dangled with sinewy necks from long tables and beef blood pooled out under our shoes. On braided twine from the sellers' stalls hung pig and goat hooves, and there were shawls and wraps and blankets, their colors stark against the pale stone, which looked even paler next to the vibrant reds and yellows and browns of the spice bins. Along one wall, a stairway led to a catwalk, squared above the market. We climbed and I saw that recessed from the walks were dark nooks, one after another like shoebox dioramas, each housing a stoic form. Their work-hardened fingers moved in a blur over the fabric, and it was then that I felt I was really subsuming Tangier. I was the pattern in the wool, the salty fishnet, the turmeric and cinnamon and saffron. I was old city and new, hash and mint tea, the stoops, the dice, the diesel, the smoke. I was the shattered wall where we gazed over Isam's world at the sparkling expanse beyond.

Then I looked at my guide and the blindfold fell away. His plain white shirt might as well have been red plaid. And where he'd taken me had very little to do with what I'd seen.

"I have only one face," he said later, before we parted. "I think of the long, not the short. What is in your heart to give, I am happy to receive."

He didn't look at the bill, just shook my hand and kissed my cheeks, and I walked back down the hill to the port.

KABILA:
THE FIRST FAMILY
OF THE DEMOCRATIC
REPUBLIC OF THE CONGO

KINSHASA, DRC

EDWARD C. DAVIS IV

THROUGHOUT MY YEARS as a young academic, I've had two passions: teaching, and the Democratic Republic of the Congo. These two passions merged once I was hired in 2006 to teach at the American School of Kinshasa (TASOK).

When I arrived in Kinshasa in May 2006, presidential elections were under way in the nation; and by August, international election observers were counting ballots, awaiting the right moment to release the results.

Although he had already served for five years, incumbent president Joseph Kabila Kabange had not yet been elected by the people. Joseph faced nearly thirty opponents, yet his main challenge came from one of his own vice presidents, Jean-Pierre Bemba.[1] The day the presidential election results were to be announced proved to be quite tense. It was

---

1 In the Democratic Republic of the Congo and throughout its diaspora, most people refer to President Joseph Kabila Kabenge as "Joseph," while his father, the former president, is always referred to as either

also the first day of classes at TASOK. I prepared to teach my group of youngsters that morning, knowing that at any moment the results could be broadcast across the airwaves. My elementary classroom represented a multinational body of expats and wealthy locals living in Kinshasa. There were children from Kenya, India, South Africa, Namibia, Senegal, the U.S., Belgium, and more.

Before she arrived, colleagues warned me of the entourage that would be accompanying my student Sifa Kabila Kabange, daughter of Joseph the president. When I spoke with her nanny and bodyguards, I wondered how I might help this young child feel normal in a world of so many uncertainties. I wondered how I would do the same for the entire class without favoring any student over another. I would need to remain politically neutral, and I would have to be respectful of her family and their privacy.

After the children all left and went home, the results of the first round of elections were announced. Joseph Kabila had received the most votes, but with over thirty candidates, he did not win with a simple majority of 50 percent plus 1. In second place, the former warlord, millionaire, and vice president, Bemba, would be Kabila's only competition in a final round of elections scheduled for November. The announcement led to armed conflict on the streets of Kinshasa, with soldiers loyal to the Kabila family and soldiers loyal to Bemba battling in all out warfare. The UN tanks that patrolled the streets of the capital city did not attempt to intervene.

The city was on lockdown. School was canceled for one week. Outside the walls of TASOK, soldiers gathered at Camp Tshatshi military base. Just across the road from the school, truckloads of soldiers loyal to Kabila organized and departed into the city's streets seeking soldiers loyal to Bemba.

"Kabila" or "Mzée," a Swahili venerable title. By 2001, Kabila was dead, and his son Joseph assumed power, at twenty-nine years old becoming one of the youngest presidents in world history.

The United Nations Organization Mission in Congo (MONUC) arranged a peace deal that would allow the two opposition leaders to make amends at least until the second round of elections could be held. When classes resumed, I faced the challenge of helping to ease the minds of young students living in a war zone.

Earlier in the year also around the time of the elections, the country held the marriage of Joseph Kabila to Olive Lembe di Sita. Although they already had a daughter together, Sifa, Joseph was not married to Olive until June 2006. The day was marked by large celebrations throughout the country. Bar owners throughout the country were given beer, perhaps paid for by Joseph himself, to celebrate the happy occasion. Several months after the presidential wedding, the new First Lady was quite nervous about her new position, although she had been in the shadow of the public spotlight since the birth of her daughter in 2000, before Joseph took office.

I first met Olive Kabila on the TASOK campus. Arriving at the end of the school day with her mother, niece, and nephew accompanying her, the First Lady made quite an impression on the local staff at the school. With my students away at after-school activities, I was straightening up my classroom when a strange knock on my door abruptly stopped my afternoon routine. In walked the school crossing guard, followed by the presidential guards and school security. A young, light-brown woman entered my classroom. Apologizing for her limited English, the woman, who introduced herself as Mrs. Kabila, started to tell me of her attempts to study the language. I began talking to Mrs. Kabila in French, which placed her at ease. From there, we sat down and discussed private matters. She informed me that she was not sure if I had been writing the class notes that went home in her daughter's folder, written in French. With many of my students speaking the language at home, I informed the First Lady that I wrote notes in French to all of my French-speaking parents. Mrs. Kabila greatly appreciated my understanding of local culture and customs. Her mother, Madame Lembe di Sita, also proved to be a most polite and respectful person.

From what I'd heard in Congo so far, most people believed Mrs. Kabila was of mixed parentage, with her mother's family coming from various regions in Eastern and Western Congo with her father reported to be Belgian. But given Madame's very light hue and Mrs. Kabila's just slightly darker, I assumed that Madame must be the one of mixed African and European parentage.

In Congo, mixed-race Africans enjoy a social space different from those of full African ancestry. Associations and social clubs for mixed-race Congolese, organized during the colonial era, still remain strong to this day. Due to the history of the U.S., most African Americans are of mixed African, Native American, and European ancestry. Thus, most Congolese classified me as mixed race, and occasionally (incorrectly) as a light-skinned member of the Luba ethnic group from Kasai. On the streets of Kinshasa, I did claim to be Luba whenever necessary. Being Western could be dangerous. Overall, I would find that my own ability to be both an insider and outsider would prove most valuable at times.

Jean-Pierre Bemba, the defeated, former vice president, is of mixed ancestry, possessing both Congolese and Portuguese citizenship. Following his defeat, Bemba hid in the South African embassy and then fled Kinshasa with his Brazilian wife and children. The family moved to one of his homes in Portugal.

After Bemba's exile, I was invited to a tennis match by a well-known tennis coach in Kinshasa.[2] When I arrived at the mansion where the match would take place, I discovered that I had been invited to watch the coach give a one-on-one lesson with Jeannot Bemba, a former

---

2 Portuguese authorities allowed the Bemba family to live peacefully; yet frequent travel from Lisbon to Brussels would bring about the end of Bemba's free movement in Europe. In March 2008, Belgian authorities arrested Bemba for past war crimes and sent him to The Hague.

senator and also the father of the exiled former vice president. As I talked with Jeannot Bemba, I nervously thought about what to say to the father of an exiled war criminal. He already knew that I taught at TASOK, but did he know that I taught the president's daughter? With this in mind, I spoke cautiously.

In our interaction, Jeannot Bemba was a very delightful and jovial man. Ironically, he looked a bit like a slightly heavier, older version of my own father back in Chicago. Mr. Bemba joked with me, calling me his twin. Many people in Kinshasa had often told me that I resembled Jeannot Bemba and now, with Mr. Bemba confirming our resemblance, it was certainly true. I suspect he had heard about the American teacher in town who looked like a younger version of him and that this meeting in his home was certainly arranged. The tennis coach would later tell me that Jeannot Bemba regularly asked about me after our first meeting, and wanted me to return to the house to play tennis and to chat with him about the United States.[3]

Although victorious and with the Bemba family out of power, Joseph Kabila faced challenges in Kinshasa. Rumors spread that he was Tanzanian and not Congolese. For this reason, many Kinois felt that the exiled Bemba was more Congolese than Kabila, and thus had more legitimacy to the presidency. Yet outside of Kinshasa, Kabila remained popular. All the same, fear escalated throughout the capital city. President Kabila ended all public appearances, and more rumors spread that he had died along with other members of his family. Each day in class, I taught the president's daughter, knowing that these rumors were untrue.

In April 2007, as Sifa's birthday approached, I received a note from President Kabila. The first family planned to celebrate with a party at the presidential residence. I was invited to attend, along with my classroom assistant, Patricia, and Sifa's friends from school.

---

3 Not wanting to ever be called to testify before The Hague, I passed on offers to return to the Bemba compound. In 2009, Jeannot Bemba died in Brussels. His last days were spent visiting his son at The Hague.

On the day of the party, Patricia accompanied me to the president's house. The compound was filled with parents, children, food, and decorations. President Kabila and I greeted each other, and he reintroduced me to his mother-in-law. Realizing that I had already met most of the members of his family, I was escorted to a table to sit with Kabila family uncles and aunts.

The dinner was excellent, and the company was quite unique. The most memorable moment of the night came as we cut the birthday cake. Sifa first cut a piece for her father, then for her mother, next for her grandmother, and the fourth slice was for me. President Kabila and his daughter both served me my plate, in a manner that displayed a level of respect. They later gave me photographs of the night for my souvenir book.

As summer vacation approached, Janet Kabila, Joseph's twin sister, made a visit to TASOK. She accompanied her niece and my class on a field trip to the Kinshasa horse stables. While the students rode horses, we spoke about the upcoming summer break and our planned vacations. I had made plans to go home to Chicago and to visit friends in the Caribbean. Before heading to America, I wanted to take a two-week excursion through Zambia, Zimbabwe, Mozambique, and South Africa, by land. Janet offered to make arrangements for me in the Congolese copper town of Lubumbashi, as well as in Zimbabwe.

I thanked her for the offer of assistance. Airports and border crossings in Congo are not easy, and government officials have been known to rob and victimize foreign visitors. I have been the victim of robbery by government authorities in Congo and Kenya, and so I welcomed Janet's offer.

When the school year ended, I flew to Lubumbashi for a most unique journey by air and land. Arriving in the copper capital at night, I got off the airplane to an interesting scene. A white sedan sat pulled up to the airplane, much to the dismay of police and airport security. Showing his documents from the office of the president, the driver pointed to me explaining to authorities in a blend of French, Swahili, and Lingala that he had been sent to pick me up.

In the dark of night, I noticed how the clean, paved, well-lighted roads of Lubumbashi differed from the littered, crumbling, dark streets of Kinshasa. The driver dropped me at the hotel without letting me know he would return for me the next day. In the morning, he urged me that I needed to return to the airport to fly to Zimbabwe immediately. Explaining my plans to further see Africa by land, I asked for help getting there by bus. But this driver did not understand why I wanted to travel by bus. He said that the airplane would be much faster, but eventually he agreed to drive me to the Zambian border and let me travel on my own.

After a drive through Lubumbashi, a trip to the zoo, and a visit to important sites, he took me to the border of DRC and Zambia. From there, I was on my own.

I certainly received a wide perception of life in Africa, due mostly to my professional relationship with the Kabila family.

THE SLAVE ROUTE

GHANA

KIM COLEMAN FOOTE

THE BUS SHUDDERS and lurches. Smoke enters the back. The passengers there are frantic and coughing. "Driver," someone shouts, "something has fallen off the bus. Go and pick it!" I groan along with everyone else.

After two weeks of vacationing in Senegal, I'm eager to return to my surrogate family in the Ghanaian fishing town of Elmina, my home for the past several months. We're about an hour away but who knows when I'll get there? The driver explains that if he stops, the bus might not start again. But the passengers' complaints keep coming so he parks and gets out. There's nothing around us but endless fields of bright green grass.

We all go silent when the driver returns. He's holding a dented metal object that looks to be the carburetor. I laugh hysterically. My seatmate stares as though I've gone insane, but soon she's chuckling and pointing at the old smoke stains inside the bus. She gasps, "These ancient buses-o. I bet this does not happen in your country." I could tell her plenty of Greyhound nightmares, but I'm tired of explaining yet again that the United States is an imperfect place.

Our driver restarts the bus but it slows to a crawl. As more passengers wail from the smoke, he calls, "Please! I beg you. I am trying to bring us to the petrol station at Apam Junction. It is just there!"

At the name "Apam," I spring upright. I recognize the curvy green hill in the distance that resembles a facial profile. Months ago, a chief I'd interviewed was giving me a ride and we stopped briefly at Apam to visit his friend, an Ewe woman. I've meant to return there ever since learning that the town has a slave fort.

I've spent the past several months in Ghana on a Fulbright Fellowship, researching the trans-Atlantic slave trade. My primary goal is to write a novel about slaves at Elmina, but I also have a personal connection, as some of my ancestors were enslaved Africans. If they did indeed originate in the country we now call Ghana, they might have begun their journey in Ghana's interior, where people were seized by rival nations mostly through warfare and kidnapping. The captives carried trade goods on their heads as they marched for months to the coast, where European traders awaited them. There they were imprisoned in medieval forts and castles that doubled as warehouses. They spent another month or so in unsanitary dungeons before getting packed into ships to cross the Atlantic.

When designing my Fulbright proposal, I envisioned trekking by foot from northern Ghana to the coast to follow in my ancestors' footsteps. That idea has since boiled down to seeing the sites individually, but I haven't yet made an itinerary. There are at least two former slave markets and over ten forts and castles to visit. Apam is on the list, so the bus breaking down there is opportune.

When the junction is visible ahead, I pull out my cell phone and call Gifty, the friend of the chief I interviewed. By the time I'm following the other irritated passengers off the bus, she and her husband are waiting by their champagne-colored Mercedes. We stare at the smoke billowing from the bus.

Her husband, who tells me to call him Uncle, shakes his head. "This bus is going nowhere."

"Kim, you will stay the evening with us," Gifty volunteers.

I'm anxious to get back to my surrogate family in Elmina but I'm too tired to protest. On the drive to Gifty and Uncle's house, I tell them about wanting to see the nearby fort. Gifty turns to look at me.

"You people feel it is important to visit the castles."

"'You people?'"

"Black Americans," Uncle says, glancing at me in the rearview.

I stiffen, prepared for the comment many Ghanaians have given me upon learning about my research topic: *That happened so long ago; why don't you just move on?*

But Gifty says, "More of we Ghanaians should go. We need to understand as well what our forefathers did-o."

"But everybody tells me I should forget what happened," I say.

Uncle frowns. "Many of us here do not know the true details of what happened. We are very ignorant. And those that do know, they don't think on it so much, because it wasn't their ancestors who suffered."

Gifty gives Uncle a head roll from the heart of black America. "Ah! But that is not all of us-o! Some of us want to forget because we are ashamed. You see, some of our ancestors sold yours into slavery, Kim. Whether or not they knew the full repercussions of their actions, it was wrong, and it still affects us today."

I haven't heard this perspective often. I unfasten my seatbelt and scoot closer. "Tell me more."

Gifty lowers her voice. "You see, I have a friend—she is an Ewe, like me. Three generations ago, someone in her family bought people to expand the family. Where they come from, there is a taboo against buying a human being. There is a rumor that because of it, every woman in the lineage would have a failed marriage. It has happened, generation after generation. The curse won't be broken until they have atoned for what they did."

"How do you atone for your ancestors?"

She shrugs. "I am guessing you must first admit what was done. And apologize."

During Panafest, a biennial Pan-African celebration that occurs in Ghana, local chiefs have done just that: they've made verbal apologies for their ancestors' involvement in the slave trade. Some people felt the apologies were merely ceremonial.

Uncle pulls into a driveway alongside their house. A spindly girl wearing a sundress jogs over. Yapping dogs follow her, frightening a pack of hens strutting across the yard. Gifty introduces the girl as Estella, her niece, who gives me a smile. I watch, still amazed after months in West Africa, as she hoists my suitcase atop her head and glides into the house. As we follow, Uncle offers to drive me to the fort at Apam and two more in the nearby towns of Senya Beraku and Winneba.

Gifty pulls me aside, telling me, "If more of us remember what happened to your ancestors, maybe we wouldn't treat you like strangers and try to exploit you today."

It's rare that I meet Ghanaians who understand our frustration at returning to our ancestors' homeland only to feel like we're being deceived, cheated, and "sold" again. Gifty notices my eyes before I can blink back the extra moisture.

She touches my cheek and says, "Aha! The chief, our friend who introduced us, told me what black Americans face when they come here. I didn't understand myself until he explained it to me."

The bus breakdown is definitely looking to be a blessing in disguise.

A humongous silk cotton tree guards the hill leading to Apam's Fort Patience. The road beyond is so eroded that I'm afraid Uncle's car won't make the climb. We park in front of a tiny fort with mildewed white walls. No caretaker is present but Uncle, Estella, and I soon discover there's nothing spectacular to see inside. Rusted padlocks that look like they haven't been opened in ages secure most of the rooms. In one of the unlocked upper rooms, we find a dingy wilting bed, evidence that the fort has been converted to a guesthouse, as has happened to a few others. In the fort's back courtyard, we find bathrooms for the guesthouse. Uncle suspects they were the slave dungeons, but a quick check in one of my history books reveals that they were workrooms.

An old woman wearing a grubby headscarf appears from nowhere, making the three of us jump. As she tells us she doesn't have a key for the locks, she stares at me. I feel like turning my back. I suspect she's not used to seeing so many foreigners at Fort Patience, which isn't advertised nearly as well as the sprawling castles at Cape Coast and Elmina, both declared World Heritage sites by UNESCO.

I tell Uncle that we're going, in Fante.

The woman grabs my arm. "Pardon me. May I ask you something?"

I shiver. Will this be my "moment?" In the 1960s, when Maya Angelou lived in Ghana, an Ewe family was about to drive her across a bridge in the Volta Region when something told her to get out and walk. Her Ewe hosts were stunned by the request. She later learned that the local residents were superstitious about driving on the bridge because of its tendency to wash away in a storm. Later in town, Angelou even came across a woman who mistook her for deceased kin. It was a homecoming of sorts.

I get excited, wondering if my whole trip to Ghana has been leading up to this moment; the seemingly happenstance bus breakdown in Apam, which would magically connect me to my ancestry.

But the old woman asks me, "Are you an Ewe or a Fante?"

I'm so startled I can't speak.

Uncle chuckles and says, "She is neither."

The woman frowns and beckons to Estella and me. "But aren't they your daughters?"

"Even if they were, they would be neither Fante nor Ewe. I am a Gã."
He puts a hand on my shoulder. "Kim here is from America. Estella
there is my niece."

"Oh, OK. But she does look so much like an Ewe."

The woman keeps studying me. When we get into the car, I flip down
the sun visor and see why the woman reacted as she did. The fine layer
of sweat on my skin makes me seem somewhat darker, almost Uncle's
complexion, but both of us are much lighter than most Ghanaians. It
must be my hair. With the thousands of micro-cornrows that a stylist
did for me in Senegal, it's hard to tell that my hair isn't chemically
straightened. Besides my skin color, my natural hair has been enough
to set my appearance apart from most Ghanaian women.

The revelation is a letdown. I soothe myself with the thought that
at least the detour in Apam has been refreshing and productive, with
the company of Gifty and her family, and visiting the forts. And I'm
finally prepared to make plans to visit the other slave sites once I
return to Elmina.

Just before sunrise, the homeless of Elmina—wrapped in faded, wax-
print cloth—slumber outside atop wooden tables and benches. The
morning air is chilly and dry, appropriate for June. My friend Ato and I
hurry from his family's house, where I've lived for the past few months,
and into my rented taxi. Ato rubs my clammy hands and flashes me
his wide reassuring smile. I'm gearing up for what might be the longest
road trip I've ever taken.

Ato, born and raised in Elmina, has been beneficial to my research,
locating elders for me to interview. In addition, a few months ago, he
encouraged his family to open their home to me when I faced housing
troubles. And recently he's solved my slave-route itinerary problems.
Some of the sites proved difficult to locate. The castles at Cape Coast
and Elmina attract the most attention and visitors, which is probably

due to their immense size and their World Heritage Monument status. They're also about thirty minutes apart and in range of hotels, which makes them most accessible. I've heard that many of the other forts are just as well preserved, but few tourists seem to know they exist. I've found only two maps indicating their locations. A vague one in my *Rough Guide* and a crude sketch in a twenty-year-old history book. Beyond the iffy directions, public transportation to the forts would be hard to arrange. If not for Uncle's assistance in Apam, I would have needed to take several *tro tros* (minibuses) and taxis.

Ato removed my worries by putting my plan into action the day I returned from Apam. He arranged for the taxi and a driver, and just a week later, we're on our way. We've decided visiting the forts in succession from west to east would be most time- and cost-efficient. We've also planned to relax for a few hours at Nzulezo, a village built entirely on water. We would finish our journey at one of Ghana's largest former slave markets at the northern town of Salaga.

On the main road just outside Elmina, morning mist rising from the grass and trees gives the landscape an otherworldly feel. The fog clears around the city of Takoradi, which once served as Ghana's main shipping port. The sky is still overcast but we spot a more ominous-looking sight, of police officers standing in the street. I've learned that Ghanaians dread them as much as Americans fear meter maids. With the exception of a Good Samaritan Ghanaian cop who once gave me a ride without expecting anything in return, I haven't seen or heard anything positive about Ghana's police. This morning, I speculate they're on the road to collect a "dash," or bribes. Apparently, it's a solution for supplementing their meager income.

The road beyond is definitely one less traveled. Public transportation is nonexistent. When we eventually come to a fork in the road, there are no signs telling us the way to Beyin, the location of the westernmost fort we want to see. Our driver waves to a lone man standing at the roadside next to his farming tools and sack of yams. He looks like he's been waiting on transportation for years. He directs us to the bottom road. After what seems like twenty miles along a bumpy unpaved road, we finally enter Beyin but still don't know the fort's location. The driver pulls over to a church, where some men sit on the steps. Ato is met with blank stares when he asks them the whereabouts of the "castle." He tries other words. "Fort." They shrug and shake their heads. "Fort Apollonia." They still look confused. "Slave trade? Slaves." More head shaking.

I urge him to say "cast-el," which is how I've heard many Ghanaians saying it. He cuts me a sharp look and admonishes me for making fun of the pronunciation. But when he repeats it as I suggested, the men throw their heads back and laugh: "Oh, you are coming to the cast-el! It is that way-o!"

Near the beach is the tiny Fort Apollonia, guarded by two cannons. A Ghanaian man in a blue shirt emerges and introduces himself as Stephen. He's filling in for the caretaker. Grabbing a computer printout summarizing the fort's history, he announces, "This place you have come to visit is now called the Apollonia Beach Guesthouse. In 1968, the Ghana Museums and Monuments Board turned it into a rest house."

As is the case with the forts at Apam and Senya Beraku. Fort Apollonia's upper bedrooms are painted pink but I'd never want to sleep there. No matter how cheery someone makes these quarters, it doesn't brighten the fact that slaves suffered in the dungeons below.

Where Stephen takes Ato and me next disturbs me even more. Right outside the bedroom of the fort's former European governor is a narrow wooden staircase. At the bottom, a cramped room with a barred peephole high in the ceiling. Stephen says this is where the female slaves were kept. The staircase gave the European men easy access to those they wished to take sexually.

I've heard this story at the Elmina castle and at a few other forts I've visited already. I'm wondering how many more times I can bear it.

By day's end, we've visited Fort St. Antonio, in Axim, and have heard about rapes again. What appalled me even more was the office desk sitting in a former dungeon, which still had its original barred door. The Board of Education had recently moved out of the fort, leaving a mess of classroom supplies and furniture. As the caretaker droned on about how the female slaves were violated, my emotion boiled over. To me, it was like placing a business office—or a gift shop or toilet or disco, as occurred at the Elmina castle and a few other forts—in a former gas chamber. Though the people caged in these dungeons weren't murdered, they experienced horrendous conditions that led to suffering and death. At the Cape Coast castle, archaeologists drilled through two feet of compacted human waste before they could locate the original stone floor.

The next morning, the thoughts weigh heavily as we enter Fort Metal Cross, in Dixcove. At first glance, I'm annoyed by the caretaker's appearance. He lounges barefoot on a bench, looking disheveled. I'm almost tempted to walk through the fort without him. He sits up and rubs his eyes when he sees Ato, our driver, and me hovering over him. He introduces himself as Mr. Cromwell and begins to narrate a story in Fante, pausing for Ato to translate for me. I quickly feel ashamed at how I've prejudged him. He gives us so many dates and historical details from memory that I can barely keep up.

He gets up from his bench, slips into flip-flops, and beckons for us to follow him. I'm surprised that the fort is very well kept, considering the state of the others I've seen. It's better maintained than the Elmina castle, even. Outside the former governor's quarters, the floor is covered with modern tiling. Someone has painted the cannons black and highlighted their crown and insignia, emblems of the British Royal African Company.

I soon discover who this someone is. Looking up, I notice a British flag flying alongside a Ghanaian one. Mr. Cromwell informs us that the Ghana Museums and Monuments Board (GMMB) has leased Fort

Metal Cross for twenty years to a British man who intends to make the fort a "tourist attraction." He has converted the former governor's quarters into his personal lodgings. To make way for guest chalets outside, he'll evict the villagers living there and move them far from the beach. *Why doesn't he just use the slave dungeons for his boarders?* I think bitterly.

The rumor is that the GMMB is in the process of reevaluating the decision to lease Fort Metal Cross, believing they've made a mistake. I wonder if any of this information has reached Dr. Robert E. Lee, the African American dentist who was denied the same opportunity in the 1970s at Ghana's Fort Amsterdam. When I interviewed Dr. Lee several months ago, he said he was denied because he refused to let the GMMB administer the money donated for renovations. A GMMB representative I later spoke with proclaimed a nobler reason: "These monuments don't belong to a single person or group but to the whole country." But money talks, apparently.

Mr. Cromwell leads us to the female dungeon. I brace myself for the familiar sight: a wooden staircase leading up to the former governor and officers' quarters. At this fort, Mr. Cromwell informs us, the only dungeons with peepholes were for the women, to aid the men in selecting them. The women were washed and taken to another holding room, which also has a peephole high in its ceiling. The room is now pristine—plastered and whitewashed—as if history can be just as easily erased.

The cargo bus hits another pothole. I squirm against the thinly padded seat and clutch the seatback in front of me. Ato, squeezed beside me in a row that barely seats four of us, looks uncomfortable too. It's the third vehicle we've taken since seeing our driver off at five o'clock that morning on the coast, where we boarded a bus headed north. We're on the final leg of our trip, headed to the former slave market at Salaga, and we've been traveling for over six hours. My old wish to walk a slave route is definitely a distant memory.

As the bus ends its route at the town of Yeji, I'm more nervous than ever about the trip, especially since our bus driver nearly drove us over a cliff a few miles back. And next we'll have to take a ferry across the Volta River. My *Rough Guide* calls the ferry unreliable.

We notice it, docked at the riverbank. It's sparkling white and looking almost brand-new. I can't quite figure out what's wrong with the picture until I realize that the ferry is tilted too far to the side. It's also far beyond the thatched-roof shelter where people are waiting. Sure enough, Ato and I learn that the ferry is "faulty" and hasn't operated in months. Our only option for crossing the river is a canoe. Word buzzes around that the last one has just departed.

A man from the bus relieves us by telling us he's also headed to Salaga and says we shouldn't worry. "They say another canoe will come. Why don't you rest here?"

The makeshift shelter does look inviting, but Ato and I debate whether to retrace our journey and take another route.

"Oh!" our Salaga friend cries, overhearing. "But Salaga is just there-o!" He guides us toward the bench, saying, "Believe me, it will surely come."

Ato and I sit. As a strong dusty breeze picks up, I look across the river again. I vaguely wonder why there are whitish poles jutting from the water. Just when our patience starts to wear from waiting, we see something in the middle of the river, making its way to our side of the shore. It gets closer, and we realize it's a canoe. It's the giant type that Ghanaian fishermen use. Less than ten of us are waiting to cross the river, so at least the canoe won't sink from overcrowding. Besides me, there's only one other woman, whose feet are decorated with henna triangles.

When our canoe sets off, powered by an outboard motor, I can see the river's pole-like structures more clearly. They're rotting trees. Our

Salaga friend explains that when Ghana's hydroelectric Akosombo Dam was built during the 1960s, the river expanded. As a result, villages built on the riverbanks were flooded.

We enter the tree grove. The boy at the helm of the canoe directs the driver so we avoid the trees. When the bottom of the canoe suddenly rumbles, the driver snaps off the motor. I hear the groaning and scraping of splintered wood beneath my feet.

When we're safely past the tree graveyard, I breathe a bit easier, but the other bank is still far away. The canoe has no lights to signal distress to either shore. None of us wears a life jacket.

The whole ordeal makes me question why we didn't just end our slave route trip on the coast. Everyone I've talked to about Salaga has warned me that I'll be disappointed. They said there's nothing left of the former slave market. More significantly, my ancestors wouldn't have stopped at Salaga. The market's activity peaked in the late 1800s, long after the trans-Atlantic slave trade had ended. Most of Salaga's slaves originated in northern Ghana and Burkina Faso and were sold locally as domestic servants or as wives to produce children in matrilineal clans. Still, Salaga had one of the largest and most significant slave markets in the area, and I want to see what it might have looked like. It's too late to turn back anyway.

I try to concentrate on my surroundings to avoid thinking about losing our lives in the Volta. In the moonlight, the guide's hand is still visible. The now-constant hum of the motor is calming. I sink against one of the canoe planks until I become aware of a tickle in my hair, at the back of my neck, along my arms. I squint through the darkness but can't see anything. I hate bugs, but after twenty hours of nonstop travel, I'm too weary to let it bother me. I snuggle closer to Ato and let the transparent dragonflies kiss my skin.

I fulfill my dream of walking the next morning. Ato and I trudge down the empty paved road leading into Salaga from the hostel where we crashed. It's not even ten o'clock and it's at least ninety degrees. We're ravenous to boot. The snappish hostel caretaker, who offered us only a hard loaf of moldy smelling bread when we asked for food, said we'd have to find a chop bar in town, a mile away. There's pretty much only one taxi that comes through the area, and it's the one that took us along the bumpy road from the river last night.

We realize we've reached the edge of the town center when we start seeing more buildings and people. There's also a large sign that reads, "Salaga Slave Market," but we're too hungry and cranky to think of sightseeing. We head for the nearest chop bar. It's not the type for tourists, which would have tablecloths, chairs, a bar, and a sound system. Instead, it's a small room with two long tables and rough wobbly benches. There's a communal bowl of murky water for hand washing. Flies buzz around. Neither of us cares at this point.

After our meal, we ask the chop bar owner where we can find the Salaga Na, the chief. We're directed to a small compound with an open courtyard. Two grown women sit there, cooking, when we enter. They introduce themselves as the chief's daughters and tell us that their father can't see us because he's deathly ill. They send one of the children of the house to search for their brother, who's filling in for his father.

A man returns not long after. He wears a blue-and-white woven *fugu* shirt and a matching floppy cap I associate with northern Ghana. He introduces himself as Brazil, son of the Salaga Na. When he learns our purpose for coming, he says he's eager to show us the local slave sites but ponders how we'll get around. Ato's and my trek that morning has killed any romantic notions I had for walking in my ancestors' footsteps. Fortunately Brazil manages to borrow a bike for Ato, but I haven't ridden in a long time. I try sitting sideways behind Brazil on his bike, as I've seen the women doing in Salaga, but I can't stay balanced. Brazil sends someone to call for a friend who owns a car. While we wait, Brazil goes into his father's room and returns with a set of rusted metal shackles. He tells us they would have secured the slaves to trees at the market. Ato is suspicious of the shackles' modern look, but I remind him that the market was operating late into the 19th century.

Brazil's friend agrees to drive us to two former slave sites. One is located off an unpaved road where a man walks a herd of cattle. Brazil cuts a path through the bush with a machete. We arrive at three-foot-wide holes, cut into the ground and brimming with water. The holes were dug deep enough to pick up water from underground streams. It was here, Brazil says, that Salaga's slaves were bathed. A short drive away, we check out a well that a volunteer recently helped to reconstruct. Brazil mentions that the slaves were refreshed with water from it.

His friend drops us off near the large sign advertising the site of the former slave market. There's nothing there but a wide stretch of unpaved ground and a young baobab tree with a twin trunk. When Brazil catches Ato and me squinting around, he says, "The market would have functioned much like they do today. Only on market day would there have been activity here, and slaves to sell. The vendors would arrive and set up their wares, then they packed them and moved on to another village."

It seems an anticlimactic end to a whole day of travel. Yet, neither Ato nor I feel we've wasted time in coming to Salaga. For one thing, Ato has never traveled so far from his hometown. Here in northern Ghana, where people are tall and slender and stare at him because he's short and can't speak their languages, he finally has an inkling of the foreigner experience I've had in his country. For me, I'm glad to have encountered so many strangers who've guided us along what could have been a crooked way. Brazil has been especially hospitable to us and is surprised when I offer him money for his assistance. I know the gesture is probably rude, but I want to leave him with something more than sincere promises to send him copies of my photos, which he says visitors never follow up on.

I still can't imagine what my ancestors might have experienced on those slave routes. My journey has been exhausting and sometimes harrowing, even with the relative luxury of an interstate bus, a cargo bus, a dugout canoe, a taxi, a bike, and a car. The trip does help me see the slaves' suffering in a new light though. As I visit more and more slavery sites, I notice that I feel less drained, depressed, and irate. Especially when it hits me that innumerable men and women underwent the loss of family and community, the lengthy march through Africa, the dungeons, the diseases, the branding, the ships, the New World holding pens, the auction blocks, the backbreaking labor, the rape, the torture, the psychological trauma. And still, centuries later, through myself and their millions of other descendants scattered from Canada to the southern tip of South America, life carries on.

Who Needs a Flashlight When You Have a Mzungu?

Msambweni, Kenya

Mike Madej

THE LATE-NIGHT KNOCKING at my door wasn't uncommon, because as a foreigner living in a coastal Kenyan village, I was something between an oddity and a novelty. When I answered my door on this particular night, it was my friend Ramisi inviting me to a mourning gathering. Through his broken English and my broken Swahili, I accepted, ready to meet up with other friends from the village and begin our journey.

To be honest, it was not difficult to get me out of my house no matter what time of day or night.

I'd rented two rooms in a single-level apartment compound. Although I could see the ocean through the bars on my windows, living in ninety-degree heat under a tin roof and with spotty electricity was nothing glamorous.

I didn't have a bathroom or running water in either of my rooms, so I fetched my water from a tap outside and shared a bathroom down the hall with the rest of the tenants. Unfortunately, the bathroom had walls that dripped with the dampness of a dungeon as cockroaches and other insects scurried about over the exposed coral stone. That bathroom was never fun to use, particularly in the dark; and at the water tap, the washing of dishes, feet, and babies, were common occurrences. That tap may or may not have contributed to my multiple weekends of 103-degree fevers.

Needless to say, I was glad to see my friend.

Venturing out into the African night never lacked excitement and this evening would prove to be no different. Since the direction we'd headed was parallel to the ocean, I asked if we could walk along the beach. I was sternly told that it was a bad idea to go to the ocean at night because that's where the witch doctors practice their magic.

With no bright moon to light our way, the local nighttime became very dark. We tramped through the coastal bush with only one flashlight among us, pushing aside palm fronds, walking through thorny patches, and tripping over broken-off reef pieces that jutted from the ground. As I followed along, I couldn't help but think about how just a couple of months prior I was sitting in my air-conditioned house back in the U.S., watching baseball, eating pizza, and drinking beer. But instead, here I was, following a group of guys through the dark night into the Kenyan bush.

Maybe the night was extremely hot, or maybe I had just taken too much chai tea earlier in the evening. When my friends and I finally reached our destination, we emerged from the dense bush into a clearing. As we walked out it seemed like almost everyone outside of this compound turned to stare at me, as if I'd walked into an unknown bar and bumped the jukebox to make the record skip. I stopped in my tracks and felt very aware of standing out like a sore thumb.

My friends made light of the moment with a joke: *"Huhitaji tochi kwa sababu tunapata mzungu."* "We don't need a flashlight because we have a white person." Indeed there was truth in this statement, as I did seem to be the only person glowing in the night. As my friends and I continued into the gathering, I could make out more details of the situation. This compound consisted of five square houses, made out of coral stone and tin for the roofs. There were no screens in the windows, just like at my place. Kerosene lanterns burned bright all around and made everyone's shadows seem to dance eerily in the dark night.

Large *sufurias* (pots) of beans and rice, pilau, stews, and chai tea, all simmered. My nostrils filled with the combination of the Indian, Arab, and African spices that make up Swahili food.

The women were wrapped head to toe in beautiful *lessos*, bright orange, green, yellow, and other colored fabric. They seemed to be in charge of cooking, serving food, caring for children, and cleaning up.

The men were also dressed in fine attire. Each wore a kufi cap and a shirt with a Chinese collar, along with a traditional *kikoi*, male wrap skirt. The men sat together on large mats eating and drinking. My friends and I walked toward the men to join them.

Greeting others in Kenya is nothing to be taken lightly, especially as a guest at an event. Ramisi and the others greeted the elder men first. As I stood by, glowing in the night and sweating from the heat, the women and children continued to stare. There was nowhere for me to hide and nothing I could do to deflect the attention; I just stood there with a clumsy smile and waited to make my formal introduction.

Ramisi eventually took me by my wrist and led me over to the specific elder whose brother had passed away. I approached the elder and let loose a garbled set of sounds: *"U-kar-a-ma-yu-we."* Ramisi, the elder, and everyone else within earshot gave me a confused look. I attempted the introduction again this time changing some of the sounds: *"U-kard-a-man-we."* Once again the jumble of sounds leaving my mouth was met with confused looks. Back during our walk from my place my friends had tried to teach me the proper words to use during the introduction, but by the time I was standing with the group of men I could only vaguely remember.

I looked toward Ramisi with a sense of desperation. After he explained my intentions to the elder everyone began laughing hysterically. People literally rolled onto their sides laughing. My failed attempt at conversation elevated me from a strange guest to the most amusing person in attendance. I was offered plates and plates of food as people gathered around to hear the mzungu attempt to say "hello." As the night went on, I slowly became more comfortable with all the attention given to me.

Most evening parties in Msambweni end about an hour before the first call to prayer. So around four in the morning my friends and I said our good-byes and walked back home through the bush. Even though the return trek was just as difficult as coming, I thought less of my feet being damaged by the rough ground and more about our evening.

My friends walked me to my door and said farewell. I checked my bed for spiders, turned on my fan, tucked in my mosquito net, and then stretched out on my bed, replaying the evening's events over and over in my head. As the fan hummed and the first call to prayer broke the silence of early morning, I closed my eyes and fell asleep.

The Impact of Oil

Niger Delta, Nigeria

An interview with Laine Strutton, interdisciplinary PhD Candidate in Law & Society at New York University

OFF TO THE DELTA:

Everyone told me not to go to Nigeria. I had decided halfway through my PhD to focus my dissertation on women's roles in the Niger Delta oil conflict, but it is an insecure region and I had no experience or contacts in the area. I felt that I really needed to see for myself if I could do research there however, so I first arrived with nothing more than an out-of-date guidebook and my backpack. I eventually stayed for a year, wading through toxic rivers, attending protests, and even sharing a canoe with a crocodile.

ENVIRONMENTAL EFFECTS OF OIL:

Since oil was first commercially drilled in the delta in 1958, there has been virtually no oversight of its environmental impact by oil companies or the government, and spills are an immense problem. After the BP and Deep Water Horizon accident of 2010, I heard several claims that the same quantity of oil released into the Gulf of Mexico in just that one spill has slowly been released dozens of times in the Niger Delta. Unfortunately, most people don't pay as much attention to the spills in Nigeria because they occur slowly over time, due to eroding pipelines and tampering, as opposed to the singular, dramatic, large-scale accidents that you hear about in the media. While offshore spills from oil rigs are certainly concerning for the local communities of this region, onshore leaking and exploding pipelines are just as hazardous because they poison the rivers from which community members fish and the land that they farm.

If you wade in the many rivers in the Niger Delta you can see the oil floating on the top of the water and dead fish washed up on the riverbanks. There are few sources of clean water in the Delta, so thousands of women use polluted river water to cook for their families, wash dishes, and bathe their children. Communities are also breathing in toxic gas flares that have been burning for years.

HEALTH:

It is extremely difficult to study the health impacts of environmental damage in a place like Nigeria. Logistically, the Niger Delta has few roads and most rural community members travel by canoe, which would be challenging for a team of health researchers with equipment. Such researchers would rarely have access to electricity and would need to bring along most of their own food and water. Secondly, it is not an easy region for outsiders, particularly foreigners, because there are serious troubles with robbery, kidnappings for ransom, and more. Even if these challenges were overcome, so many other factors there would make it problematic to identify environmental damage as the sole cause of certain health issues.

For instance, the Niger Delta has an extremely high infant mortality rate. Although that could be due to, for example, babies and pregnant women consuming oil-polluted water, the water could also be harmful in ways unrelated to oil—a lack of indoor plumbing in homes or waste seepage into shared water. On further speculation, the infant mortality rate could result from poor nutrition, lack of prenatal and postnatal care, unidentified genetic birth defects, or anything else. So, any study certainly could yield a correlation between oil spills and health problems, but proving causality would be complicated because there would be so many other variables to take into consideration.

DIVIDED RESPONSIBILITY:

I would say that the average Niger Deltan community member would identify the foreign oil companies, the largest one being Shell, as the main culprit of conflict and pollution. They see the oil company vehicles on the roads, they may have passed the guarded compounds where companies house their employees, and they see the logos on oil equipment. The companies are clearly outsiders, so an "us versus them" mentality easily arises. However, in my longer discussions with both individuals and groups, the matter of government accountability also came up. That is, one could argue whether the nature of capitalism does not require companies to be morally accountable in the same way that democracy requires governments to be morally accountable. The primary function of corporations is to make profit, but the primary function of governments is, simply put, to stop bad things from happening to their citizens. Isn't it the government's responsibility to monitor the activities of the companies?

Niger Deltans know that the federal government, in conjunction with foreign oil companies, is enjoying immense oil profits—yet the people themselves live without electricity, clean water, reliable roads, access to hospitals, and funded schools. They wonder among themselves, "Where is all the money from oil going?" People are frustrated and angry that government representatives, or others who they call "Big Men," are not engaged in economic development at the local level. They feel that such development is particularly important because of how oil activities have negatively impacted their traditional forms of livelihood. There is a sense that the government and oil companies together should offer some type of compensation for the environmental destruction that now hinders local economies.

WOMEN AND MOBILIZABION:

I became interested in women's resistance to the Niger Delta oil industry because it seems to have emerged quite suddenly, although women's protests in West Africa are certainly not new. After Nigeria's transition to democracy there was a spate of female-led marches and sit-ins against oil companies in Rivers and Delta State, starting in 2002. The biggest protest occurred at Chevron's Escravos oil terminal for ten days that July. For the first time on such a massive scale, some 600 Itsekiri women of the Niger Delta staged an anti-oil occupation of the extraction site. They made claims against Chevron and the government, alleging illegal appropriation of property, broken economic-development contracts, and environmental damage caused by oil spills and gas flares.

This particular demonstration received a lot of media coverage because during the occupation the women exposed their bare bodies to shame male officials with the "curse of nakedness." Behind the curse, there is a belief that the breasts of a mother are sacred and that showing them to a man in protest is like saying, "Look, I gave you life from these breasts so you must listen to me." In some places in West Africa they say that seeing the bare chest of a mother can make a man go crazy or blind. An employee who was there during the Escravos takeover also said that women had left symbolic branches and leaves on the oil equipment to curse the company.

This occupation immediately inspired additional takeovers, which involved over a thousand women at six different sites.

Away from the oil terminals, female vendors in the region responded to the call for anti-oil action by closing their market stalls and cutting off urban food supplies near extraction sites. Male workers joined in the occupations with their own labor stoppages and women forced out unionized workers who had refused to strike. It is significant to note that men sometimes liked to bring women into marches because soldiers and police are less likely to use force if women are involved. There is a strong cultural taboo against using public violence against women, especially older women, so females may march in front of men to act as a buffer.

WOMEN'S GRIEVANCES:

These protesting women had communal and sometimes nonspecific demands. First and foremost, they wanted jobs for their husbands and sons. Aside from that, most told me that they wanted the companies or government to provide electricity, water, and roads, as well as build schools and hospitals. To a lesser extent, they also were asking for the company to clean up the environment so that they could continue fishing and farming (although by some scientific assessments the Niger Delta ecosystem may not fully recover in our lifetimes). The more ardent protesters, specifically the Ogonis who followed Saro-Wiwa, said that if companies can't do these things then they should leave Nigeria altogether.

THE CHIEFS:

There are chiefs of varying levels of power in the Niger Delta, from low clan chiefs to the kingdom chief, and they are powerful enough that I could not enter a village without paying a visit to at least the local chief if not also those above him. In the first community I visited, a local taxi driver called ahead to tell the chief I was coming. I then had to show up with *kai kai*, or locally distilled palm liquor, as my offering. I sat in the chief's living room as he and his men asked me questions about why I wanted to walk through his community and what my financial stake was there. After explaining that I just hoped to gather field data, he poured a capful of *kai kai* over the threshold of his front door and sang incantations to the spirit in the local language, Ogoni. This means he prayed to the ancestors for my safety during my visit. Then we drank the *kai kai* together, meaning that I had his permission to be there. He sent out word to community members that it was all right with him that they talk to me.

I had to repeat this kai kai ceremony at several other higher chiefs' palaces, until the king said that I didn't need to see anyone higher than him. This was all very important to gaining access because as such a clear outsider, community members would have been very suspicious of me talking with them.

A COMPLEX REALITY:

Something that's interesting is that my conversations in the field about oil protests indicated that local chiefs had a heavy hand in instigating these demonstrations. In rural areas, the law of a chief is far more powerful than that of the government, and as my interviewees said, "Chief's law goes." In many instances the chief sent a town crier through the community announcing the day and location of the march. A protest may serve the chief's interest as much as the community members' because he may be rewarded by the company or the government for ending the demonstration and for keeping the peace. Also, even if the company or the state offers concessions, such as funding for social amenities, those funds are going to be controlled by the chief. In this sense, whether the women or other protestors succeed or fail, the chief may benefit. Since these leaders hold so much power in daily life, it isn't necessarily surprising that those same power dynamics would be reproduced in the social movement.

So essentially, I went to Nigeria looking for a story of increased political activity among the women, but what I found was far more complex.

RUNNING

SOUTH SUDAN

S. IMRAN ALI

WE HAD BEEN driving for about five hours along one muddy road, going north from the Doro refugee camp, headed up to a place called Guffa at the border of the two Sudans. We were a small exploration team looking to see if any refugees were coming down now that the dry season was approaching. I had been in the refugee camps of Maban County, South Sudan, for three months now, working to provide aid to refugees fleeing fighting in Sudan's Blue Nile state. This was my first time headed up to the disputed border zone. It was here, about ten kilometers from the border, where the thin road had closed in even more between the tall grass and it felt like we were standing in a long, narrow room, when we finally met them, some refugees coming south.

They were members of a single family—a man and woman in their forties, a girl in her mid-teens, and four young boys from about three to twelve years in age. The man wore a thin beard on his chin and a tattered shirt in brown over his body; the customary knife and scabbard of the Ingessana tribesmen lay against his arm sticking out from beneath the torn sleeve of his shirt.

The woman of the group carefully adjusted and balanced a wicker basket, covered with a wicker lid, upon her head.

The younger girl too carried a basket, this one open and holding a muddy jerrycan half full of water from a stream just up the road. The girl had a solemn, quiet beauty; around her neck she wore a pink plastic compact on a string, hanging open and reflecting the world back at itself, a straight crack running across the surface of the glass.

Two of the older boys moved past us and went into the tall grass after their goats, gently rustling it, as the wind did too.

Atop a donkey sat two younger boys, who maneuvered the animal with ease and control beyond their years. Between the boys lay a tiny newborn goat, its umbilical cord still attached and slowly drying out.

Upon spotting this family on the road, we left our vehicles and approached to see how they were doing. The nurse on our team did a quick check to see if anyone was injured or unwell, and fortunately, they all seemed to be physically fine.

We asked them where they were coming from, about what had happened.

The man told us that their village had been bombed. They had fled and been on the road ever since, walking for four days now. He explained that when the bombing began all of the households of their village scattered into the bush, carrying what they could. He didn't know what had become of the others; his family hadn't encountered any of them since.

As we spoke to the family, the woman bounced gently on her knees, rocking the basket above. Her movement wasn't enough, and the shrill cry of a newborn rang out from beneath the wicker lid. The woman cajoled the basket until the baby within fell back to sleep.

We filled up the family's jerrycan with our clean water and told them of a village some ten kilometers down the road. They continued south and we remained on our way north, up toward the border.

We arrived at Guffa at about midday. That left a quick half hour in the village before we had to leave so that we could make it back to base before nightfall. The team quickly carried out an assessment of the village's health-care facilities, water points, and airstrip. Military authorities in the town told us they had been seeing aircraft in the skies to the north for the past week, streaking in and leaving plumes of smoke rising from the earth behind them. Refugees had been coming through the town sporadically, but the authorities couldn't give us a number of how many had passed through recently.

With time running short, we loaded up to make the run back to base.

On the road south it wasn't long before we came upon the refugee family again. As we slowed down to pass them, not so far from where we had first met, the woman gestured for us to stop while the man yelled something to us in Arabic. But our lead car kept moving. I was confused and asked the logistician riding in front what was going on. He told me that the family had called for us to stop and transport their kids with us down the road to the village. I asked him why we didn't. He said our security procedures prohibited us from picking people up, notwithstanding a medical emergency. But there was none here. We had done an assessment and they were physically fine. They would reach the next village on their own by the end of the day. Also we only had space for a few of the kids; if we took them, we would split the family up. And what would we do once we got to the village...just leave them there? I nodded in assent and turned back to the window to watch the tall grass whip by. Still, the thought of that baby in that wicker basket made me question our decision. The family was fine and would make it to the village by the end of the day, but still, it just felt strange to pass by refugees, having fled what they had fled, and keep going. I guess sometimes you can't react to everything you see, and that's a hard lesson to take in.

AGATO

TOKYO, JAPAN

YUKI AIZAWA

I REMEMBER MY auntie Yumi from my childhood as the thin figure at the edge of our family reunions at my grandparents' house in Tokyo. She often appeared alone and late, wearing stiff, narrow jeans tucked inside high-heeled cowboy boots, her arms crossed, shouldering an oversize white sport coat with the collar flipped up. Yumi's hair smelled like perfume and smoke, and ended in loose coils in the middle of her back. She spoke very quickly and glanced at me from under darkly lined lids that rarely wavered in intonation. Her long bangs swept over her brow like a slab of onyx. She often tossed the room a deliciously concealed excuse, "They're waiting, so..." and would skip out early.

Auntie Yumi was not always warm and inviting toward me when I was little, whenever my parents and I had returned to Japan for visits from our own home in the U.S. She had divorced her husband soon after their daughter, Atsuko, was born. Mother and daughter had a rocky relationship throughout Atsuko's adolescence. I would occasionally overhear my mother's soothing Japanese over the phone late at night as she comforted her niece half way around the world in Japan. I sensed that Yumi resented my mother's closeness to Atsuko and reacted by distancing herself from us.

The few times we were alone together, however, Auntie Yumi took great pleasure in teaching me things. On one of my childhood visits to Japan, she spent days showing me how to make miniature stuffed animals from colored felt and cotton wadding. We sat at the vanity table in her bedroom, the heavy brown drapes shutting out the afternoon sun (she never rose before noon), and she taught me how to thread the needle and make the stitches identical. These were skills I already knew, but I copied her carefully, nervous and thrilled by the intimacy of this lesson.

On some occasions together, Yumi would simply impart imperatives: "You received this straight black hair from God, so don't dye it or perm it, and keep it long." While I would later impulsively cut and dye my hair throughout high school and college, her words always remained like little pearls stored in the back of my mind. It wasn't terribly important advice, but being the tomboy that I was, Yumi's voice rung with a feminine wisdom as though taken from an age-old canon of womanhood. From others, I've heard scraps of it before: "Don't leave the house without lipstick," or "Eat a light snack before the barbecue." But her instruction was something I could hold on to, something I felt was meant for me.

When I was an older teenager and in town, Yumi began to invite me to her house under the pretext of watching a television special or a baseball game. We would sit at the kitchen table, under a dim hanging lamp, together in front of a diminishing bottle of champagne. The kitchen was also Rikka's domain, the pet bird that resided in a white cage. Yumi also took care of Momoko, the cat who lived upstairs in her bedroom. Atsuko had brought the cat home from the street when she was in high school.

"I bought the bird so that Atsuko could learn the value of life when she was little. It was a way to teach her that suicide was not an option." Yumi gazed at Rikka as he danced in front of his mirror, which was plastered with little broken seeds. "Rikka thinks the reflection is his wife. When he eats, he feeds her too. And he jerks off on it."

On my first return to Tokyo after college, I went to work for Yumi at Agato, a small members-only bar and snack club she had started by herself ten years earlier. Since Atsuko moved to Paris five years before, Yumi had been living alone. Daily she shuttled from her house to the grocery store, to Agato, and back. She worked Tuesday through Saturday, from six in the evening, late until the last guest left. Her only employee was a college senior who was about to embark on the grueling job application process and would be quitting soon. Since I was only working part-time at an English-speaking newspaper and teaching English at my grandfather's factory, I felt obligated to come in and help Yumi once a week.

Agato was in the Azabu-Juban district of Tokyo, the more subdued and posh neighbor to Roppongi. The latter was notorious for catering to foreigners and businessmen with its many nightspots, where men could come enjoy their drinks in the company of pleasing women employed by the bar. Some places hired only Japanese women, others Russian, Australian, or Southeast Asian. When the drinking nears an end, a man and a woman may leave together, or he might pay for her hefty cab fare home, or they might simply go their separate ways. Yumi liked to remind people that Agato was not that type of establishment. It was a place where her friends could come to drink and relax after a hard day's work, where even women could come alone to drink in peace, like an extension of her living room. "A salon," she'd say.

The interior of Agato was long and narrow, with one heavily frosted window by the entrance, and a dark gray carpet with splatter stains of the occasional drinks spilled. Near the door stood a small television on rollers, wired to a large black karaoke machine. Upholstered sectional couches and polished black tables lined the facing wall. Between the couches and the tiny kitchen in back ran the wooden bar, dotted with little glass bowls of candies and pickled plums from the tree in my grandmother's garden. There were champagne flutes stuffed with forgotten cigarettes. Behind the bar, the shelves were lit from below by soft fluorescent beams, which set the rows of spotless tumblers and high-ball glasses purring, illuminating the colorful liqueurs that were gathering a film of sticky dust. Square Suntory whiskey bottles sat behind the bar on the far end, little gold chains around their necks carrying the nametags of the regulars.

Opposite the bar, a tall chest of drawers housed an assortment of party toys for Agato's more adventurous guests: blond wigs, Afro wigs, party hats, a tambourine, sequined bow ties, and a pair of green swim briefs with a gold faucet sprouting from the crotch. Those briefs were once donned by a drunken Honda executive, over his slacks, during a particularly inspired karaoke performance. Yumi also kept several old photo albums and yearbooks on hand, which she sometimes pulled out to show her more frequent clients, many whom were fellow classmates or graduates of Keio University, one of the best schools in Tokyo.

In the club's dim interior, under the guise of work, I felt comfortable with Yumi. When she found herself in a position to disclose information to me, her eyes lit up. On slow nights, if the weather was bad and no one came in, she would stand behind the bar and nurse her favorite drink of whiskey diluted with iced oolong tea, and she would let me sit at the bar and drink my beer. We smoked Mild Sevens and as her inebriation deepened, she turned nostalgic. Sometimes we would put the television on and work together on various craft projects Yumi had accumulated: gluing champagne corks to the outside of cardboard tubes to make an umbrella stand, or cutting up old calendars to use as notebooks.

"I can't throw things away," she would say. Other times she showed me the old pictures of her and her sisters playing on riverbanks on summer vacation, or wearing tidy dresses in a tableau in the garden. I was shocked to see how plain she always looked. In these photos, Reiko, the eldest sister, is a brooding waif, my mother is a beaming tomboy, and Miko is clearly the adored baby of the four. But Yumi is nearly invisible. Even the picture in her college yearbook, where she received a master's degree in library sciences, shows a sober and sullen girl with no trace of make-up and a thin smile. She took delight in my surprise at seeing the picture, "I was so studious! I never went to parties."

One day Yumi relayed the story of her ex-husband, whom she had married almost immediately after she graduated from college. She liked him because he was gorgeous, brilliant, and tall.

"Over six foot you know," she would say, uncrossing one arm and marking his height in the air above her head. While they were dating, he would pick Yumi up in a sports car and drive her out of Tokyo to the Kamakura coast and strum guitar for her on the beach. She quit her job when he proposed. It was her first relationship, and she was blissful. But it was not long after she gave birth to Atsuko that he began to verbally abuse her.

"Do you want to know what he said to me?" Her speech was slurred now but her eyes were glinting beneath her dark lids. "He said, 'I married you so I wouldn't have to pay for sex.' Unbelievable, isn't it?"

She remembered going to his mother's house for the first time, to help him move into an apartment. His mother handed him a plastic bag with a handful of rice. When she saw that, she said she realized for the first time how poor they were.

After he hit her for the first time, Yumi divorced him and took Atsuko, who was only five. He was never present in his daughter's life again.

"*Never* let anyone hit you."

"No, I know." It seemed like an obvious answer, but later I've thought how easily I have stayed in relationships for the wrong reasons, and how days can mount into years. Perhaps, if I had been born a generation earlier, I may not have replied with such certainty.

Several years ago, Yumi's ex-husband had heard about Agato and dropped in unannounced with his two sisters. "Do you know what I did? I looked him straight in the eye and said, 'I'm sorry, have we met?' Because I honestly didn't recognize him, I had just blocked him out. He gave me his business card. They had a drink and then left."

After their divorce, Yumi changed her and Atsuko's name back to her maiden name, and went to work for my grandfather's company. She started going out at night and dated a string of men. Once, when we were drunkenly going through her closet at home, she pulled out a gorgeous black floor-length coat with an asymmetrical collar. "This is so cool!" I exclaimed, hoping she would offer it to me.

"That was from my partying days. You know how to wear that? You wear it on a date with some heels and nothing underneath." The coat was never offered. It was too tight anyway.

It was also around this time that tensions began to rise between the sisters. For as long as I can remember, my oldest aunt, Reiko, and her husband, Tsuneyo, have been the least visible of my relatives. They were strangely distant and cold. If I saw them at all, it was usually when my parents weren't around. Growing up, Reiko would sometimes pop up in dinner conversations between my parents and my aunts Yumi and Miko. In my presence, the topic would inevitably be cut short with, "She doesn't need to know. This is between our generation," though I often begged my mother to tell me. As an only child, the fierceness of sibling rivalry was somewhat of a mystery.

Even in recent years Reiko has made up thin excuses to avoid seeing us. "I would invite you in but somebody's taking a nap on the living room couch," she once said to my mother and me through the half-opened front door when we dropped by on our way to my grandparents' house. Reiko only maintained regular contact with her parents, dropping off chocolates or a homemade pound cake wrapped in a doily every week.

"Tsuneyo-san is the cancer of the family," Auntie Yumi once said. He started working for my grandfather after he married Reiko. He was smart and ambitious, from a working-class family, and put himself through Keio for a degree in business. At Tsuneyo's request, my grandfather sent him to earn a master of business degree at Stanford under the agreement that he would return back to work for the factory again. Husband and wife enjoyed their new life in California and started a family, all with the full financial support of my grandfather. When they returned to Japan, Tsuneyo wanted to pursue his doctorate. My grandfather refused to pay for this degree, a master's was plenty for his company. Tsuneyo was hurt and began to slander my grandfather to other employees, some of whom believed him. Tsuneyo was asked to leave the company.

Reiko and Tsuneyo highly disapproved of Yumi's divorce. They frowned upon her newly acquired freedom, and they were embarrassed by her late-night outings and boyfriends, and even the way she dressed. Tsuneyo was infuriated by the fact that Yumi was now working full-time for the family company and had even taken over some of his old affairs.

"They used to say I looked like a prostitute." Yumi raised her eyebrows and smiled down at her drink. "But you know what? When they were first married, I know Tsuneyo liked me. Once when Reiko was away, he was staying with his mother. I dropped by to bring them some rice cakes or something, and she said to me, "Tsuneyo should have married you Yumi. And he just smirked!"

One night, a few years after he left the company, Tsuneyo called my grandparents saying he had urgent information about Yumi. He claimed she had been sleeping with Miko's husband, and my own father, and even one of our cousins. They easily dismissed the accusation. Tsuneyo insisted that he had photos of these men leaving her house. "Of course they come by!" Yumi said in reply. "We're family, we visit each other!" Since then, Reiko and her family rarely come to visit my grandparents.

Learning this, I could scarcely believe that the incident dividing the sisters was something so childish. I had imagined far worse.

Reiko never spoke up in her sister's defense. Neither Yumi nor her sisters could completely forgive her for it. But they couldn't totally blame her either. Something had happened, they all thought, some change in Reiko since she got married. Yumi told me that when Reiko was in high school she painted incredible pictures. "Just amazing," she said, in that memory finding some forgiveness.

When the little gold bell on Agato's front door jingled, Yumi would drop her cigarette and walk toward the entrance with a smile, "*Irasshaimase! Welcome!*" Her normally low voice immediately rose in pitch and she waved them inside. I would come out from behind the bar so she could introduce me.

"This is my niece from America. She just graduated from Columbia University." This received "oohs" of recognition as Columbia had become popular recently; and after the Japanese pop idol Utada Hikaru enrolled, there seemed to be a surge in Japanese tourists on campus.

After guests were seated, I would fetch a hot towel from the electric towel warmer and offer it unrolled. I'd set down the little chopsticks on holders Yumi made from old champagne corks. Then I'd bring out small dishes of candies or nuts, a glass bucket of ice, and their bottle of whiskey with water or tea to mix. I was always concerned that the drink I mixed was too watery or too strong for the discerning businessmen, or if I had forgotten which way the chopsticks need to point.

Often the customers wanted us to sit with them when they drank. "*Mama-san!*" they would say, which is the endearing term for the female proprietor of bars and clubs, "Come have a drink with us!" "Sing with us!" Yumi would always happily oblige, but she would say to me, "It makes these old men happy to drink with a young girl. Just smile and nod, and say things like, 'Oh really, how interesting.' But you don't have to if you don't want." I usually obliged and sat with them, keeping constant watch to make sure their drinks never went empty and that their ashtrays never grew too full. In Japan you never pour your own drink.

This specificity of custom and decorum was a constant source of anxiety for me. The strangest part was that it did not seem to matter whether I was visiting a Shinto shrine or in a smoky bar. I always felt to some degree that there was a slackness in my mannerisms that gave me away as being foreign. I could have been more natural, revealed more of my own personality rather than stubbornly emulating my idea of a proper Japanese girl. Still, I wanted to show that I could grasp the qualities of this country I so greatly admired.

When I met Kataoka-san, one of the Agato regulars, he had just returned from a business trip overseas and was praising, obnoxiously, the features of Indonesian women to my aunt. "They have big, round eyes and perky butts," he said, and then he thrust his hands, palms up, towards his chest. Yumi nodded and laughed politely. Then without looking at me, Kataoka-san asked her, "She isn't...is she?"

"No. This isn't that kind of place." Her response was uncharacteristically stern.

When Kataoka-san discovered I was American, he insisted that I sing with him. Yumi hoisted up the karaoke songbook from behind the bar. It was thicker than a Bible. We sang a Beatles medley. It was one of the few English selections in the outdated system that I could sing along with, but the songs kept changing so quickly it was difficult to keep up. Kataoka-san snapped his fingers and flicked his wrists steadily to an imperceptible beat, booming the words while he inched his rocking hips closer to me.

In Japan I had come to accept karaoke as an important social function and had been doing my best to improve. I could sing in pitch but my voice didn't seem to project.

"Hey, you've got to sing louder! And get into it a little more, move your hips like this." I squirmed out of Kataoka-san's grasp and kept singing. He seemed to think I was incapable of having fun because I was not having fun with him. He kept trying to hold my hand.

Yumi came out from the bar to bat his hand out of my direction.

"You can't touch her, understand?" Then to me she said, "You don't have to sing anymore, you can rest for a while."

Kataoka-san turned his back to me and kept singing at the monitor. Yumi joined him and let him take her hand.

I retired to the cramped kitchen to smoke and stare at the stacks of little dishes and plastic bins, which, though numerous and slightly mismatched, were faintly organized on the metal shelves. The yellow light in the kitchen was refreshing after the dimness of the bar, and I picked up my Japanese character textbook and practiced some *kanji* until I heard the door chime again as Kataoka-san took his leave.

A very different man, Terada-san, was my favorite of the regulars. He would sit hunched over the bar eating Yumi's curry with rice or her pork cutlet sandwiches. I'd watch him twist his gentle face into complaints of how "awful" her cooking was, saying, "This sandwich is so *mazui*! Why do you put so much butter on? You're going to kill me." He would make her laugh.

When other clients came in to sing and drink at the tables, Terada-san did not join. I never saw him in a suit, and his calm demeanor encouraged me to prod him with general questions.

"How was golf today?"

"Golf? Terrible. No good courses around Tokyo."

"How is your son?"

"Aw, he's no good. He's with his mother. She spoils him."

If no one else came in, Terada-san insisted on buying Yumi and my drinks, even though we always had a drink in hand regardless. Once, Yumi flipped the news on and together we all watched footage of the tsunami that hit Indonesia. The news clip showed the wave after it reached inland. It was a slow moving wall of debris.

"Every day I think, 'I'm so lucky just to be able to live life normally.'" Yumi ashed into the self-cleaning ashtray. "I hear those islands were like heaven on earth. I wish I could have gone there."

"A lot of other beautiful places to go on this earth," Terada-san said. "Close the bar for a week. Take a vacation."

"I can't do that," Yumi told us. "I have to take care of the bird and the cat. They're so particular. They've never left the house."

Another regular, Keiko-chan usually arrived at the bar early, just after dinner. She was a close friend of Yumi's. Keiko-chan had recently survived uterine cancer and also divorced her husband, a well-known economist. She'd pop in whenever she was in the neighborhood and slip behind the bar to help out or pour her own drinks, sometimes she'd have a light smoke. She was a slight woman who dressed in flashy, girlish clothes while still exuding a sense of charm and sophistication. She was easy to talk to, and her smiles spread and faded slowly.

One evening another woman, Choko-chan, came in on Keiko's heels, already drunk and in a glittering black outfit that seemed to serve her the opposite effect as Keiko's, but she was so loud and grating that it wouldn't have mattered. She had a daughter a little older than me who lived with her in a sand-colored gated condo nearby. The daughter often called Choko-chan while she was at Agato late at night and demanded that she come home. Like many successful young "career girls," as the Japanese referred to them, the daughter threw herself into work and desired the comfort of awakening to a home-cooked breakfast before entering the corporate world each day.

It was the end of April, just before the string of national holidays that make up "Golden Week." Yumi was closing the bar for the week for a much needed break and had invited several of the regulars to celebrate. The three women sat at the tables and discussed their holiday plans. I brought Choko-chan her usual bottle of wine, chilled in a bucket of ice.

They soon unhitched the microphones and began to sing their favorite songs: melancholic lyrics of lost love within simple melodies from the '70s and '80s. Keiko and Yumi had taught me a few of these ballads, including *"Jinsei Iroiro,"* "Life Is So Varied." They delighted in hearing me sing lyrics about complicated emotions.

"It's sexy when you sing these songs," my aunt would say, "because you're so young, and you can't possibly know what they mean."

Then the little bell rang, and I heard Yumi's greetings strained over the singing. "Oh, what a surprise! Please come in!"

Two short, plump women conservatively dressed stood in the entrance. I recognized one as Kazuko-san, an old friend of my parents' who first introduced them back when they were all studying at colleges in Pennsylvania. Kazuko worked as an interpreter at an office nearby. She was not very close to Yumi, but they had met several times over the years.

The two ladies sat at the other end of the couches, and brief introductions were made. The other party was well into their drinks. Kazuko explained how she knew Yumi and me, and how she had set up my parents. Hiraoka-san, another regular and an old classmate of Yumi's who had slipped in while I was in the back, replied, "Oh, so in other words, you are the person who made Yuki." He raised his glass to her and went on drinking.

A tall, heavy-set man who Yumi apparently knew very well came in soon after. His shiny hair was slicked back to show a widow's peak. He sat down alone at the bar and seemed amused by the singers.

The night deepened and Yumi was in high spirits. Then on her way back to the bar Yumi tripped on a wrinkle in the carpet and fell face down on the floor, her thin legs folded neatly behind her. Her eyes were crumpling and she did not get up for what seemed like a couple minutes. The room fell silent and I suddenly felt the weight of sinking drunken revelry on my shoulders. I remember going to her but do not recall whether she needed my help, or if she leaned her weight on me to make it back to the tables. But once she sat down again she began apologizing to the guests and to me.

"*Gomen ne.*" She was rubbing her little knees and started to cry, "I'm sorry. I'm sorry."

"What are you talking about?" Choko-chan blurted. "I fall down drunk in my bathroom all the time! Yuki, go get your aunt another drink."

The table continued to drink and sing at a lower tone. Yumi went back to the man at the bar and sat on the stool next to him. It was almost one in the morning, and I started cleaning out ashtrays and soaking empty glasses.

Yumi was crying on the man's shoulder. "My sisters, they all have good husbands, but Yumi is all alone. But I have this place, I have Agato, you see?" She looked at me over the bar with swimming eyes. "*Wakaru?* Do you understand?"

I nodded as sympathetically as I could.

"What are you telling her for? She's just a kid!" The man scolded, not unkindly.

Yumi went on, "I work so hard. I come here every day. I clean my whole house to show my gratitude and respect, you know?"

Yuko-san approached me to settle the bill. I had never written one up. Yumi always calculated it toward the end of the night, scribbling down the drinks and dishes from her memory with her little reading glasses on. I was only vaguely aware of her pricing system, and I was flustered after my aunt's fall. I eased my own brief panic with a thought that perhaps it was customary not to charge if the proprietor falls down drunk and starts weeping. But I wrote up a slightly discounted check, for which she handed me her cash with a grave look. It seemed to suggest less concern for Yumi and more offense of her behavior. I scowled at the back of Yuko-san's round head as I followed them out, and then held the door for her, bowing, thanking, and apologizing as she left.

"Good-bye, person who made Yuki," Hiraoka-san called out.

Yumi, after lamenting with her good friends, was in a jovial mood again and had finally resolved to pour more oolong tea than whiskey in her drink.

The guests, recognizing that Yumi was back to herself again, started handing me bills. The man Yumi had been crying on gave me a 5,000 yen tip.

We took a cab home with Hiraoka-san and Keiko. The driver, a young man in his thirties, was a former barkeep at Agato. Yumi kept in touch with him and gave him customers, and in turn he reduced their fares.

Yumi sat wedged between Hiraoka-san and me in the backseat. Keiko, in the front seat, leaned her own head back and dozed off. Yumi and Hiraoka elbowed each other and played like children.

"What'd you say?"

"I didn't say anything."

"What?"

"What?"

My stop was first and I stepped out of the taxi into a cool, misty night. I padded silently up the stairs of my grandparents house and passed out on my bed. Yumi probably did the same, stopping to greet her bird in the kitchen, then flopping down on her bed without changing.

She would sleep soundly through the night, with Momoko the cat curled at her side.

A HAIRCUT

AUSTRALIA, INDONESIA, CAMBODIA, AND TAIWAN

LISA DAZOLS

FOR THE PAST five years, I've gotten my hair cut by Julie at Nice Cuts in the heart of San Francisco's Castro District. The whole process takes little effort on my part. In the gayborhood, Julie probably cuts about eight fohawks every day. I can drop by without an appointment, she takes fifteen minutes to do her magic on my head, and I fork over the usual twenty dollars.

When I decided to backpack around the world for a year, I knew that I would have to let go of many comfortable routines, but I had no idea that getting a haircut would lead to such a cultural experience each month. I got my last haircut from Julie a day before leaving San Francisco, so that it would last the maximum time.

My hair starts getting shaggy in Sydney, where I have difficulty finding a haircut for less than forty dollars. Luckily, I find a young woman in a mall salon who says that she watches a lot of *Ellen* and understands what I want. She charges me twenty-five dollars, and I like what I see. I'm reminded how much I feel indebted to Ellen for making the butch lesbian look so cool these days.

Four weeks later I'm in Java, Indonesia, and have two hours to get a haircut before leaving for the airport. I walk into a spa where there's a sign that advertises a two-dollar haircut. A young man seats me in his salon chair and studies my head. I point to a man's haircut on the wall, among all the sample photos of hairstyles. The stylist tells me that because I am a woman I should not have a haircut like that one. I tell him not to worry.

The stylist doesn't wet my hair or use special scissors. He looks at me, and starts to sweat nervously. He confesses that he has never cut a Westerner's hair before. I wonder to myself why all the sample photos of hairstyles on his wall are of Western models.

With great pains, this man cuts about five of my hairs at a time. The only time he starts cutting fast is when I point to my watch, and then he decisively cuts off my lady burns, the one area around my ears that I've asked him to keep. He can tell by my face that he has made a mistake, and he gives me a look of panic. The social worker in me tries to console him. "Don't worry, it is only hair. It will grow back." He takes a full two hours to finish.

My hair grows back and one month later I am in Cambodia. I walk into a salon, this time with a new strategy for my three-dollar haircut. I whip out my laptop and show the young woman a slideshow of photos of me back home in San Francisco. She snips away furiously fast. She also takes off far more hair than I expected. I can see how Cambodians get their money's worth for each haircut.

This stylist leaves the back of my hair very long, so I make a *bzzz* sound and mime shaving the back of my neck. She doesn't have an electric razor and takes out a handheld blade that looks like something my grandfather would have used in 1920. After shaving the back of my neck, the woman then moves on to shave little hairs on my ears that I didn't even know I had. Before I can blink, she proceeds to shave my face. As the stylist scrapes away on my cheeks and forehead, I wonder if she knows I am a girl. I am shocked at the thirty-two years of peach fuzz she has managed to collect.

Having pretty much given up on ever having good hair during this year abroad, I dread getting my hair cut in Taiwan. On my own I had already accidently dyed my hair black when I bought a box of hair color with the instructions all in Japanese.

Anyway, I decide to give it a try with a young guy working at a salon advertising twenty-dollar haircuts. This guy, he gives me one of the best haircuts of my life. First he starts with an amazing fifteen-minute shoulder and neck rub, done with Tiger Balm. Then he walks me over to a massage table where I lie down for full-body vibrations. After, the stylist pulls a visor over my eyes so I can rest while his coworker massages my head and washes my hair with three different shampoos. I then sit in a chair where the receptionist hands me a latte and turns on MTV on a personal flat-screen TV. I feel like a movie star when this man blow-dries and then styles my hair with spritz, gel, and hair spray. High on fumes, I don't want to leave his chair.

Many times, I've considered giving up on getting haircuts while traveling. I've thought about saving money and taking my own stab at it. But then again, a haircut can be one of your most intimate interactions with other people when you travel. And really, isn't that the whole point of going abroad?

LIVING ON THE EDGE OF CHANGE

CHINA

SIERRA ROSS GLADFELTER

THE RAIN, WHICH has been falling all day in the lower villages, crystallizes and coats the ground with a thick sheet of ice. Glacial mountains morph in and out of the gloom behind shagged yaks that nuzzle through the snow to graze on the remains of late autumn stubble. In the valleys below, herders' tents are pitched. A whisper of dung smoke rises on the damp air as the only evidence of their presence. As our bus descends into the valley where Taktsang Lhamo is cupped in a yoke of snow-encrusted mountains, the rest of China raises its flags in honor of the National Holiday.

This week, the Chinese pay homage to the People's Republic of China (P.R.C.), glorifying Mao and other Communist revolutionaries. It is ironic that as the rest of the nation celebrates, my boyfriend, Eben, and I are fleeing the city to find peace on the Tibetan plateau. We have heard that more than a thousand nomads still herd yaks on the plains above Taktsang Lhamo and live in tents for three seasons of the year. We imagine that if any place has escaped the thrust of China's development, it is here.

This village is not like the city where we live and teach. In Mianyang, a city swollen with more than five million people, the skyline is dominated more by cranes than by the ragged teeth of finished skyscrapers. The sound of steel being cut announces each dawn, and lakes of poured concrete harden every day across Sichuan Province. Whole cities have risen overnight, like slumbering giants standing up and stretching toward the sun. Still, this region has only recently become China's "heartland," as the government summons settlers into the country's core. For centuries it was fringe, the margin on which the Han people traditionally lived.

We are searching for this limit, as the motor of our bus strains against the incline. Our hope this week is to reach the borderland between the Sichuan and Gansu Provinces, and then descend back to our city through a circuitous string of Tibetan villages tucked into the eaves of mountains.

The towns in our guidebook are listed in both Chinese and Tibetan: Xia He, *Labrung*; Langmusi, *Taktsang Lhamo*. Here, there are almost no P.R.C. flags flying, and many residents would never identify themselves as Chinese. The people who live, and have lived here for centuries, are Tibetans. Their country, which once included the territories of Kham, Utsang, and Amdo, is now politically fractured between the borders of Nepal, Bhutan, the Tibetan Autonomous Region (T.A.R.), and other less-restricted western provinces of China.

The Tibetans in Sichuan and Gansu, though not from Tibet as the Chinese define it, are for the most part, less constrained; this is due to their incorporation into China's heartland and their lack of "rebellious" status as an autonomous region. In fact, in several temples across the region we find pictures of the Dalai Lama tucked away into quiet chambers where the Chinese soldiers will not come looking.

On the outskirts of Taktsang Lhamo, hotels have risen along with the Chinese middle class. They provide accommodation for the Chinese tourists that have begun to roll into town during the last few years with their digital cameras and designer wilderness gear.

Alongside the rising hotels is another form of construction—or, perhaps more accurately, a rebuilding of the past. High on the hills at either end of the village are the fortress-like temples of two monasteries. Their gold and silver roofs gleam in the afternoon light, and as we walk around the grounds, the air burns with the smell of fresh paint.

Although their footprints are ancient, these monasteries, like most of China's religious structures, were razed during the Cultural Revolution. Only in the 1980s and 1990s did the people of Taktsang Lhamo summon the necessary freedom and funds to start rebuilding their most sacred temples. The hillsides are trampled with mud from constant construction, as structure by structure, ancient scenes are brought back to life.

In the vicious afternoon sun and gentle breeze, prayer flags undulate overhead as we wander up the packed, red-dirt alleys through the monastic quarters. Huge, curtains painted with the bowed heads of deer billow in the falling air. The sun is out and flashing off the snowy mountains and gilded eaves of the monastery. A monk, moved by the fact that we remove our shoes before ducking into his temple, leads us through the shrines. Before we leave, he has us pose before a vibrant fresco for a photo on his iPhone.

It is here in Taktsang Lhamo that we find the front on which the ancient and modern meet.

Tired of the crowds of tourists, we stumble across a sign—WIND HORSE TREKKING—painted on the wall of a shop stall. Three minutes after we dial the number, a Tibetan man comes to meet us on his motorcycle and escorts us back to his office to work out the details. Within an hour, we have made plans for a two-day horse trek into nomad country around Taktsang Lhamo.

The next morning, we are delivered to our horses and young guide, Tendor, whom we are told nothing about except for the fact that he does not know a word of English. His face, despite the raw red lick of sun and cold, shows the youth of a teenager.

Once on horseback, we follow Tendor out of town, weaving upstream along the White Dragon River. He is dressed in a *chupa* (the traditional Tibetan fleece-lined robe) and a black mask that makes him look like a pirate as he rides ahead, slumped over on his steed. Later, when he grows warm and sheds his sleeves, we discover that beneath his traditional garb he is wearing a Phoenix Suns basketball jersey.

Tendor is constantly bowed forward, talking into his cell phone, which blasts back static. I imagine he is talking with his sweetheart back in the village. Occasionally, he lifts his gaze to assess our progress or to catch the attention of his dog, Japo, who limps at our side.

We stop for lunch at the neck of the valley where spring water gushes from limestone formations. This is the source of the White Dragon River. White *katak* scarves have been knotted around the stones, and tattered flags trail into the stream. There are two herders' tents pitched in a meadow, sides painted with never-ending, blue Tibetan knots. A lone man brings noodle soup and tea to us, as we draw bright yellow plastic chairs up to a little table. The cook has a solar panel hooked to a battery and a stereo, blasting Chinese rap music. We assume this is more for the two Chinese tourists who hiked up the valley this morning, than it is for us. With so many tourists to cook for, we wonder how much herding this man does.

From the herder's tent, we turn cross-country and ride through hills that roll like green waves into the distance. Our destination is a pass, high above the soggy meadows where blue trumpet flowers bloom.

In the afternoon, Tendor hangs up his phone. Even though he cannot speak English or understand much of Eben's Tibetan (Tendor speaks Amdo dialect, and Eben speaks Lhasa dialect), he makes an effort to interact with us. Tendor drops from his horse to fetch us boughs from a shrubby bush, which is covered in leathery, orange berries. He motions for us to pluck them off and pop the sour, half-fermented capsules into our mouths. The prickly twigs cut our faces as we try to imitate Tendor, who removes the berries with his lips.

We communicate to Tendor the English word "slowly" when he attempts to comment on Eben's old horse dragging in the rear. Promptly, Tendor switches from singing his lilting herding songs in Tibetan to adapting the phrase "slowly, slowly, SLOW-LEEE!" for the tune. Later he serenades us, proud of his repertoire of English songs, which includes Justin Bieber's "Baby" and The Alphabet Song. We laugh heartily and even join in with only yaks to judge to our singing.

On the other side of the pass, the landscape opens up to wide, uplifted plains of auburn grass. Mountains rise like tables in the distance, and an alpine stream carves a deep ribbon into the black earth. The valley is swollen with animals feeding. Black bodies of bowed yaks are sprinkled across the fields into the horizon. I cannot help but think that this is what bison must have once looked like, grazing on the plains of Montana, before the American West was settled and hunted bare.

The bruised sky threatens to storm as we weave among the yaks. Some are shy and snort, startled by our horses. Others stare, perturbed by our intrusion into their mountain solitude. It starts to hail. Ice pellets bounce off our saddles and into the dense wool of the yaks' shoulders.

Lowering our heads, we cross to the first nomad camp. As we approach, large dogs roped to stakes begin barking and we skirt the margins of their claim.

Tendor's tent is last in the cluster. It is raining by the time we dismount and unsaddle the horses. Tendor motions for us to enter the flap door to his tent. I notice that the poles supporting his home are held together at their joints by the vertebrae of perished yaks.

Inside, an iron stove occupies the center of the space. At the far end, a few wooden planks have been arranged on wads of sod to create a kitchen. The bed is made from sheets of earth that have been piled up, more at one end to compensate for the incline. A padded tarp has been laid down on top. All that is missing is a sign: HOME, SWEET HOME.

We are invited to sit as Tendor scoops a shovelful of dried yak dung from a massive pile and starts a fire in the stove. He places a large teakettle on top to hold in heat. Occasionally, when the flames begin to die, he shovels more manure in with his bare hands.

The dung heap has quite a presence, consuming at least a quarter of the tent and serving not only as a readily accessible source of fuel, but also a counter upon which clothing, phones, and large bricks of yak butter wrapped in cloths are stored. I notice that Tendor's solar panel propped outside the tent is attached to a battery, and that he even has a satellite dish and small flat-screen TV.

Passing us two empty jam jars, he pours us tea when the water is ready.

Not long after we arrive, a woman kicks up the door flap and ducks into the tent. It is Tendor's young wife. She is beautiful and wears a full chupa, silver-studded belt, and chunky coral earrings. Her long black braids are bound together at the tips. She bears a bag of assorted biscuits, grapes, and a two-liter bottle of Pepsi that she has brought from town. They insist on pouring out our tea and replacing it with Pepsi. I cannot help but wonder if this is what they drink themselves or if it is a kind gesture to the assumed taste of two Americans. Perhaps this was all decided over cell phone conversations earlier in the day.

After a snack, Tendor and his wife duck out of the tent to collect and secure the yaks before dusk. The herd has already gathered where the grass is burned with urine, but each calf and cow must be tethered to a long line running between wooden pegs planted in the hillside. A few of the yak calves prove difficult to catch, and we chase them through their mothers' legs until someone can grab hold of the calves' fleecy necks and fasten their toggles to the line.

Tendor's wife cooks us dinner when we return to the tent. Replacing the teapot with a wok, she fries cabbage, scallions, and noodles, which are served over rice.

As night sets in, Eben and I try to bridge the language gap by fumbling with the few words of Chinese and Tibetan we know to ask about our hosts and their lives. We discover that Tendor is only nineteen, and his wife is twenty—and five months pregnant. Already humbled by the intensity of their demanding lifestyle, we are moved by our hosts' youth. Only twenty-two ourselves, and still "kids" by American standards, Eben and I find ourselves struggling to fall asleep as the two of them and the two of us lay on opposite sides of the woodstove. Despite our proximity in the tiny tent, the difference between our lives and theirs cannot feel vaster.

The dogs bark all night as frost glazes their fur.

Tendor and his wife rise at 6:30 a.m. and put away the bedding. It is time for milking.

This is a job for Tendor's wife, who has fifty to sixty animals to tend to. Her method is to unclip one calf and let it run to its mother, until its suckling causes the cow's udder to descend. Then, she yanks the calf away and pegs it to the half-frozen ground a meter away. Squatting by the cow's shaggy belly, she grabs the udder—squeezing a stream of thick milk into a metal pail. As Tendor's wife works her way up the string of yaks, we watch with numb fingers and stamp our feet against the cold.

Still steaming in the bucket, Tendor's wife brings the milk inside to separate later with a hand-cranked strainer. Grabbing headphones and an iPod, which she tucks inside her chupa, she shoulders a basket that is attached to a strap around her collar. The basket is for collecting dung to dry and store for fuel, that the animals have dropped overnight. She slings manure over her shoulder with a pitchfork, and it lands each time with a heavy smack as her pregnant frame buckles briefly under the impact.

Meanwhile, her husband is up on the hillside counting sheep. He and another man are running the herd across the hillside, counting as the animals run through the bottleneck between them.

When he has finished, Tendor warms us bowls of fresh yak milk over the dung stove. He prepares bowls for *tsampa*, a Tibetan staple meal. First, Tendor brings out a wooden box divided into two chambers: one with the powdered barley flour and the other with yak butter. Using a wooden scraper we shave ribbons of the pungent fat into our bowls and then sprinkle in dried yak cheese from a bag sewn out of goat hide. The hair is still imbedded in the leather. We mix this with warm milk and knead the flour into a dense paste.

Our kneading does not meet Tendor's standard, so he takes our bowls and digs into them with dung-rimmed fingernails. In the end, he forms a potato-sized wad of dough that we bite into like an apple between slurps of yak milk. Neither Eben nor I can finish, so we are given the blue baggie that the biscuits came in, while Tendor's wife saddles the horses outside.

After saying farewell to Tendor's wife, we ride down the valley to the highway that leads into town. It is hard not to feel disappointed leaving the mountains. From the shoulder of the road trucks and buses roar by, and carloads of tourists nearly cause accidents as they hang out of their windows to take pictures of us. Two Americans and a Tibetan on horseback seem as much of an attraction as the magnificent landscape. We try to leave the road, but are blocked by fences where the pastureland has been divided among villages by the Chinese government. We return to the road. It is our only way back.

Gold-toothed Tibetan men with thick, black hair licking their ears and dense chupas belted around their hips fly by on motorcycles. Many nomads, we learn, have taken to herding their yaks on motorbike rather than horse for the same reasons we find ourselves on the road. With an expanding highway system, swelling traffic, and land fragmentation, riding a motorcycle is increasingly safer and more convenient than a horse.

Finally, we reach Taktsang Lhamo by cutting across the mountain behind the village sky burial grounds. The ridge is covered with tattered prayer flags and the shreds of souls.

At the end of our journey, we return to the monastery. The paint has not yet dried. As we walk *kora* around its base, I think of Tendor and his wife and all the things we were unable to ask them. I wonder what their hopes and dreams may be. Although they grew up in tents, following their families' herds up and down the valleys, I wonder what their own son or daughter, born this winter, will grow up to choose. Will the child continue to find sustenance in the mountain pastures, or move to a city like Mianyang where life is kinder?

Knowing that this question can be asked of millions across China, I thrust my weight into spinning the heavy, prayer wheels pressed from tin. It is hard not to feel the weight of time spinning along with our weightless prayers that drift over the Plateau.

SABAH

MALAYSIAN BORNEO

ADAM KARLIN

SIGNAL HILL GIVES you a sniper's view onto the port of Kota Kinabalu, second largest city on the island of Borneo and capital of the Malaysian state of Sabah.[1] The simple grid of streets is easy to follow, if deceptively dubbed. Beach street crosses Fashion street, which is ironic, as Kota Kinabalu, which everyone calls KK, has neither, unless you count Foot Locker knockoffs as fashion and the *E. coli* dip off Tanjung Aru a beach. Still, there is a cerulean band of the South China Sea out there, layered under a matching ribbon of turquoise sky. Breast-ish humps of jungly overgrowth, the islands of Tunku Abdul Rahman National Park, blot the horizon.

But mainly what you see from Signal Hill is buildings and poor urban planning and buildings and McDonald's and KFC and buildings and new-car lots and buildings. You can see spindly *kampong ayer*— water villages, the traditional stilt-like dwellings of the Malay people— and the effluence that comes out of them, contaminating the nearby sea. You see old Chinese brothels sandwiched between empty malls, and you see cars: many, many cars.

---

1 Quick geography lesson: Borneo is an island divided between three countries—Malaysia, Indonesia, and tiny Brunei. This story takes place in Sabah, one of the two provinces (along with Sarawak) that makes up Malaysian Borneo.

Locals say there are ghosts on Signal Hill. I never asked what kind. Maybe they're the indigenous *balan-balan*, a detached female head that flies about trailing its guts in the air, snacking on placentas and menstrual lining (there is a lot of Freudian psychoanalysis waiting to be applied to the invention of such ghosts, but I am not the man to provide it). More likely, the ghosts here are the wandering souls encountered across Asia, the disturbed dead who were never given proper veneration and now heckle the living for a lack of respect.

I think it likely the ghosts out here are an iteration of wandering souls. Not the spirits of those passed on, but the old, original animist energies that crackled across this land, the powers of the indigenous people of Borneo. Those ghosts did not die per se, but if a soul has a body, the corporeal form of these *kami*—the actual land and sea, forests and mountains that make up Sabah, one of the most beautiful places in the world—is being killed, quickly and efficiently. That said, if the ghosts of this land are mad about its systemic destruction, then they aren't angry enough, because every day the wild spaces of Sabah shrink, and from Signal Hill you have front row seats to view the catastrophe.

At the time of this writing, Swiss investigators were looking into corruption charges at financial services company UBS, accused of laundering some $90 million of illegal timber money connected to Sabah's chief minister Musa Aman. Sabah is often upheld as a success story within Borneo when compared to the neighboring Malaysian state of Sarawak and the Indonesian provinces of Kalimantan, but I found things were not so bright in the place the Malays call "The Land Below the Wind." Ethnic tension, corruption, irresponsible land development and environmental degradation were increasingly common, but so were efforts to battle all of the above. The winners of this war will determine if the KK skyline is built on something sustainable that complements the Eden that surrounds it, or paves the jungle into a concrete, waste-tainted scar.

Joel runs a successful motorbike rental business in Kota Kinabalu. He's a good guy who is positively ferocious when it comes to loving Sabah. Born and raised in Kuala Lumpur, he came to East Malaysia in his early twenties. If you're familiar with American historical-cultural tropes, understand that for many Malaysians, especially those from places like Kuala Lumpur, "East Malaysia" codes as "Wild West." It's the frontier but with more jungle, complete with scary natives in loincloths (who are quite rare in Sabah, but more on that later). In any case, Joel fell in love with this Southeast Asian territory ahead and has never looked back to what he calls, with a bit of derision, "the mainland."

"Look, I grew up in KL [Kuala Lumpur]. I'm a city boy. Then I come here to Borneo, to Sabah. I'd never seen blue sky and blue ocean like this, man. Never seen mountains like this, going so far, right up to the beach. This is paradise. This is heaven. How can I leave?"

Not only did he not leave, he married a local woman and started a business that has the express purpose of showing off Sabah to tourists. You can tell, Joel *loves doing this.* He loves the land he emigrated to, and even more so the chance to promote it. But right now, the city-boy-turned-Sabahan hates his country. He's even reconsidering, à la Fort Sumter, 1861, whether the state of Sabah should remain in Malaysia.

The straw breaks the camel's back while we're driving and listening to a recap of the London 2012 Olympics on the radio. Lee Chong Wei, Malaysia's great Olympic hope, had lost his gold medal badminton match against China's Lin Dan.[2] The morning radio talk shows react to this news with an odd mixture of mourning and delusional optimism.

"Hey. Hey. Look here-la," says the announcer in an accent that muddies American drive-time morning show with Straits Chinese Singlish, "I just want to tell everyone listening to not give up. Don't give

---

2 Wei plays badminton, which at the time of this writing, and along with cycling, was the only sport Malaysians had a chance at medaling in. They are crazy for badminton in Southeast Asia. Matches between Malaysia and regional rivals such as Singapore draw huge crowds—folks stop work to watch the event on outdoor screens and go through mood swings that would shame the most zealous Raiders or Red Sox fans, which is crazy, because it's badminton, and even at a high level of play, it's a little boring.

up hope. *Datuk* Lee Chong Wei is still a hero.[3] A national hero, man. He is a hero to all Malaysians. And you know what? You know what-la? I hear the gold medal is only, like, 10 percent gold. The rest is silver. Ninety percent silver! I'd rather have 100 percent silver, OK?"

I start laughing, but Joel looks annoyed. He flicks off the radio, says, "That's what's wrong with this country, man. We tell ourselves we've won after we've just lost." He's quiet for a minute, then snorts and changes tack on his rant. "Malaysia. Everyone comes out to love the Chinese guy during the Olympics, but if he wasn't good at sports the Malays would treat him like they treat the other Chinese."

"Which is how?"

"Which is shit."

Joel's shift in gripe is unexpected, but not by much. He is a member of Malaysia's most prominent minority, the Chinese Malaysians, a group with no shortage of grievances. To understand them, it helps to know that since the 1970s a series of affirmative action policies known as *bumiputra* laws have been in effect in Malaysia. Their ostensible goal was to create economic and educational parity between the majority Malays and the ethnic Chinese; the latter have traditionally dominated the local economy. The laws created opportunities for Malays that shifted thousands from rice farms to IT offices and high finance in the space of a generation.

But today, even beneficiaries of the bumiputra movement admit the system is abused, and that the ways bumiputra status is determined has become problematic at best, if not downright plagued by corruption at worst. Stories abound of "professional bumiputra," ethnic Malays who hire themselves out to sit on various boards or ink their names on founding charters so companies can claim bumiputra, government entitlements. The biggest beneficiaries of the system are a small segment

---

3 "Datuk" is an honorific in Malaysia.

of politically connected *Taikong*—"captains of industry"—who are as needy of affirmative action as the characters of *Gossip Girl*.

Worse, for Chinese Malaysians like Joel, is this: bumiputra status is not just an economic privilege. It's an assertion of identity and belonging that ethnic Chinese feel they can never possess, short of converting to Islam, marrying a Muslim and rearing Muslim children.[4] Bumiputra means "sons of the soil," and if a Chinese Malay cannot be bumiputra, the implication is they are not of the soil.

This indignity rubs at Joel in a thousand small ways. He acknowledges that the Chinese have played a disproportionate role in the economy in the past, and that they are largely paving the way (quite literally) for the timber and palm oil industrial interests that are ruining his beloved Sabah's environment today. But he hates making a dirty deal handshake with "professional" bumiputra. He hates that the history of Chinese Malaysian resistance to the Japanese during World War II is glossed over in school textbooks. He hates that during an election year, the government-backed film *Tanda Putera* is being released, which seems to blame the violent race riots of 1969 on the Chinese, who were largely victims of said riots, in a transparent bid to gin up animosity (and votes) from ethnic Malays. He hates that athletes like Lee Chong Wei are referred to as "datuk" and that's somehow supposed to make up for all this. And finally, he hates that his family has been in Malaysia longer than mine has been in America, yet are still considered, in some very important ways, foreigners.

And on top of all this resentment, Joel is annoyed with the Chinese. Not Chinese Malaysians, but visiting Chinese from the People's Republic and Taiwan, who by far constitute the largest segment of tourists now traveling in Sabah.[5]

---

4 For various reasons—modernity, ease of travel to the Middle East, and good old zealotry, among others—Malay ethnicity and identity have become increasingly linked to Islam, to the point that the two are now inextricable. Article 160 of the Malaysian Constitution defines who is an official Malay; the first condition listed is one who "professes the religion of Islam."

5 Joel calls people from Hong Kong "honkies," which I love.

"I watch these Chinese, man, and I can see why the Malays don't like us."

"But you're Malay," I say, and then to correct myself. "No, not Malay. Malaysian. But if you say 'us' to refer to Chinese but don't want to be thought of as Chinese..."

Joel laughs. "Yeah, I know. We're confusing."

Well, not that confusing. If Joel loves Sabah for its wild spaces, I can understand why he feels a bit of animosity toward the tourists who come here to be ferried around in huge tour buses, which by necessity vomit huge clouds of exhaust and require the paving of new roads that asphalt the very wild places said tourists visit for the sake of their wildness. The more tourists, the more paving, the more construction, and the more of Sabah that resembles a post-industrial scar, as opposed to the verdant jewel it once was.

And the tourists themselves seem to be unaware of the wilderness travel mantra of leave nothing behind and take nothing but photos. At worst, they seem to passionately do their level best to spit on the guideline. When the guides tell them to be quiet on wildlife walks, they answer their mobile phones; when they are told of endangered species, they order shark-fin soups, birds nest, and aphrodisiacs culled from god knows what fauna.

A German engineer who was called in to consult on sustainable building practices for a seaside hotel told me how investors from China eventually grew tired of his recommendations for maximizing the place's snorkeling potential. Eventually, in an effort to rush the construction process, they parked a trawler full of cement *on the reef* that was to be the resort's main draw. The coral died, of course. "It was a disaster," he said, shaking his head sadly.

The hotel example is one of greed, but greed's sibling, ignorance, is often along for the ride. On a beach on Pulau Sapi, a small island off the coast of Kota Kinabalu that is technically part of the protected Tunku Abdul Rahman Marine Park, the entire beachfront has been given over to litter-strewn barbeque stands built for Chinese day-tripping groups. I see one kid pick up a starfish from the ocean floor and slam it onto the ground, over and over, in front of his bored-looking mother. A local Malaysian runs up and screams at the mother frantically; she looks basically unperturbed, but tells her son to stop doing what he's doing. I ask the local what happened afterwards.

"She thought the starfish wasn't real. She thought it was like a plastic decoration," he says, stunned beyond further words.

Or as Joel puts it to me, as we continue our drive, "The Chinese from China who come here don't know what wilderness is, so they don't care if they come here and destroy wilderness when they want to see wilderness." The irony, I gather, kind of kills many people who work in the local tourism industry, but there's so much money to be made from engaging in cheap, unsustainable tourism practices, like hastily erected hotels and huge tour bus transportation unsuited to Sabah's delicate ecosystem, that most travel industry professionals laugh off these issues all the way to the bank.

The Mari Mari Cultural Village, located just north of Kota Kinabalu, is a sort of open-air living museum of Sabah's different tribal groups, complete with authentically designed traditional housing and actual *orang asli*—"the original people"—dressed in actual tribal regalia.[6] This is another major selling point for Sabah as a destination—"See the jungle people and their blow pipes"—and a fundamental way Sabah is conceptualized by the rest of Malaysia: wild frontier populated by just-tamed headhunters.

Except this is all a load of bunk. Even the fiercest Murut warriors I have encountered, the ones who still hunt wild boar with dogs and a knife, don't wear loincloths or feather headdresses. They wear T-shirts

---

6 *Orang* is Malay for "person," so to say your nationality, you would say *Orang America*. Hence the word *orang-utan*, which literally translates as "person of the forest."

and shorts. And if anyone out there *does* wear full-on traditional garb, they're probably not donning things like a full headdress while brewing rice wine, which is what the Mari Mari villagers do, which is the equivalent of doing your laundry in an evening gown. And while many people do still live in longhouses, not all longhouses are built out of thatch. Many incorporate concrete and other modern building materials into their design, and plenty have electricity, even satellite TV and Wi-Fi. All in all, the cultural village does not treat Sabah's tribal people as members of a living culture, but museum pieces frozen in time, forever brandishing spears at outsiders (there is even a part of the tour where visitors are fake ambushed by near-naked warriors).

There is a depressingly predictable "traditional dance" where the participants seem embarrassed to be traditional dancing. And it occurs to me, as I consider my earlier conversation about the ethnic tensions of Malaysia, that this is another example of easy ethnic stereotyping in this country, a way to simplify the uneasy ethnic balances of the nation via cartoon caricatures. I mention as much to a Malay friend. Isn't it ironic, I say, that so many Westerners easily stereotype Malaysia as a jungle backwater when Malaysians do the same to Sabah? He smiles in a way that clearly says, "Hey. Stop thinking of all this and have another Tiger beer."

The Mari Mari is just a few miles north of Kota Kinabalu, but it takes almost two hours to drive back to the city because my way is delayed by construction of new hypermalls like Suria Sabah: seven floors of garish retail space, built around the same time as thousands of transplants from mainland Malaysia, lured by subsidized housing and promises of jobs, moved to Sabah. The mainlanders bring their culture, customs, and religion with them; West Malaysians are friendly folks, but their version of Islam is far more conservative than the one practiced by Sabah's indigenous Kadazan and Dusun. There has been some tension as a result, often around the issues of drinking and homosexuality; the former is embraced by the party loving Kadazan and Dusun, while the latter has historically been winked at, if not discussed publicly. In addition, many Sabah natives are Christians who remember the attacks on churches perpetuated in mainland Malaysia in 2010 by hard-line Islamists.

Against this potentially volatile backdrop, new mosques pop up with as much frequency as the malls. "Religious fundamentalism and consumer capitalism, together at last," one lawyer tells me—all built with the mainland ethnic Malays in mind. The newcomers are largely supporters of the ruling United Malays National Organisation (UMNO) political party, which makes no effort to hide the fact that they are shifting voters to Sabah in an effort to shore up their political support in the region. Their electoral platform is one of undisguised political pork. In one fishing village, locals tell me they must vote for UMNO if they want the government to finish constructing a new set of docks which were half-built during the last elections.

In the meantime, revenue generated from the extraction of Sabah's vast natural wealth—timber, oil, and rubber—flees the state for Kuala Lumpur. Sabah is one of Malaysia's three top oil-producing states, and was the second-richest state in Malaysia during the 1970s. Now it is the poorest, with the highest unemployment rate in the country. Ask Sabahans why this state of affairs exists and invariably, someone will grumble about economic exploitation from the mainland, even as more mainlanders flood into the state. The Mari Mari is entertaining, but if you want a real cross-section of the demographics of Sabah, don't look for tribal people with spears. Look for gleaming mosques springing up next to shining shopping plazas, and the squatter camps that spread between them as poverty in Sabah worsens.

It's hard not to like Howard Staunton. He's big, he's friendly, he's a good storyteller and jokester, and he can drink like a tank. He used to be an international rugby player for England and later became one of the first white international-level players of kabbadi, a South Asian rugby-esque sport that frankly makes no sense to me however many times Howard explains its rules and gameplay.

Mainly, I like Howard because he is passionate about Sabah and life in general. (This state, it becomes clear, is the kind of place that attracts eccentrics.) One of Howard's good friends is a retired merchant marine sailor who now makes a living diving for artifacts, from World War II Japanese Zero parts to chests of old spice-trade gold.

"So you're an underwater treasure hunter," I say to the diver.

He pauses, considers this. "I really should put that on a business card."

Howard and I meet in Kudat, on the northern tip of Borneo. The shore here is a puzzle's edge of forest and cliffs; low, sharp grasslands grow up the slopes of the high hills and past a certain altitude, are blanketed under dark cloaks of jungle. Look to your periphery and on either side, always, is water, specifically the South China and Sulu Sea. Out at sea the water is a deep blue, but as it approaches shore it lightens into bands of teal. But where the waters of the two adjacent seas meet, they meet violently, and the waves become almost purple.

All across this beautiful land—not just here in Kudat, but across Sabah—farmers are encouraged to sell their property by timber and palm oil companies. Usually, the property is cleared for timber first, then "reforested" with palm oil plots. That kind of reforestation is unfortunately as environmentally beneficial as leaving the plot empty; the staggeringly diverse wildlife of Borneo cannot effectively function within neat rows of palm oil trees. In the meantime, the farmer who has sold his land for several thousand U.S. dollars—more money than he has likely seen in his life, but only enough to live on for a few years— has lost the one income-generating piece of property he owns.

Then along come guys like Howard, an expat who married a local Rungus woman (because he loves her, clearly, but perhaps also because, during a wine fueled binge at a longhouse, her brothers made it eminently clear that it was time for Howard to step up and do the right thing or risk the anger of some of Borneo's fiercest warriors). Howard and his wife live in a modest jungle home adorned with a tilting sign that reads "fawlty towers." Nearby is Tampat Do Aman, a jungle camp that accommodates volunteers, backpackers, families looking to get a little off the beaten track and travelers interested in exploring Sabah's environment.

Trails web through the jungle, over the mountains and onto beaches, all on land purchased by Howard. By buying the property, he keeps it preserved and beautiful for tourists. His ecological travel initiatives all involve some form of partnership with whomever he purchases land from, so while Sabah's green spaces are preserved, they also become a source of entirely renewable income for locals. After taking in a sunset from a cliff that overlooks the Sulu Sea, and then watching locally employed village boys play a laughing game of soccer in front of a new mangrove walkway attraction, it is hard not to love Kudat (even if, I find out later, some of the largest saltwater crocodiles in the world swim just off the coast).

In the south of Sabah, the valleys of Sapulut, Silas Non Gunting is putting his ice cream empire to work.

Silas' father is a Murut, a member of one of the bravest warrior tribes of Borneo, people who only embraced a settled lifestyle free of constant warfare and hunting in the last few decades. And to be frank, Murut still like to hunt. Silas considers himself an inheritor of his people's warrior heritage, and in this battle, he is fighting for the future of the tribe. He built his fortune running a popular chain of ice cream stores in Kota Kinabalu, and now invests that money into Orou Sapulot, an eco-tourism project that reflects the best of Howard's Tampat Do Aman. It just happens to be located in, if anything, a more stunning location.

Silas has purchased land from the same Murut villagers who now operate Orou Sapulut ("Orou" means "sunrise," and Sapulut is the area of Southern Sabah Silas operates in). Most of the employees work in a small *kampong*, or village, located on the banks of the Sapulut River, a waterway that is so stupidly beautiful and postcard perfect it should be a screen saver on an old Windows PC.

I sit watching this perfect ribbon of blue snake around fuzzy green banks overlaid with virgin rainforest with the village headman. He's a skinny man with hard hands, an avid hunter who still loves to take down boar, with a knife if possible, even if he largely lacks the teeth to eat them. His chocolate-brown skin turns into walnut shell wrinkles whenever he smiles, which is often. As we smoke cigarettes together, he points to the muddy tidal flats near the village and tells me the Murut are the people of the crocodile.

I already knew some traditional Murut kept a representation of a crocodile in their front yards, but I thought this was a relic of ages past, done more out of memory than of memorial to the beasts. The village headman shakes his head.

"I had a dream," he says. "I dreamt there were crocodiles, so many crocodiles, basking in the moonlight. They called me down. So I woke up, and went down to the river, and there, where I am pointing, there were crocodiles. So many. So I sat with them in the moonlight. And they eventually left, and the next morning I knew the Murut would have nothing to fear from crocodiles in this river."

I want to believe that the reptiles are benign, but within hours I am wading through the river, and while the setting is stunningly pleasing and attractive, I am also wondering: if the crocs have some spirit totem pact with the Murut, does that mean they consider me a tasty alternative snack?

I don't have time to ponder this for too long, because Silas leads me and Charlie, an American who runs his own excellent jungle camp near Mount Kinabalu, deep into a cavern that somehow exploits my fear of tight spaces, the dark, and heights all at once. To walk through this cave, which is hot and sweaty and feels like the womb of the Earth, is to play a game of fecal slip and slide with yards and yards of bat shit tarred floor. Stumble on one rock and end up in a tight crevasse; lose your footing on another and you stare over the lip of underground pits I had heretofore thought only existed in video games. I bump my way down one guano-crusted slope and cut my hand, and wonder how long before my arm needs to be hacked off to prevent gangrene.

"What do I do, Charlie?" I ask.

He shrugs. "As long as we get you a Band-Aid in about forty-five minutes, you should be fine."

I do not, of course, want to continue spelunking, but I'm glad we do. We wade past blind albino crabs and blind black frogs into an underground river; Silas turns around and tells me the village elder I met before believes a dragon lives at the end of this wine-dark waterway. Given the size of the cave complex, that seems a reasonable proposition.

I do wash off my wounds and Band-Aid them. I decide to stop worrying about crocodiles—they vowed not to attack the Murut, and I am a guest of the Murut (also, Charlie pulls me aside and explains crocodiles only get this far up river during floods, and even then it's kind of rare to spot them). And as I float down this water, shaded by cathedral arches of virgin rainforest that could have sprouted out of the opening chapter of Genesis, trees from groves that I am paying for with money that goes toward their preservation and the livelihood of the natives of this corner of Sabah, I am struck by how, sometimes, the universe just gives you a kiss.

That night, the local Murut prepare dinner. It's a joyous occasion. One of these fierce warriors goes so far to tell us he would not have his job, would not have anything but the money from selling his ancestral homeland to timber and palm oil barons, would not have the fresh jungle he hunted in and wants his children to hunt in, were it not for people like Silas. We eat well and get a little drunk, and I share a delicious meal among Chinese, Murut and ethnic Malays, and I am struck by what Malaysia can be when she lives up to her highest ideals of tolerance.

Being a responsible traveler in Sabah is relatively easy. There are lots of volunteers here, attracted by orangutan sanctuaries and jungle camps in constant need of willing labor. This sort of behavior does admittedly confuse locals, though.

Ed, a Chinese-Malaysian friend in Kota Kinabalu, asks me quizzically, "What is with all the young Westerners coming here to dig toilets and build village huts on their vacation? I don't get that." I had to laugh; for noveau riche Chinese, vacation is exactly that, a leisurely reward for working long hours, and perhaps at a deeper level, an assertion of success for a demographic that is perhaps a generation removed from poverty, a generation that may have merely dreamed of having enough to eat, let alone the possibility of foreign travel. Many would say travel is about experiencing that which we don't get to experience at home. This theory doesn't account for the hordes of tourists who seek out the same Starbucks in whatever country they're in, but it has some merit when you consider the phenomenon of Western volunteerism in places like Sabah.

Western privilege has allowed Western travelers to essentially close a circle of experiential wandering. Our lives are so comfortable some of us don't seek out additional comfort; we seek the manual labor our ancestors worked so hard to keep us away from. That sort of sentiment is probably rooted in a good place—yes, some students on volunteer programs are fattening their résumés, but in general they seem to want to do good—a *noblesse oblige* state of mind that acknowledges privilege and wants to return the favor in some way.

But all this is hard to explain to Ed, so I just shrug and buy him another shot of Black Label. And in any case: you don't need to volunteer to responsibly travel in Sabah. Plenty of folks have found grassroots ways of preserving Borneo while employing her natives; it's just a matter of patronizing the right businesses.

I see the potential, all potentials, from Signal Hill. I can see local politicians who want to make money and earn votes quickly by exploiting ethnic differences, building largely empty retail space and clear-cutting Sabah's green forests for their own gain. According to the *Yale Environment 360* blog, roughly 75 percent of the Yayasan Sabah forest—an area slated for protection by the state government—has been intensely logged. According to Yale's blog, "Following a pattern that has devastated tropical forests in much of Malaysia, Indonesia, and Southeast Asia, politicians have used the Yayasan Sabah forest as a personal honey pot, logging it to enrich themselves, finance their political campaigns, and reward their patrons."

And I see the potential of camps run by guys like Howard, Charlie, and Silas. Ecological attractions that require a little more work to set up, but are still priced way below resorts, where you have to be willing to rough it a little (leeches love Borneo) but as a reward, you get to float down sparkling rivers amidst primary rainforest that has never felt the blow of an ax. That's an opportunity few people have, especially when said opportunity is combined with the ability to give back to the local community.

All paths can be seen from the hills overlooking Kota Kinabalu. It's nice to think the spirits will select the right way forward for this beautiful corner of Malaysia, but if those spirits are tied to the wild places, the ones under threat from greed and short-term development, it may be time to give them a helping hand.

ANYTHING IS POSSIBLE IN INDIA

INDIA

CECILIA HAYNES

TRAVELING TO INDIA is a rite of passage. It is the most vibrant, explosive, defiantly confrontational country in the world. If you can survive India, you can survive anything that the rest of the world throws at you. A nation of extremes, it is not uncommon in India to feel elation in one instant and intense dejection in the next; to see a land so breathtakingly filled with beauty and then bordering on decay. India cannot but help make a strong impression. You will leave India either bursting with a relieved aversion or burning with desire to return and immerse yourself once more.

I grew up amidst the chaotic backdrop of Kolkata, New Delhi, and Chennai. My one- to four-year stints in these cities added up to a total of eight years, the longest I have spent in any one country. My time in India was punctuated by yearly visits to the United States and Hong Kong, which served to contrast the distinct lack of normalcy in my life in India. When most elementary school students were learning about deserts, I was falling off camels in Rajasthan. When for many kids a long car ride to visit grandparents served as the vacation of the year, my family and I were hopping off rickety sleeper trains to go to tiger reserves. Other children were forced to clean their rooms, while I had a maid, a cook, and a driver. Before leaping to any conclusions of overwhelming opulence, keep in mind that India's labor force is inexpensive. Services that most people find unaffordable in most countries are commonplace in India. I was spoiled and privileged compared with the vast majority of the local population, and yet, in some ways, considered deprived by most Western societies.

My skills in caring for inevitable bouts of food poisoning left me healthier than my brother. To this day I cannot stand to drink water out of a tap, and I hesitate when ordering uncooked food at a restaurant. Shots were my best friends, and by the age of seven, I was adept at mixing electrolytes for rehydration. I am more in tune with exactly how my body feels at any given second than anyone else I know. My idea of luxury was the commissary on the embassy compound, and my image of the U.S. consisted entirely of Kool-Aid mix and Fruit Roll-Ups, unavailable in everyday Indian supermarkets. Power outages were the norm, and I swam in the swollen monsoon waters in the streets of New Delhi.

Through all of this I never complained. First of all, my dad had no tolerance for complaints, but, in all honesty, I loved every second of living in India. After staying in the U.S. or Hong Kong for more than two weeks, I started to get bored. The novelty of sitting through a movie *without* whistling catcalls and an intermission wore off after a little while. I was ready to go back to my real life of oppressive heat, unceasing noise, and streets full of cow dung. I returned to my multinational friends, one of whom owned a menagerie of animals, including a camel and a deer. Imagine being able to ride a camel whenever you wanted after school. I went back to festivals, including Holi, the most colorful, powdery interaction that you will ever have with another human being. Never wear anything that you care about on Holi unless you want it dyed in a cacophony of color. I cradled my dog when Diwali, the festival of light, came around and the unending fireworks blasted like bombs. This was my life, and I would not have traded it for any other.

The first time I ever traveled alone I was fourteen years old. I flew from Chennai to the Philippines to visit a friend. It was a major step in autonomy, even if the only time I was truly alone was on an airplane. This gave me the confidence to approach my parents with an even more independent trip the following year. I wanted to go with two guy friends, one fifteen and one fourteen, to the hill station Kodaikanal. Kodaikanal is a ten-hour trip from Chennai, requiring a combination of trains and taxis. My friend T used to live there, and his stepmother invited us to visit her over a long weekend. My parents consented because they believed quite strongly in my freedom to explore. Also, T had lived his entire life in India and was as close to native as a foreigner could get. With permission granted, bags packed, and tickets in hand, we were unprepared for what would become one of the longest nights of our lives.

If I had to condense the whole of incredible India into a single experience, I would go with train rides. They are everything that is terrible and wonderful about the country all rolled into an exhilaratingly horrifying journey. I have ridden on many, many Indian trains. My advice: always try to get into the first-class sleeper cars. Mostly hygienic and less run down, they have the luxury of a curtain to draw against prying eyes. Plus you have the advantage of a wide window through which to gawk at the flowing scenery. Villages, splashes of green fields, and laughing crowds of waving children pass by in a riotous stream of motion. There is something undeniably alluring about being able to observe snapshots of daily life while being removed enough to escape unscathed from any trickle-over mess.

However, you should never let your guard down on a train, because the minute you do, something will go wrong. My first encounter with the truth of this adage was when I was eight. My family and I were headed to our fifth attempt at seeing a tiger in a wildlife preserve.

Confident that the train crew would know when to stop, since we were four passengers all going to one destination, we slept peacefully through the night. Luckily my dad set an alarm so that we would be ready to hustle onto the waiting platform; he was awake when we reached the station and watched it pass by as the train kept on going. He quickly got the attention of the crew, who alerted the engineer, and the train screeched to a halt only a couple hundred feet past our destination. We then had to trudge back along the rail tracks. Little known fact: there are giant trenches between the rail lines. These trenches are difficult to navigate in the predawn darkness of five in the morning, and even more so for a sleep-deprived eight-year-old. I ended up falling in one, panicking because I felt skittering rat-like paws on my feet, and then being hauled out by my dad. Despite the shaky start to the trip, that was the one time that we actually saw a tiger in the wild. The whole experience seared into me the need to over-prepare when dealing with transportation in India.

With that hard-won lesson firmly in mind, my three friends and I arrived at the train station two hours in advance of the time printed on our ticket. The train station welcomed us with wide-open doors and a decided lack of air-conditioning. Painted in blacks, browns, and grays, it was a bleak halfway house. Fellow weary passengers stretched out on the floor and on benches, contorting their bodies to fit the space. They avoided spots stained orange with chewing tobacco and concentrated in areas covered only in a light layer of dust. Loaded down with duffel bags and enough chips to feed a small army, we strained our eyes looking for our departure time on the giant board in the middle of the concourse.

It was not there. Growing frantic, we started scanning the train numbers. Eventually we found our train, only it had left two hours before our arrival. The ticket agent had misprinted the time on our ticket. At this point we returned our eyes to the board anxiously searching for another train to Kodaikanal. There was only one, and it was leaving in ten minutes. We scrambled to the ticket booths, only to find out that everything was sold out. I doubt my friend T is proud of this now, but he mustered up enough tears and somehow this six-foot-two upset blond boy persuaded the agent to sell us a few third-class, unreserved tickets. As Indians are so fond of saying, *Anything is possible in India.*

Third-class, unreserved tickets are the worst of the worst and the absolute bottom of the barrel. This realization did not hit us at first because we were caught up in the adrenaline of coping with furious disappointment, and then overwhelming relief, before being swept up in stressful anxiety as we sprinted to make our new train. When we arrived in front of one of the third-class cars, we were greeted with a rusty exterior half hidden by the sheer amount of people hanging off the sides. People talk about clown cars but that joke is nothing compared to the reality of a heaving mass of bodies overflowing doorways and windows. It felt like they melded into a single breathing entity, all too ready to envelop unsuspecting passersby.

Since third-class, unreserved cars are on the ends of trains, this left us in a mad dash across the length of the surprisingly long train. Each section passed by in a blur of dirt-stained blue sides and the occasional markers for classes more fortunate than us. Luckily the other third-class car wasn't as crowded and we piled in just as the train began to roll. Breathing an enormous sigh of relief, we turned our attention to seating. But as the last passengers we lost out in the lottery for seats. In spite of the fact that this car was filled with unpadded wooden bunks, all available spaces were filled; those went to the people who clearly had the correct times printed on their tickets. Loath to spend the next eight hours standing, we scoped out possible spots to roost. The only empty area was an alcove nestled between the only two toilets of the car. In fact, the dull green rusted doors of the bathrooms formed the walls of the alcove. Reluctant to sit on the floor, we gingerly placed our bags and sacrificed their cleanliness for ours. There was only space for two so we got on a rotation cycle and became a lot more comfortable with cuddling that night.

Armed with a deodorant spray and a portable fan, we battled the drifting tendrils of stench the whole night long. Wind took care of most of the smell while the train was in motion, but as soon as a new station was announced and we felt the telltale drag of a slowing vehicle, we whipped out our weapons. The deodorant bathed us in a fragrant cloud that chased away any encroaching smells of urine and other bodily waste. While resting our pointer fingers, we split our time between laughing at our predicament and watching those around us attempt to sleep while standing. Men in stained white *lungis* stared straight ahead lost in their own thoughts, swaying with the rhythm of the train. A calm pervaded the entire car as we all resigned ourselves to surviving the journey.

Upon arrival in the wee hours of the morning, we prepared for a winding two-hour taxi ride up the mountain. I was in a daze as the car wound through the mist. Verdant growth cloaked in gray patchy fog and giant billboards advertising the latest Bollywood hits provided the backdrop to our surreal trip. We even stopped at a gushing waterfall before the driver deposited us safely at the home of T's stepmom. The relief was overwhelming and I looked forward to three days of adorable puppies, great food, and good company. Unfortunately at this point we learned that the reservoir, which provides all of the running water for Kodaikanal, had burst. It was a good thing that I was already handy with using a bucket to flush the toilet. The secret is to toss the water in one powerful thrust instead of a slow trickle.

While some people would likely consider this an unbearable turn of events, it was not so bad, until we got to my third day of not showering. I drew the line there and decided to go back to nature. Kodaikanal is quite a rainy place and I used what I had to work with. Even though the temperature was around fifty degrees, I ran outside in a T-shirt and shorts and proceeded to scrub the goose bumps off. It was invigorating.

During the periods when I was not coping with a new disaster, I was mesmerized by the mystery of Kodaikanal. Imagine a movie set for an Edgar Allen Poe production mixed with the nature from a *Lord of the Rings* film. We spent our days wandering the numerous paths that litter the area. Towering trees with knotted branches crept toward us and caught at our clothing. The soft white caps of mushrooms sprouted from the brown mulch that covered the ground. In our explorations we never encountered other people. It felt like we had stumbled into our very own Grimm fairy tale, complete with a lack of adults and a moody atmosphere.

Through this whole experience, I never once regretted the fact that we pushed forward. It was such a feeling of accomplishment and no one will ever be able to take that away from me. India will test you in every way imaginable. Your tolerance for comfort, smells, cleanliness, and food poisoning will come under siege until something gives way. Either your tolerance continues to stretch like the top of a drum or it snaps and you run screaming for the nearest airport. India is not an easy place, but it will reward you for your stubbornness.

A Memory of Seoul

Seoul, Korea

Sara Cooper

I ARRIVED IN Seoul with a carry-on, some thank-you cards, and an acute sense of worry about how my work would be perceived by a Korean audience.

My collaborator Zach and I had been flown in on Korean Air to see the opening night of our musical, *The Memory Show*. His music would stay roughly the same, but my script and lyrics had been translated into Korean, which is difficult when the characters occasionally throw in little bits of Yiddish. I had been told that one pivotal moment, a song about Yom Kippur, had been made into an Easter lyric. We weren't sure what to expect.

We were greeted at the airport by our good friend Jiyoung and our friend-to-be, the producer, Moon. We were exhausted. They took us to an Italian restaurant and then to the hotel where we collapsed, visions of Tiffany-blue-scarfed stewardesses running through our dreams.

The next week was completely mind-blowing. Seoul is the kind of city you never want to leave. The food is delicious. The people are generous and kind. There's no shortage of entertainment. And the streets are clean and safe and beautiful.

Seoul is divided into north and south by the Han River. At the city's center is a series of mountains that look stunning in the day and literally took my breath away at night. Standing on a mountain at night, and looking down at the city, was one of the single most incredible moments of my life.

I am not well-traveled. In fact, this was only my third time out of the country. Yes, I am one of those obnoxious New Yorkers who thinks New York City is the center of the universe (truly).

But looking out over those mountains, I had a sense of the world as a larger place. I left a little piece of myself there.

The rest of the trip was a dream. Zach and I watched our show, in Korean, and it was spectacular. The direction and set were wonderful, the actresses were beautiful and amazing, and, even though we didn't know exactly what they were saying, we recognized it and embraced it as our show. The audiences on the nights we were there were receptive and engaged. We were humbled and moved.

I hope to go back to Seoul. I would like to see other productions by the company, and to see my friends, old and new. I want to visit those mountains and the river and the coffee shops that line the streets five to a block. Next time, I'd like to bring my long-term boyfriend Jim, who was the only thing missing from the trip. I want to show him everything I saw, and together, to do the things I didn't get to do in my brief trip this first time. But until then, Seoul lives on in my mind and my heart, a city that welcomed me and my work, a place where the characters I wrote on a piece of paper came to life on the stage, different, similar, beautiful, real.

WHEN
COCONUTS ATTACK

HYDERABAD, INDIA

SARAH KHAN

MY GRANDPARENTS IN India live on a tidy little estate called Palm Grove. It's a whitewashed house with a red Spanish-style tiled roof, a marble courtyard with a swing, a pint-size pond and rose garden, and, of course, the soaring trees that give it its name. It was my second home, and I spent many a leisurely summer challenging Raju, the caretaker's son, to never-ending cricket, badminton, and hopscotch matches on the circular driveway; playing cards and sipping fresh mango juice in the veranda; and reading Nancy Drew books on the seating area shaded by guava trees. It's where some of my most idyllic childhood memories are from.

It's also where I developed one of my greatest fears.

One day, while strolling aimlessly across the courtyard—the very same place where, years ago, I would vigilantly steer my tricycle over rows of marching ants—I suddenly noticed the coconuts littering the ground. This was not out of the ordinary; Palm Grove is home to many palm trees, and these lofty trees begot coconuts galore. Somehow I'd never paid them much attention before, but on that afternoon, I became consumed by their existence. They looked so harmless, lying there idly at the base of the mammoth tree trunks. But wait—how had they gotten there in the first place?

Just like that, I developed a fear of falling coconuts.

Yes, coconuts. Falling. From the sky. A terrifying prospect indeed.

Now I'm sure you're thinking I was just being silly. But would you think the same of a noted University of Florida shark researcher? Because according to him, fifteen times more people die of coconut-related injuries each year than from shark attacks. But you don't hear about *those* victims on the news, do you?

When I was living in Saudi Arabia during the Gulf War, I had more substantial fears, like bombs. However, at my grandparents' home, coconuts were a bigger threat. All those hairy brown shells lying on the ground didn't walk their way down the tree trunks. They had to have plummeted. And judging by their numbers, they were committing suicide by the masses. I wasn't about to stage an intervention with my head.

For the rest of that summer I refused to set foot outside the house, unless it was to go directly into a car. I was subjected to ridicule by my grandparents, siblings, and even the servants. But I would not budge. I had no intentions of lounging lazily on the swing, minding my own business, only to be mauled from above by a stray shell. No, sir. I was not prepared to die. And certainly not in so unglamorous a fashion.

Everyone tried to convince me of the absurdity of my newfound phobia. If I hadn't been struck by one in so many years, they assured me, I probably wasn't about to start being assailed now. "When has a coconut ever hit anyone in the head?" they implored. Their logic astounded me. Just because by some blessing of God I'd thus far avoided being in the unfortunate trajectory of one of these destructive orbs didn't mean I should flagrantly tempt fate.

Then one afternoon, in the summer of 1997, when I was comfortably ensconced within the house watching MTV, word suddenly came from outside that a small coconut had dropped from somewhere—

presumably from up above—and hit one of the servants in the back. Fortunately she was fine; she escaped unharmed and lived to tell the tale. Or simply to forget all about it (she did seem rather unfazed for someone who had survived such a brazen act of food-borne violence). However, not every coconut-attack victim may be so lucky.

Many years later, in the safe, coconut-free confines of my Boston College apartment, I tuned into CNN in time to catch a brief glimpse of a headline: SCIENTIST WINS PRIZE FOR RESEARCH ON INJURIES CAUSED BY FALLING COCONUTS. Aha! All my fears came flooding back to me, but it was comforting to finally see my concerns validated by science.

I've since devoted many hours to learning more about the perils posed by these plummeting balls of terror. Apparently coconuts can weigh nearly nine pounds and tumble from up to eighty feet at speeds of fifty miles per hour. In many island destinations, resorts even hire people whose sole job is to knock coconuts out of trees to keep guests safe. Because let's face it, few things say "honeymoon from hell" quite like a fruit-inflicted coma.

Some might feel pity for the coconut itself—after all, should it survive its plunge and not bring harm to an innocent bystander, it lasts just long enough to have its own skull fractured and its insides devoured. But I am not one of these people. I don't even *like* coconuts. So if I don't knock open its noggin, the least it can do is afford me the same respect.

BUNKING
WITH THE ENEMY

CHINA AND THE NORTH KOREA BORDER

KAITLIN SOLIMINE

THERE ARE THREE things you need when boarding an overnight train from Beijing to the North Korean border: strong elbows, toilet paper, and an understanding of international soccer.

Luckily, I have all three when I stand in the unheated waiting room outside the platforms of the Beijing train station on a frigid winter evening. I'm heading to the Chinese border city of Dandong to research a story. Although I've traveled by myself by train in China dozens of times, I've forgotten about China's train station mayhem. Thousands of my fellow train mates swarm the entrance, rice bags and canvas luggage held like prayer offerings above their heads. I plow forward, dragging my carry-on suitcase behind me. In the five years since I last traveled by Chinese train, I've already abandoned Rule One: bring only luggage you can grip to your chest.

Somehow, I make it on board and settle into my bunk. Music filters through the train speakers. The curtainless cabin window is fogged, but outside I still see the masses jogging down the platform, shouting at their compatriots to hurry. In China, the modern day pace of life is exacerbated by the fact there are over 1.4 billion others eager to overtake you. Missing a train could mean an unending string of failures—you don't get that job, can't afford rent, your husband leaves you, you end up on the streets begging for spare change, you're arrested and never able to return home again. In China, restlessness is not a choice, but a necessity. Without a social safety net, most Chinese fear being trampled by a society moving at such a fast pace—you either keep up or are swept away by the current.

As I'm thinking, I hear my cabinmates boisterously enter. Cracking, teenage-boy voices filter down the aisle. The language isn't Chinese, but Korean. The boys drag with them deflated Adidas soccer bags. They don matching black-and-white uniforms with the Democratic People's Republic of Korea (DPRK) flag proudly silkscreened on their backs, and red pins featuring the face of Kim Il-Sung on their chests. *Holy shit*, I think. *I'm the only American on this train and I'm surrounded by North Koreans.* Immediately, the cold-war-era films my father loves spring to mind and I hear the squealing "Yee-haw!" of Slim Pickens in *Dr. Strangelove.* My father: an ex-Navy pilot, a Republican, a diehard Yankee. Me: alone, American, bleeding-heart Liberal, bunking with a group of North Korean boys. The last time I was so close to verifiable North Koreans was at a World Cup first round soccer game in South Africa a year earlier—Portugal: 7. North Korea: 0. Surely, I shouldn't use this anecdote as an icebreaker.

In China, train travel is a class-based experience. The options start at "standing-room only" and, as the term suggests, that's bare bones at best. Next, there's hard seat, which, if you've traveled by that service for any number of hours, will make your sit bones wish you were standing. The next level is soft seat, then hard sleeper—which is where I find myself, my preferred service for its middle-class feel and camp atmosphere. The top rung of Chinese train travel is soft sleeper, featuring separate closed-off cabins of only four beds, fancier window dressings, and, I can only assume, plusher pillows and blankets.

My bunkmates in this open-concept hard sleeper cabin politely arrange their luggage in the racks above the beds and below the bottom bunk. I sit on the bottom, even though my ticket assigned me the top—there's no way thirty-one-year-old me is squeezing into that space for the next fourteen hours. I figure I'll sit it out on the lowest level until I'm asked to move, or the rightful owner of this bunk wants to sleep.

Before the train's wheels chug northward, the North Korean boys have somehow signaled to their friends in nearby bunks to check out the woman who will soon sleep alongside them. They inspect me the way one would a specimen of cattle, although I suppose I'm equally guilty of probing glances. They remove their shoes, then their socks, sniffing each as if judging for authenticity then lie in their bunks, hands behind heads, several joining from nearby cabins to stare at me as I unpack and settle in, arranging my instant noodles, books, and magazines, on the small, shared fold-down table.

One of the boys, handsome and clean-shaven (or, more likely, prepubescent) with a long face and calm eyes, pulls out his ticket to show me. It's his bunk I'm sitting on.

"Me, move?" I speak the English of a traveler attempting foreign conversation. I wish they knew I'm fluent in Chinese, as if this would give me credibility.

"No," the handsome boy shakes his head, thumbs his chest, and gestures he'll sleep in the top bunk, chivalrously offering me the better night's sleep with less climbing per bathroom visit.

"Thanks," I say in Chinese, smiling. This he understands and smiles back, both of us gracious for the brief, coherent exchange.

After some tense silence, a rounder-faced boy with thick thighs (surely the team's defensive player) makes his move. He is confident in the way of a child who comes from a well-connected family.

"You," he points. "Where home?"

I feel like I've been found out. Everything I've been taught by American news tells me North Korea is the enemy: *North Korea*

Threatens Merciless Strike on South; North Korea Claims U.S. Is Within Missile Range. I sit back and bite my lip.

"America," I say, immediately wishing I hadn't.

Their eyes open wider. "Ahhh, Am-er-i-kah," they repeat, drawing out the syllables in a surprising enthusiasm.

I want to explain I'm not a stereotypical American, whatever that means to them. I want to say I believe nationalism is just as dangerous as religious fanaticism. That humanity is tied by bonds much deeper than skin color. I want to tell them I have a Chinese family who I lived with when I was in high school—didn't they see my Chinese "father" sending me off at the station? I want to tell them I write fiction about China because I believe seeing a place from the outside can be as valuable as from the inside. I say none of this. I wish, for the first time in my life, I spoke Korean. *My iPhone!* I think with glee, and quickly find an application that translates from English to Korean. The app is a failure: mostly, it teaches me inane words like "apple," "student," and "bathroom." This is not useful.

Within minutes of leaving the Beijing station, fourteen hours remaining, there's a crowd of at least ten North Korean boys surrounding me on the bunks. They are obsessed with my iPhone the way most people were years ago when it debuted. They preen past one another and over me to see what I'm browsing.

"Internet!" They crow. I'm surprised by their technological savvy. Last I read, North Korea had no broadband data network and only one Internet café in Pyongyang. Still, the boys persist. "Messi! Beckham!"

I find them photos of their heroes, offering the device to the rounder-faced boy, who then hands it to the handsome skinny boy who gave up his bunk for me earlier. The two quickly adapt to the phone's touch screen, scanning the images, and smiling and pointing and remarking something in Korean I don't understand. Despite the fact the vast majority of North Koreans don't own personal computers and very few have smart phones, these boys are a fast study.

"Girl!" They shout emphatically. "Messi girl! Beckham girl!"

Suddenly I understand. They want to see the girlfriends of their soccer idols. I'm not up on the pop culture of soccer WAGs, but I find Victoria Beckham, and a shot of Ronaldo and his girl *du jour* lounging on a Spanish beach.

"Ahhh," my bunkmates coo, as if watching fireworks for the first time.

One of them, with young, rosy cheeks, jogs to a nearby cabin to retrieve a camera. He shows me photos of the team's trip to Kunming, their training regimens, a video he recorded of their flight from Kunming to Beijing. He motions that it was their first time on a plane as he reenacts the sound of takeoff. I motion that my father is a pilot and he bows his head in a surprising show of approval.

While the boys decipher how to zoom in and out on my phone, I open my laptop. Two Apple products in one day. The boys act like it's Christmas morning. One obsessively runs his fingers over the transparent trademark white apple on the outside of my computer. They take turns rubbing the sleek edges of the phone and computer.

I point at the Apple trademark and ask, "You know it?"

They shake their heads, raising their shoulders. Could it be they've never seen the world's most ubiquitous logo?

"Macintosh," I say, pointing at the icon, and they nod, repeating my phrase studiously. Several of the boys wear clothing with the Adidas logo, and while there's a chance their gear is fake, it's strange to see these kids, so utterly unconnected to global capitalism, eagerly supporting one of soccer's most successful and lucrative brands.

The boys' enthusiasm is quickly infectious. I can't help myself. I open my iPhoto application, running through recent travels—Costa Rica, South Africa, Singapore. I want to show them I'd seen their team play in the World Cup, but, strangely, they're either not interested or too embarrassed by their national team's performance. I know that access to the outside world is severely limited in North Korea, so I want to show them everything I can in the brief amount of time we're together.

But they're not finding the pieces of my life exciting. Instead, they yearn for more images of soccer stars, and Korean celebrities whose names I can't spell. The same rosy-cheeked boy who showed me his camera is the only one who enjoys my photographs. He closely examines the screen anytime there's a shot of a friend who's black. He brings me a SIM card, gesturing he'd like to transfer some of my photos to his device, but then another boy says something snippy to him and he shirks from the cabin, embarrassed, it seems, by his overzealous attempt at seeing the world through an American woman's eyes.

It's dinnertime and the boys offer me their instant noodles. I motion I have my own (a vegetarian version to their beef). There's a tenderness in the altruistic kindness of boys with families whose monthly salaries are probably less than $2,000 per year. These boys were likely born during one of the world's worst famines—from 1994 to 1998 as many as 3.5 million North Koreans died from malnutrition—and yet my bunkmates would have gladly given the supposed enemy their only meal.

As we slurp our noodles, a man in a black sweat suit walks the aisle of the train, eyeing me suspiciously. He says something to the boys and a few scurry like scolded mice to their assigned bunks. A cluster remains, likely the older, or more privileged, or more talented. Either way, they are for some reason allowed to stay and the older man returns to his bunk, although occasionally I notice him perusing the aisles. I craft elaborate fantasies about the nature of his work, which leads to anxiety he'll consider me a spy and snap my neck in the middle of the night while I'm asleep.

After dinner, I open my iTunes app and play American music for the boys, then switch to British classics like the Beatles. They don't recognize a thing. Not even hits like "Yesterday" and "Let It Be." They want to hear Korean music, but I have no idea what bands they're talking about.

I also realize they likely haven't seen an episode of American television. I only have a few downloads, and choose an episode of

How I Met Your Mother, a popular CBS show about a group of friends in New York City. Most scenes take place in a bar, where the group crowds a table, drinking beers and talking about life. My bunkmates, likewise, crowd the computer. They haven't been watching for more than a minute when one of them points at the screen and shakes his fist angrily. I lean closer to see what he sees: in the background of the set, there's a small American flag posted on the wall of the bar. Although I've watched every episode of the series, I am only now, for the first time, noticing the flag.

I point at the flag, my nation's symbol of freedom and democracy, and cock my head, raising an eyebrow at the boy, who makes another gesture of anger: eyebrows pinched, mouth angry. The other boys nod knowingly, raising their fists in angered solidarity, as if theatrically acting out a role assigned from birth. The flag they hate. But what about me?

For the first time since our encounter, I feel awkward and confused. As if a teenager myself, I wonder if the boys actually like me or if they're merely interested in the trappings I bring with me—the iPhone, laptop, and photos of soccer stars with their WAGs. How can I possibly find the words to talk with them about how we don't have a choice where we're born? That my country's policies have a lot more to do with power and self-interest, as do theirs? Or do they already know this? Is their dramatic gesture of American loathing merely a display they put on for one another, worried that if they don't, they will be shunned from the group? Is it any different from my singing the national anthem at a baseball game or hosting a Fourth of July barbecue?

After the flag disappears from the scene, they don't show much interest. It's close to bedtime; the conductor has already switched off the overhead lights, music replaced by the endless clacking of the train's wheels, the occasional warning whistle. We are somewhere in the Chinese countryside where most of the world is dark, just specks of light in clustered villages we pass in the span of a breath.

As I search for something else of interest to show them, one of the boys who'd displayed anger toward the flag sighs then settles into the bed across from me, his mouth pulling into a frown, a pensive look on his face.

I watch him watching me, neither of us speaking, the clack of the train seemingly unending below us.

In the days before I meet the North Korean soccer boys on the train, the U.S. had sent an envoy to Beijing. Chinese and foreign news outlets were abuzz with analysis of the upcoming six-party talks that aimed to persuade North Korea to abandon its nuclear weapons program. The state of U.S./North Korean relations was tense, especially with North Korea's plans to launch a ballistic missile (two months after my trip, North Korea launched a "weather satellite" into space; it exploded ninety seconds after launch).

I've been living off and on in China for nearly two decades, but spent most of the past few years in Los Angeles, living with my husband and writing a novel about China. Recently, I was offered a job as a television host for a Chinese station, but turned it down for many reasons, not the least of which was the fact I'd be working for a Communist, party-sponsored propaganda machine. Now I return to China on a strange mission: to revisit the city of Dandong on the North Korean border, a place I'd traveled through more than a decade earlier. I can't name what calls me to return, but here I am, alone in a bunk, speeding toward a destination without a purpose.

As the boys ready for bed, a middle-aged man in a sporty white jumpsuit enters our cabin. He introduces himself as "Coach Park" and speaks near-perfect English. He is polite, soft-spoken, and clearly eager to practice his conversational skills with me. He appears well-fed (with a slight gut and a pleasantly round face), much to the contrary of the images of stark famine that American news outlets regularly report. (The nation's youth soccer program must be worthy of funds not allocated to the masses—I wonder if the ironies of Communism aren't lost to the boys and their coach, or if they're just grateful to be beneficiaries.)

Coach Park tells me he's been leading the under-16 North Korean team for many years. He says he's traveled to China and "Chinese Taipei" (the Communist world's name for Taiwan). He studied in university and loves watching television dramas.

"What did you study in university?" he asks.

When I tell him Chinese language, history, and culture, he perks up.

"I love history!" he says excitedly. "You know King Arthur?"

I nod, but my knowledge of the Knights of the Round Table is embarrassingly scarce; I hope he doesn't ask more. I tactfully redirect the conversation to speak broadly about the dangers of historical accounts.

"I always liked history," I say, "but it's difficult to know what's a true historical account because often survivors are the only ones who leave their stories."

"I know," he says, nodding his head, his thick well-combed hair waving along. "History is written by the victors."

Coach Park pauses and I realize he's indicating we've reached the end of our conversation on this topic. We can speak in vague generalities, but the specifics are shrouded in nuance. This is something I learned in China in the mid-'90s as a high-school student in Beijing: when your companion stops adding to the discussion, the topic is making them uncomfortable or they feel they're being watched.

Before I can offer a new perspective, he says, "It was very nice to meet you." He stands, extending a hand in the Western tradition of greeting and farewell. "What do you say in English? 'Good night?'"

"Yes, that's correct. Good night," I say.

The boys above me parrot the phrase they've likely heard before. "Good night," they say from their bunks, like in *The Sound of Music*, a film that, given its anti-Nazi Germany undertones, feels strangely appropriate here.

As I fall asleep, my iPhone's battery precariously low, I keep one eye open for the man in black who marched the aisle an hour earlier. I'm still paranoid I could be considered a spy (film references of spies dragged from train cabins in the middle of the night abound), but the boys around me don't seem at all perturbed by my presence. The presumed DPRK secret service operator must be fast asleep in his bunk while across the aisle, my bunkmate dreams in a language I do not speak, of places and worlds I'll never know.

Awakening on a train in China is a jarring affair. Ninety minutes before reaching the train's final destination, the overhead lights burst on (particularly uncomfortable if you're on the top bunk), and music resumes its ear-bleed-inducing synthesized saxophone squeal. Vendors pass the aisles pushing clanking carts filled with instant noodles, shrink-wrapped hotdogs, candied haw, and spiced sunflower seeds: China's breakfast of champions. The vendors repeatedly shout their offerings to sleepy-eyed passengers, who exasperatedly cover their heads with train-issued starchy wool blankets, hoping for a few extra minutes of stolen sleep.

Outside our window, the world awakens with us. Farmers slap at donkey's haunches, schoolchildren march to class. We pass villages, then long stretches of barren, snow-encrusted brown fields. This area of China, Liaoning Province, is known for its iron and steel resources, its maize, apples, and petrochemical factories.

The last time I was here was in 1999. Back then I didn't have a cell phone (and certainly not a "smart" one), and I carried my heavy Toshiba laptop in an overstuffed backpack with a Canadian flag stitched to the canvas (the U.S. had just "accidentally" bombed the Chinese embassy in Belgrade and I wasn't taking any chances). I don't remember a landscape like the one outside my window now—in fact, I took few photographs in 1999 because my camera required film, an expense I couldn't afford except to chronicle places I wrote about for the guide.

The boys wake, shuffle sleepily to the shared unisex bathroom at the end of the cabin to brush their teeth and slap cold water on their faces. By now, I know the squat toilet is a disaster and I consider waiting until I reach my hotel in Dandong, but I can't—instead, I carefully avoid the spilled urine surrounding the toilet hole that empties straight onto the tracks. In the bathroom's corner stands the ubiquitous shit mop that train attendants use to "clean" the floor—aiming one's bodily refuse on a shifting train is like hunting for a deer while drunk.

As I pack, I'm compelled to snap a photograph of the scene outside my bunk window: snow-capped mountains and brown villages, chimneys puffing black coal smoke into the cloudy sky. I'm about to upload the image to Instagram, when I look at my bunkmates. They did not bring books with them on their several-month-long journey, nor smartphones and laptops. Instead they remind me of a long-lost American youth; they banter with one another, mock karate fight, and devise games to play with their hands. Some sit in pensive silence, watching the same scenery I do, but without the impulsive need to chronicle it, to announce to the world where they are or what they're doing.

I, however, am slave to my devices. I sit on my bunk to take notes about the night, brainstorming plans for my research in Dandong. I open Microsoft Word, typing into the blank white document so utterly familiar to writers everywhere.

A Night with the North Koreans.... I title the file, but how can I write a story that's still unfolding?

The skinny, long-faced boy who gave me his bunk sits across from me, watching me type. I can tell he's formulating thoughts in his head—that he wants to say something, but how? We don't share a language other than the names of international soccer stars.

Finally, he breaks the silence.

"My mother," he says, then makes a gesture of writing in longhand, something I never do anymore.

I say slowly, "Your mother is a writer?"

"Yes," he says. "You?"

Yes, I nod.

He gestures to my eyeglasses, a hipster pair framed in tortoiseshell and made in Italy.

"Do you want to see these?" I ask, removing them from my face.

He takes them, holding them to his face and shuddering at how the prescription lenses make his vision blur. He smiles. "My mother, same" he says, pointing at the frames and gesturing that his mother's pair is even more enhanced in prescription strength. I understand: *His mother wears glasses larger than these. His mother's eyes, incapable of seeing distances. His mother, the writer.*

"My mother, same," he repeats, as if worried I will not understand the importance of this, before handing me back my glasses. I reposition them on my face, look to the Word document staring back at me, dark words bleeding into the digital page. I wish I had a language in which to tell him his mother must be an exceptional writer, that she must love him very much. I wish I could say that writers everywhere are the same, compelled by some foolish instinct to trap the experience of life in words. Instead I smile politely and resume my work while he watches me for several minutes with a strange, unspeakable comfort I imagine is because he has sat like this, watching his mother type, since he was a baby.

We are already on the fringes of Dandong, a brown city where the sun barely pokes through the wintery polluted haze. The train slows; the tracks cut through a crowded part of the city, 1980s Soviet-style buildings crammed against red-brick two-stories constructed during the Japanese occupation of Manchuria over half a century earlier.

As the train squeals to a stop, we gather our things, our legs reacquainting to solid ground. I am compelled to give the boys my e-mail address, a mailing address in the States, but would they be able to write me? Would such a gesture, common in the social media age, make me look desperate and overreaching to them? Could a friendship with an American cost them their spot on the team?

Before I can bravely hand them a business card, we disembark together, the boys huddling in a group, all of us equally shocked by the colder temperatures in this more northern, more humid, city. I could stand and wait for their next directive, following them away from the train, but I know this would be inappropriate; I don't know what else to do—so, like a teenager in love incapable of making the next move, I wave good-bye to them, and they smile and wave good-bye as well, proudly shouting their newly learned farewell. I walk down the stairs to the busy, teeming station lobby, their echoing voices lingering behind me, feeling unexpectedly alone.

Later that evening, I stand at the window of my hotel room with a view of the city's famed Yalu River, the watery border cutting between the DPRK and the People's Republic of China.

There are two bridges in sight—one, the Sino-Korea Friendship Bridge, with an endless line of trucks waiting to cross the border back to China after a day collecting inventory for import (China is North Korea's largest trading partner).

The other, Duan Qiao, or "Short Bridge," (also known as the "Bridge to Nowhere") is familiar from my last stay here. Its iron arches stretch only halfway across the river: during American airstrikes in the Korean War, fighter jets dropped bombs the size of boats into the river, slicing the bridge and cutting off what was then the only link between North Korean forces and their Chinese allies.

In the distance, North Korea is a brown, mostly empty landscape. I only see as far as a forested embankment, the border town of Sinuiju where a few shoddy buildings poke their roofs above leafless trees.

Pyongyang, the country's bureaucratic heart, is a little over a hundred miles away and where my erstwhile bunkmates are returning home after several months abroad. They're likely greeted by caring mothers and fathers, escorted back to urban apartments where a home-cooked meal, of the family's most expensive goods, awaits their growling stomachs.

I wonder if they turn a westward gaze to think of me looking for them, watching and waiting—or if they quickly settle into the familiar routines of a childhood now far beyond reach for me, out of sight.

Eleven Months, One Week, Four Days: Japan in Fragments

Japan

Brenna Fitzgerald

1

soliloquy

on

the seasons

The corners of my mouth seem to rise and fall with the weather. The days are getting shorter. My eyes linger longer on the sunsets. The nights are cooler. I'm snuggling deeper into my comforter. I think there's a print of my body in its folds. I crave steaming pots of tea and soup. As I succumb to this new season, I know I have to shed old habits. There's a hole where traces of summer used to dwell.

As a foreigner in Japan, I can't find my usual autumn comforts. Sweet beans become my chocolate, figs my fruit of choice. There's an unidentifiable smell in the air. I can't tell if it's a flower at its peak or a plum tree beyond its prime. Winter looms too close. When the wind blows, the leaves rustle at my feet. I'm callously blown around.

Then one day I ask my students what their favorite season is. Everyone always says fall or spring.

"Winter," he says.

"Why?" I retort with an edge of defensiveness.

"It's peaceful time."

"It's A peaceful time," I correct. But I have a gnawing feeling that I'm the one who has been corrected.

2
knowing how
to
not know

In Japan, I don't know many things. I don't know precisely how deep to bend my upper body in a "greeting bow" versus a "thank you bow" versus an "I understand bow." I don't know what type of sauce goes with what type of noodle. I don't know what all the buttons on my toilet do.

I look again at the ordinarily overlooked. In the list of ingredients on my flu medicine, I see ornate calligraphy. The handmade paper wrapping on my box of sweets is worthy of a frame. My gooey food spirals playfully around chopsticks and sometimes falls in the space between my bowl and my mouth. I think I said "you're welcome" instead of "thank you." I think I asked her where her nose is. I think I burped instead of slurped. I don't know many things. But sometimes I think I know. And that's where I get stuck, closed off to the unknown, blind to possibility.

Yes, I remember winter. I know cold. I know rain and its snowy incarnations.

Kanazawa has thunderstorms in winter. This I didn't know. This I wasn't exactly happy to know. Typhoons sweep across the valley, breaking branches, tossing hair, stealing umbrellas. An incessant rain pelts the pavement. My breath shortens. My body tightens. The thunder sounds like an angry animal. My heart pumps harder in its presence. I pull my covers tighter around my neck.

To end class one day, some chitchat about the weather:

"Bad weather this week, eh? So much rain! So many violent storms! Winter's coming." My voice lowers in disappointment.

"I like thunder," he says. The class laughs. I shoot him a quizzical glance.

"You know buri?"

"Buri...??" My voice rises in bewilderment.

"Yellowtail fish."

"Yes, I know yellowtail."

"You can eat best buri in winter season." The class knows this. They nod in agreement. I stare blankly.

"Thunder makes fish move to shallow waters. Easy to catch. So I like thunder. Fish is most plentiful in winter. Very fresh. Very delicious! Kanazawa most famous for winter buri."

"Oh, I didn't know." He smiles. I pause, taking a moment to soak up his explanation. Hmmm...thunder and buri...I like that.

The time is up, and we exit the classroom. Filing hesitantly out into the cold. There's a faint hum of thunder today and a gray, expansive sky cut dramatically by snow-capped mountains. Winter brought a change in air pressure that lifted the heavy fog of summer and fall, revealing these rocky landscapes. Massive. Majestic. Mysterious. I take a deeper breath when I see them in the distance. I can see my breath. It joins the wind that blows to the mountains. On the other side of those mountains is the sea. In the sea, thousands of buri are thrashing around to the rhythm of thunder. Somewhere a fisherman smiles.

In all my experience of thunder, I never considered its positive effects. My shivers and shutters at its boom-bang-cackle made me think I knew all there is to know about thunder. I'm not sure I know what bad weather is anymore, and I'm glad.

3
is it a bird?
is it a plane?

The pink has descended on Japan. As the country prepares for sakura, or the infamous spring cherry blossoms, a pink commercial explosion introduces flower-shaped sweets, blossom-printed backpacks, spring-style school uniforms, all in shades of pink. I never thought I'd embrace a color most girls in America are pigeonholed into accepting. "It's a girl" is code for, "Now I can buy that adorable kid's pink pajama set." I used to run from pink like it was the devil.

"Oh, I don't want it. It's pink."

"Do you by any chance have this in another color?"

"It's too pink for my liking."

"I'd take purple over pink any day."

"It looks like a flamingo threw up in here!"

In Japan, pink is a gender-neutral color. It's the color of spring. The color that marks the end of snowy days and frigid nights. The color that cracks a smile on everyone's winter mask. Most kids know how to say pink before they can say hello. It's a friendly color that can warm timid children to a scary-looking English teacher putting on her silly face in a desperate attempt to win their affection.

"Head, shoulders, knees and toes, knees and toes..."

"A, B, C, D, E, F, G..."

"One little, two little, three little elephants...four little five little six little elephants..." Blank stares. A tighter grip on Mommy's leg. Wrinkled faces. The quiver of a tear. Oh no, this isn't going so well...

Time for pink.

I whip out the old color flashcards. Like magnets, the kids are pulled toward pink. They start to smile. They start to high-five me back and detach from their parents. I look into their eyes, and I know I've won them over.

The sun sets a little later these days. Today I go for a walk without a jacket. Suddenly, I hear a voice. "SUGOI!!!!!!!" You only need to spend one day in Japan to know what this means...("AMAZING!!!!!!!"). I look up. A family of three is pointing at what looks like an ordinary tree. I wait for them to leave before I take a closer look. There before my very eyes are the first rosy buds of a sakura tree. Stretching toward the sun. Lengthening against the last winds of winter. My heart leaps at their insistent pink. The sakura are coming!! The sakura are coming!! I'm five again. And I skip into spring.

4
nature's
paradox

Three weeks ago the late winter sun splashed its brilliance across the Kanazawa sky. I walked home extra slow that day. Two weeks ago I opened my curtains to let in the morning, and a white heron skirted past my window. It left me breathless. One week ago, on March 11, 2011, a 9.0 magnitude earthquake hit the Tohoku region of Japan. Shortly afterwards, tsunami waves over twenty meters high hurled themselves onto the land. Fear turned to shock. Shock turned to sadness. Sadness turned to compassion. Yesterday morning a swallow followed me to work, dancing to the rhythm of its tweets. I gave myself permission to smile. I'm confounded by the paradox of nature—simultaneously playful and dangerous, continually giving and taking life.

Today the air smells of melted snow and new earth. Spring has come. The weight of wool clothes and sting of whipping winds has lightened. I'm liberated. I'm also chained. Chained to the news. Every day the death toll rises. Every day more people are displaced. This year, spring has ushered in new shoots and the promise of pink in a landscape haunted by fear.

"I'm sending food to my family in Yokohama."

"We're worried about radiation, but we can't leave."

"I feel guilty hoarding canned food and bottled water, but I'm afraid."

"I'm angry at the government."

"The Japanese media is hiding the truth."

"Will people stop buying Japanese goods?"

And then one day, through a smile that's really more of a wince, he asks me a question.

"Do you want to go back to your country?"

"No," I say. "I'm going to Sendai."

5
three stories
from
sendai

Her house will be demolished, yet we are shoveling out the mud. She is tossing what look like important, official documents, yet keeping little key chains and bookmarks. I just spent hours pulling paper off dead trees while she pulled weeds from a desolate landscape. We're sweeping the dirt from the sidewalks. We're cleaning the rubble. What's the use? Her house is going to be demolished. Nothing really makes sense. Her house is going to be demolished because a tsunami stimulated by a massive earthquake destroyed it. Nothing really makes sense. She squints under her hat. The sun is bright and intense. A dark, cloudy sky would be better suited to this scene. Debris scattered everywhere. Her old neighborhood is an apocalyptic wasteland. We are helping her pick up the pieces and hold on to a few memories from the past.

No one is here, only rubble. The laundry rack is still hanging in the window, the clothes dried with mud. Trees, furniture, dead fish, old food, mud, and dirt jammed into the apartment building. Junk. But as we pick away at the layers of this waste, we begin to see the scattered remnants of people's lives. A phone off the hook. Kids' backpacks still stuffed with notebooks and pencil cases. Wedding certificates. Polaroid pictures of little boys eating noodles at the table we just chucked onto the garbage pile.

"They're still alive. Everyone from this apartment building escaped. They're all living in evacuation centers. I'm sure this family wants their memorabilia back."

We put those irreplaceable items in a separate pile. I slide my goggles off my eyes, onto my head and scan the scene with unobstructed vision. I keep doing this every hour. I can't grasp the reality of it. Closets full of closet things. Flip-flops in the bathroom. Torn teddy bears. A Nintendo DS player. A busted bag of rice. Cabinets with dishes. Baskets with toys. A full refrigerator. Life frozen in an instant of terror. A teapot precariously propped on the stove. I empty its liquid contents from the spout and turn my head away as the overpowering scent of old water and dead fish contaminates the air.

"There's that tsunami smell," he laughs. He's been doing this for a month. I only came yesterday. It's hard to smile. I'm in shock.

As the weekend unfolds and we go from house to house shoveling mud, scraping oil, picking up the pieces, the same smell haunts us. It lingers on our clothes. I can even still smell it in my hair after showering in the evenings.

We walk the path to a doorway, stepping on shells and bones from the bottom of the ocean that now lay caked in the yard. Oil marks deface the outside of their relatively undamaged home. In our old clothes, rubber boots, gloves, and goggles, we set to work scrubbing, wiping away traces of the tsunami.

The job is mostly a cosmetic one, but it would have been difficult for this elderly couple to do alone. Her eyes are soft and smiling. She works diligently beside us, bending as low as her frail body will allow. He continually circles the perimeter of the house, refilling our buckets and replacing our sponges. She brings us tea and coffee and fruits as we work. He helps us take down the screens and lengthen the hose.

They only returned home from the evacuation center yesterday. She explains her situation in Japanese. I can't understand all the words she uses to tell her story, but her voice trembles and her breaths are ragged. I can see that the house next door is unsalvageable. Her family was lucky. She pauses abruptly, perhaps to recount a painful memory. I don't understand her words, but the story written on her face tells me everything.

Cherry blossom buds continue to stretch and grow. Soil is turned inside out. The cycle of the seasons. An old woman hobbles past kids playing ball in the street. The cycle of a generation. I inhale everything and sweep my arms up to the sky. I exhale everything and bend forward. Elongate my spine. Arms extend, palms facing upward. Hinge and fold. When I give to Japan, I'm also thanking Japan for its many gifts to me.

6
under
the
ume

> "Is it crazy over there in Japan?"
> "How are the Japanese people coping?"
> "Are people scared? Anxious? Sad?"
> "What's the mood in Kanazawa?"

Last weekend, I went to Kenroku-en Garden to see the plum blossoms, called ume. Like sakura, ume are one of the first signs of spring. Cotton-candy-like. The flowers stay close to their branches, hardly altering the shape of the tree. The garden is alive with people marveling at the flowers, using macro lenses to capture anatomical details. In Japan, a flower is like a rare Picasso, and this photography frenzy, like the buzz on a gallery's opening night.

Under the ume, couples cozy up on benches and stones. Children dance. Families picnic. A respect for renewal. A sigh of relief at regeneration. An appreciation of impermanence.

"So, what are you doing this weekend?" I ask before our lesson is over.

"I'm driving to Fukushima."

Surprised, "Really?"

Silence.

"Yes." He bows his head and continues, "Driving truck of food and medical to shelter. My company give to Fukushima."

Silence, but my heart weeps in awe at his generosity.

"The other day I talk to shelter person. Very difficult situation. Many old person."

Silence.

Worried, "What about the radiation warnings?"

Silence.

"Japan is small country. We have to support each other. My name means protector. I live up to my name." He bows his head again, glasses slipping off his nose.

Silence. It seems unreal that my heart with these exploding sensations can fit into a cavity called my chest. Silence...because what I will say is better expressed with my eyes. But I say it anyway.

"You're a very good person. I respect your decision."

Silence.

"Thank you."

Silence.

Two smiles. Four eyes. Two hearts. Two currents of breath spiraling around each other. I teach English, but in these moments, the body prefers to speak its own language.

Silence...and then a smile.

"April is happy time in Japan. Hanami, cherry blossom viewing. Will you see sakura with me when I get back?"

Immediately with a smile, "I'd be honored to."

In less than one week, the cherry blossoms will bloom in Kanazawa. People will eat and drink and laugh together under the trees. They'll walk their dogs on paths of pink petals. The wind will continue its inhales and exhales, tossing old flowers this way and that, making way for new shoots.

7

walk on the other side
of
the river

How can I be a traveler in my own town? How can I see the freshness of every day? How can I reroute myself from old habits? Seasonal changes are built-in mirrors. When spring brings warm weather, and I can't remember where I stashed my sandals or how it feels to let the wind touch my skin, I become aware of my winter routine.

"Oh yeah, it's just Kanazawa Castle, and this is just Kenroku-en Garden, and that's just Oyama shrine." They stop and stare in awe. I catch myself getting impatient. I'm madly crossing the sights off our list. We've got so much ground to cover in so little time.

"What's that?" She points excitedly away from where I'm leading her. "Look at that garden! Look at that bridge!"

I shrug. Turn my head nonchalantly.

"Oh yeah, that's just...just...um...that's...um..." I'm speechless. It's beautiful. It's breathtaking. It's tucked away in the corner of the shrine grounds that I've traversed many times before, too quickly to notice the details. It's a magical garden. Where was it before? Where was I? I'm ashamed of my blindness. Thank you, Family, for opening my eyes to the new in the old. Thank you for taking me by the hand as you travel slowly.

Today is a perfect sunny day. Cool breeze. Cloudless. The city in bloom. It's hard to imagine the destruction on the other coast of the country. My family departs Kanazawa, leaving insignificant remnants of their presence in my apartment. A button. A gum wrapper. A strand of hair on my tatami mat. In the corners of every room, a fading hint of laughter. It's hard to imagine my life without them.

In my family's honor, and in honor of those who lost theirs in the earthquake, I decide to reroute myself. I decide to take a walk on the other side of the river. Simple. Profound. There on the other side is a path I never took with a statue I never saw and a pond with koi fish that I never introduced myself to. Where was it before? Where was I?

I sit on a flat rock at the edge of the pond watching koi fish come toward me. Like clockwork, they sense my presence and suck the surface of the water with ferocity. People must feed them often, I think. In a predictable pattern of classical conditioning they expect food and hover near my feet. Their scales like abstract paintings. I follow the glimmer of sunlight that bounces off their wet bodies, slips onto the skin of the water, and fractures when the wind blows ripples in the pond.

I continue my walk about town, taking paths untaken, discovering shrines and parks I've never seen before. After nine months, I thought I knew Kanazawa in and out. I was mistaken.

I loop my way back to the koi pond, expecting the fish to swarm again at my feet, the sun to dance again on the surface of the pond. Only ten minutes have passed, but the scene has changed. There, standing still on a rock, four feet from the edge of the pond is a

great

blue

heron.

Watchful.

I hold my breath, afraid to move, afraid to disturb the sublimity of this image. All the people passing by carry on as usual. They walk their same walk. Paying no attention. No one seems to notice the heron. My heart beats faster. I've never been so close to a heron before. I sit again at the edge of the pond trying to soak it all in before it changes. The koi fish come over. The sun reflects in the water. The heron stays motionless. I become aware of beauty and fragility and the waves of impermanence that bring freshness to the familiar.

Suddenly, the heron turns its head and looks me in the eyes. It spreads its wings, leaps into the air, and soars above my head. Between its wing beats I hear a message.

Wake up Brenna. Wake up. Travel slowly and you'll see.

8

turning time into moments
instead of
moments into time

It's a funny thing about time. Time slows down in waiting rooms and train stations. In the pulse of summer heat, time looms languid. So it goes when we're uncomfortable, when we want something to be over, or when we focus on what we lack. One motion becomes one hundred tedious movements. The second hand on the clock moves in lead-heavy strokes. There's a visible pause between the back and the forth of a fan.

These are the little moments, I tell myself. Let them drip-tick-tock. Let them let you breathe and appreciate. When we want something deeply, time lengthens so we have an opportunity to reach for it.

When I think of time, I think of the seasons. The seasons are so integral to Japanese culture. With this connection comes a perpetual celebration of change, an awareness of the temporary, and a respect for the old. Every season has its special fruits, meals, activities, clothing, and festivals. It's been like this for centuries. I notice the passage of time more in Japan. Perhaps because it's all so continuously new. Perhaps because life and death aren't polar opposites here.

Now it's summer again in Kanazawa, nearly one year after my arrival. I constantly feel time. Slowing down. Speeding up. I thought winter would never end, but now the cold summer noodles I used to eat are back in the grocery stores. Walking home from school at night, I am once again enveloped by the swell of cricket songs and the hot, humid air that sings with wind chimes. I remember how that air hugged me when I arrived last summer.

I see the change in Japan, the change a tragedy ushers forth. I see images of grass growing in unsalvageable apartments and the reconstruction of a school. I see people in evacuation centers smiling as they go home. I see young college students with spiky hair and rainbow stockings marching in protest before a nuclear power plant.

I see the change in me. I am more patient. I am more aware. I have let go in order to embrace. I have discovered that, like life, time unfolds in cycles of destruction and creation, the end of an hour, the beginning of a moment. You choose how to perceive it. There is no waiting for something to be over or for something else to begin. A year, two years, ten years, fast, slow…fluctuates with thought, and everything in between continues to wilt and renew.

Fandom
International

An interview with
Daniel Ketchum, editor at Marvel Comics

WHAT HE DOES:

A comic book editor is charged with managing the process of getting the stories from the creators' heads to the readers' hands. This entails everything from creating and maintaining the overall vision for any given book, hiring talent, line editing scripts, providing feedback to artists, setting and enforcing deadlines, making sure freelancers are paid, and producing auxiliary print and digital content for each issue. And more and more, Marvel editors serve as a face for the company, promoting our titles online and in real life, at comic conventions. It's a demanding job, but made totally worth it by the fact you tell stories for a living...and decide who Captain America is going to fight each month.

FAVORITE WORK-TRAVEL MOMENT OF ALL TIME:

Since so much of my life has been tied to comics over the past seven years, it's hard to pick just one. But I do have what I might consider a "coming of age" moment in my career. In 2011 I was one of only a couple Marvel editors sent to C2E2 (the Chicago Comic and

Entertainment Expo) in Chicago, and I was the only editor from the X-Men franchise in attendance. It just so happened that C2E2 decided to host an X-Men-specific panel that year. So it ended up being virtually just me on a stage in front of a room full of fans for a full hour.

WHY THIS WAS TERRIFYING:

At that point in my career, I had only sat on a couple of panels previously, and yes, was terrified by them. If you've never seen a Marvel panel, it's pretty much this: for fifteen minutes the editors and comic creators present a slideshow that informs fans about the exciting developments in various titles and what they can to look forward to reading in the coming months. After that, there are forty-five minutes of free-for-all where the folks onstage take any question the audience throws. You never know what to expect. Some personality types may thrive on that, but me, I am a planner. So an open format scares the bejesus out of me. Maybe I think about it too much, but when you're onstage at a show you have to balance so many things. You need to answer questions as fully as possible, but without giving away anything that hasn't yet been announced by the company. You must remember all of the correct shipping dates and creator names attached to a project, and ramble through all of it without cussing (this is a problem more often than you might think). And all while keeping the room entertained and not looking like a doofus. These are not skills I typically think of as being in my wheelhouse.

THE BIG MOMENT:

After the slideshow at this panel we moved on to the question-and-answer period. Of course, I was initially filled with terror, but then...I don't know whether I felt cornered by the fact I was on my own, or if instead I was completely freed by it. But what followed was later described by someone on the Internet as "Daniel Ketchum QUEERED. IT. UP." This Zen feeling came over me and I just started chatting with the audience like I would with my fellow "White Queens" (the Marvel gays) over Sunday brunch. It was great. The audience rolled with what I gave them and the panel turned into more of a discussion—one that culminated in a disclosure of my fantasy dream project: editing a series about my favorite character, Storm, titled "Storm: She Beats Bitches Up With Weather." See, I told you it wasn't easy to keep from cussing.

HOW HE GOT THERE:

I attended a really wonderful undergraduate program that I affectionately refer to as "The School of Choose Your Own Adventure." My adviser encouraged me to study whatever lit my fire, no matter how far-flung or unconventional it may be. So I chose to pursue something I had been passionate about since the third grade: comic books. In my final year there, I thought I should do something to legitimize my years of reading comics for school credit, so I applied for an internship at Marvel Comics. I had been teaching at a private school in Brooklyn at the time, suspecting that I would probably go on to become a teacher following graduation, but the stars sort of aligned and I ended up on a very different path. I landed the internship at Marvel. I interned there for one semester in the spring of 2006. On my last day of the internship, the associate editor I was working for told me that he was leaving the company and asked if I wanted his spot. I graduated from school two weeks later, and then just two weeks after that I was at my desk at Marvel. I've been on the editorial staff ever since, now seven years later as a full editor in the X-Men Office.

THE GROWTH OF FANDOM:

Comic conventions have long been an odd hybrid of trade show, professional conference, and comic fan extravaganza. But they've grown even more eclectic in recent years, as they've expanded to encompass other industries as well, such as gaming (both video games and tabletop gaming), film, and television. I've attended every New York Comic Con at the Javits Convention Center, in Manhattan, and I've witnessed it explode in size as comic conventions now cater not only to comics, but also to many corners of geekdom.

So, the recent Madrid Comic Expo was a nice change of pace for me, as it was almost exclusively focused on comics. I've attended a handful of different shows in the United States, and Madrid was smaller than any, in floor space and guests. The booths were occupied by vendors from all throughout Europe, and they carried everything from mainstream American comics, to anime, to the beautiful oversize and hardbound albums that are typically found in Europe.

IN TRANSLATION:

Virtually all the work I did at the Madrid Expo was reviewing portfolios. Prior to the show, the organizers allowed aspiring artists and writers to sign up to have samples of their work critiqued. About one in every four artists I met with spoke one of the same languages as me. I took seven years of French in school, but unfortunately the only Spanish I know comes from restaurant menus. And it's sometimes especially difficult to communicate at a comic convention, where so much of the language is specialized and specific to the comics medium. I was lucky enough to have the help of a translator to facilitate communication. Even then, we would run into trouble where the specific usage of a word didn't quite match up with what would logically be its Spanish counterpart. Interestingly, trouble words included "perspective," "panel," "layouts," and "storytelling."

Really though, at the heart of it, the experience was the same as it's always been anywhere else: sitting with an artist and discussing their craft. This truly is one of my favorite parts of the job.

THIS ONE GIRL:

I was reviewing a young artist's portfolio and while she was incredibly talented, it was apparent that she was drawing from her head rather than referencing real life. When I suggested that she draw from life, she gave me a confused look. I was unsure whether it was because she didn't know what I was suggesting or if my restaurant menu Spanish was failing me. So I pulled out paper and a couple pencils right on the spot and said that we'd take a minute to draw the man sitting across the table from us. And as we sat there drawing, it became like a little bubble of calm and creation amid the hectic convention environment. It was a really cool moment, and we were bonded on a fundamental level by our mutual love for comics and art. When we finished, she told me that she was excited to do it again. And just recently actually, she sent me a bunch of sketches she's done since we met. I love that!

THE INTERNATIONAL COMIC BOOK COMMUNITY:

My experiences at conventions like this one have left me with the impression that the creators and fans in Europe are not so dissimilar from those in New York or anywhere else. Perhaps it's because these events all spring from the same storytelling medium and a love of the same properties, be it Spider-Man, Skywalker, or old-school Mario. In broader terms? I think the comic offerings in the U.S. aren't as diverse as they are abroad. While U.S. comics are typically associated with superheroes (though that does seem to be changing quickly), that isn't the case in other countries, where comics span every imaginable genre. I think the readership reflects that diversity.

A CONNECTION:

Though geek culture has further found its way into the mainstream in recent years, there is still some profound connection felt when you find someone else who also rolls a healer in "World of Warcraft," or who played in the most recent "Magic: The Gathering" prerelease. The same is true of comics. Growing up, I would regularly find myself asked, "You read comics?!" I was made "other" by my love for comics. But it was always nice to find someone else who read them, because—and I believe this is a truth applicable to most things—when you find someone else who loves something that you love, it makes you love it that much more. Traveling abroad to attend a comic convention is the feeling of finding someone who loves the same thing you do—but times a few thousand. Sharing this common ground means that you always have something to talk about. But even more than that, you feel a kinship, like you've found your people. You get to be "other" together. Even though I didn't speak the language and I was in a city I'd never before visited, I was always at ease in Madrid because I was with my people.

FINE ART AND HAM:

In Spain, there was one other thing I knew I absolutely wanted to do while I was there: visit the Prado Museum. Luckily, one of the Spanish artists attending the convention also happens to be chair of the Illustration Department at the Maryland Institute College of Art. So not only was I able to go to the Prado, but I was given a tour by this incredibly talented and knowledgeable artist. It was a fantastic experience afforded to me by my work in comics in more ways than one. As a totally unrelated bonus, he also took us to the famous Museum of Ham—a restaurant that's directly out of the fever dream of anyone currently on a low-carb diet.

WHY HE LOVES THE COMIC BOOK INDUSTRY:

At its heart, it's fueled by creative people who want to tell stories. It's inspiring to be surrounded by people who are actively contributing to an art form and a community that you love.

NYClopedia

New York City

Ian Bardenstein

Anonymity, Part 1: We pass Ben Stiller at Hudson River Park. Behind steely, blue-tinted aviators, his face betrays a naked desire for anonymity.

Anonymity, Part 2: I am only able to have a perfectly ordinary conversation with Joni Mitchell's ex-husband because I don't recognize or know anything about him. Then a friend whispers to me. Normalcy crumbles.

Balls: Will's roommate takes us to an art show sponsored by a crudely-named vodka company. The art—pictures and looping video of the ocean—is no better than the vodka. Dollar tips wilt in sticky heat. Finally, we're drunk.

Birth*day*: How long from your actual day of birth is it still appropriate to accept happy birthday wishes without correcting people? I don't want to be one of those people who abuse the scarcity of a birthday by stretching one day into a prolonged self-celebration.

Brooklyn Bridge: After waiting for a nice day to give way to a nice night, we walk across the bridge toward the earthbound constellations of Manhattan. Ella somehow keeps disappearing despite her turquoise pants.

Brunch: I order chicken salad, envisioning chunks of brined chicken, celery, mayo, walnuts, grapes, a little salt and pepper. A green salad topped with chicken strips arrives at my table.

Color: The bruising between broken toes is a nice shade of purple. For a second, I forget they're mine.

Dedication: On the weekends, Brian spends long hours rehearsing with his band in Brooklyn. In high school, his abrupt exits often concluded our band practices in his basement. "I gotta shower," he'd say, discarding his drum sticks.

Dogs: Men who need a lot of attention are very much like dogs.

Dress code: It's too humid to wear anything but shorts the first weekend, even to the bars. Friends plead my case to impassive bouncers. The second weekend, we go to a lounge where the dress code is simply "No fur."

Dumbo: Sasha wants to move to the cohabitation-hip neighborhood in the shadow of the Brooklyn Bridge, when she gets married. That sounds far off until I realize it's been six years since high school.

Face-off: Sasha, Cat, and I wait outside Cat's apartment. Finally Michael emerges in a maroon V-neck and sees that my sweater is the same color. "This can't happen," he says. "I'm changing."

Fat Cat: People come to this bar for Ping-Pong, shuffleboard, even chess. A pick-up salsa band plays. It's an oasis because no one is here to be seen.

Frohawk: It's been a couple years now that Aaron's had his frohawk. It didn't use to seem like an enduring hairstyle. Now there must be a growing population of Brooklynites who don't know him without it.

Frontier: In Manhattan's Alphabet City the buildings grow dense and narrow. A siren that almost fits in with the music from the bars lends a tinge of urgency to the Saturday night revelry.

Grown-up: Seeing how other people have matured since high school makes me feel undeniably adult. When I was younger, I never thought that one day I would be friends with a teacher.

Joseph Leonard: A knife from the neighboring table falls onto the floor, almost stabbing my foot. Ten minutes later I unwittingly return the favor. The waiters laugh and threaten to separate us.

Manifest Destiny: I'm walking around Williamsburg, Brooklyn. Gentrification seems inevitable, a natural process whereby Money always follows Cool like an annoying little brother.

Murray Hill: Irish bars and sushi restaurants abound in Manhattan's halfway house for college grads transitioning to the real world.

Naïveté: It's Fleet Week. Young naval officers in pristine white uniforms weave through the streets in search of girls and free drinks. Something about their attitude concerns me.

Pizza: For some reason in Brooklyn all I eat is pizza.

Perspective: "You should probably stop doing that," Cat says. We're on the roof of her apartment building. Skylights protrude from the roof like bubbles crossing a membrane. It's fascinating. I've never seen our human habitats from above, and so I peer into living room after living room.

Projectiles: Playing catch is an evolutionary impulse that helped our ancestors attract mates and develop hunting skills. At least, this is how I justify my insistence on playing Frisbee at Long Beach. Amanda indulges me while Ella sprawls out beneath the graying heavens.

Real-life J-Date: On nice Saturdays, young Orthodox Jews gather on the north side of Central Park's Great Lawn to mingle, hoping to find their *bashert* (Yiddish: destined soul mate).

Rental dogs: It costs Seth five dollars to rent a woman's shaggy black dog for twenty minutes at Central Park.

Reversal: In Brooklyn, do visiting Manhattanites become the bridge-and-tunnel crowd?

Shake Shack: The Shack Stack burger sneaks in a whole fried and breaded portabella mushroom. The crinkle-cut fries are definitely tasty, despite a resemblance to the soggy specimens from my elementary school's cafeteria.

Shed: Michael tells me that in Australia, maintaining a shed is a legitimate hobby for a middle-aged man. The shed is a sanctuary and base of manly operations. Inside its modest frame the shed owner might tinker, drink beer, listen to old records, or watch sports. He might also occasionally lean outside to brandish a shotgun at the nearest young person.

Size, Part 1: "Just to warn you, he's short," Erin says. Her boyfriend might meet us in Central Park. "I'm pretty sure I can handle it," I say. "No, like really short. Like my height." I've always thought of Erin as petite. Her boyfriend doesn't show.

Size, Part 2: I'm five foot ten: about average height. In many nights of couch surfing, I don't encounter a single average-size couch. My feet seem destined to dangle.

Sound: On the back patio of Carmine's in Brooklyn, Aaron and his coworker from the studio discuss the tradition of jazz musicians recording whole takes live, solos and all. The inevitable imperfections are watermarks of sorts, testaments that true improvisation has taken place.

Speechless: "Got the old-school beeper," I say, noticing her fidget with a small device at her waist. "Actually, it's an insulin pump," she replies.

Spontaneity: Ella and Amanda conduct an impromptu yoga session on the grass looking across to New Jersey. I excuse myself.

Steak Sandwich: It takes three tries for the proprietor to get Will's order right. One attempt involves a hard-boiled egg between two slices of bread. Soon we're all laughing hysterically. My clothes are soaked through after a late-night sprint during a storm. It's just good to be out of the rain.

Times Square: People flow around me, but I feel no connection to them.

Zoo: New York is more zoo than jungle.

NO REGRETS

NEW YORK CITY AND ISRAEL

DOC HALLIDAY GOLDEN

I COME FROM a racially mixed family. My mother is African American and grew up in the South. My dad is Jewish, and his family is from Austria. My parents took me to Israel as a little girl. As an adult, I desperately wanted to return. In 2004, when I was twenty, I had that opportunity.

My Israeli roommate in college told me about an organization that led trips to Israel for college kids. I thought to myself, *Why not?* It sounded like a great opportunity to learn firsthand about my rich heritage. Even though I was not brought up in a religious Jewish family, I had heard so many stories and traditions of our people from Dad.

I took a chance, made some calls, filled out an online application, and went in for an interview. Soon, I was signed up and on my way to Israel. I was unspeakably excited.

The day came for me to gather up my things and head to the airport. I did not know anyone going on this trip, but I was more than ready for the adventure. Oddly enough, when I was in the security line at New York's JFK airport, someone approached me who claimed to know me. So now I knew one person going on the trip. Either way, I was ready to go to Israel. I was ready to grow.

Once I got to my seat, I met some other college kids in our group and we became instant friends, as if we had known each other for years. It was a great flight. After about ten hours we touched down at Ben Gurion airport, in Tel Aviv. *WOOT WOOT!* There was cheering and applauding throughout the plane—from those returning home as well as those visiting for the very first time. It felt like coming home for many of us visiting as well.

From day one in Israel, it was like living a dream. They call it the Holy Land for a reason, and there truly is a holiness in the air. Driving through Jerusalem, particularly the Old City, it is breathtaking to see the land spoken of throughout the Torah, the Qur'an, and the Christian Bible.

One of the first places we went was the HaKotel, commonly known as the Western Wall, right next to site for the Dome of the Rock. This area is sacred to Christians, Jews, and Muslims alike. My introduction to Israel was magically beautiful.

Each day was an adventure and a blessing. We traveled all over Israel by bus, with armed Israel Defense Forces soldiers, learning and trying new things everywhere. Listening to music we don't regularly listen to, eating foods we don't normally eat, and doing things we don't generally do.

The first few days we stayed on a Kibbutz, which is often (but not always) a cooperatively owned farm. Members are not paid but are provided with housing, clothing, food, medical care, and education, by families within the community. Everyone has roles/responsibilities and works to maintain the community. In two days of staying there, I was convinced this was the way to live. I loved that everyone worked together, with and for one another, rather than how things seem to operate in New York—with everyone trying to outdo the next guy and put themselves on top.

A couple days into the trip was Shabbat, the Jewish day of rest. I knew about this observance, but did not observe it growing up; something else exciting for me to experience for the first time. That evening we went to a Shabbat service and enjoyed a lovely Shabbat dinner. We continued the night talking leisurely and sitting around the fireplace in the Kibbutz.

We told stories and shared laughs. We were very comfortable with one another by this point, and some of my new friends, noticing that I looked different than most of the people on the trip, started to ask me a few honest questions. "So, how are you Jewish exactly?" "Were you raised Jewish?" "What do you believe?" "How does that all work?" None of the questions offended me. In fact, I quite appreciated that they seemed genuinely interested to know about me. They listened intently as I explained my upbringing. Most of them were fascinated because in the families they came from few people married outside the Jewish culture.

After we'd hung around the fireplace for several hours, past the stroke of midnight, our larger group branched off into smaller groups of three or four that went on to hang out in people's rooms. Why not? We were young and in Israel and it was the Sabbath. We were very limited in what we were permitted to do on the Sabbath, but we could talk all night and learn about each other.

Sure, Judaism is a religion, but being Jewish is a culture, an ethnic identity. If that weren't so, the Holocaust would not have taken place the way it did. To me, if you have one parent from Brazil and one parent from Germany, you are just as Brazilian as you are German. Likewise, if you have one Jewish parent and one non-Jewish parent, you are fully both. If I tell you the names of my family members who perished in the Holocaust, no one can tell me they are not my family.

Although it was a good amount of our conversation, we did not talk solely about race, religion, and culture. We talked about everything. *Who are you? Who am I? What do you like? What do you want to do with your life?*

The next afternoon many of us went for a nice, long nature walk through the woods to a local mountain. It was great; rest and fun at the same time. As we walked, we learned more about Israel's history, enjoyed our new friends, some of whom already seemed like family. When we returned, it was just about time for Havdalah, the ceremony that marks the end of the Sabbath, welcoming the new week.

Over the next few days we continued our adventures. Jerusalem, Tel Aviv, the Golan Heights—we were going to see and do everything we could in our two weeks. One night we went out to a place where we ate and did some traditional dancing. If there is one thing I am not known for, it's dancing. But this particular night was different. To the rich melodies and harmonies of traditional Israeli music we danced the night away. Not only do they use instruments that we don't generally use in the U.S. but they also have notes that don't exist in Western scales. It was beautiful. I was sweating, laughing, and having a blast.

In between group dances and celebratory yelling, I was pulled aside by one of our leaders, it happened to be the young lady that had interviewed me for the trip. She asked me if I was having a good time. I said, "Absolutely. I am having the time of my life." She continued asking me a bunch of simple, small-talk questions. It started out as a pleasant conversation. Then the questions continued and increased with intensity until I heard, "Is Jesus your Messiah?" I responded, "Yes." She continued to ask me several more times in a few different ways. Then she proceeded to tell me that I might have to leave Israel. I reminded her that she and I had spoken at length in New York about how I was not raised in a religious Jewish home, and that she had assured me this was not a religious trip but one "made for people just like me." People who wanted to learn about their heritage and experience Israel for themselves.

The next day it was confirmed. I was to be sent back to the United States immediately—and alone.

My heart was broken. I was devastated. I had been having such fun, learning so much about Israel, my people, even myself; I'd made several good friends and now, suddenly, it was all being stripped away from me. The organizers allowed me to say good-bye to everyone that night before dinner. With tears pouring out of my eyes, I told them I was leaving and how much I enjoyed my week with them. I didn't have much more to say because I didn't understand what was going on or why. I just knew I was leaving.

After my tearful good-bye, I met with some of the other leaders on the trip, two in particular, who apologized profusely for what was happening to me. They said that they really appreciated me being on the trip and were outraged about how it was being dealt with. One of them, a man in his mid-twenties, was so livid that he actually cried tears with me in the stairwell of the hotel. He did not have the authority to change the situation, but his tears meant a lot.

That night, in the lobby of my hotel, I met up with one of the soldiers who had been assigned to our bus as we traveled throughout Israel. I told him about what happened and that I was being sent back to New York the next day. I don't know why, but he was devastated. Devastated at the idea and the hypocrisy, I suppose, of what I was experiencing. I met up with him around 10 p.m. that night. He comforted me in the lobby of the hotel all night, listening to me and holding me as I cried. He sang to me in Hebrew, knowing I couldn't understand the words, but I could the comfort. Shortly after the sun came up, I had to return to my room to get ready because the taxi to the airport would be there soon.

I was on my way back to New York, traveling alone with way too much time for my mind to think about everything that happened—the good, the not so good, and all the whys.

When I returned to New York, I didn't tell anyone I was back. I was back a week early and I was ashamed that I'd been sent home. I was angry and confused about what seemed to me to be wrong. I had been upfront with the organizers about everything from the beginning, and was reassured that I was absolutely welcomed; I abode by every rule they had, and yet I was asked to leave because I was apparently a disgrace, or was a threat? Why exactly was I sent home to America with such haste and intensity?

It took me a bit, but after a while I let go of the shame; after all I was in fact innocent. My hands were clean and my heart was pure. My words were honest. The shame turned into pride. I was tremendously grateful for the time and the experiences that I had, the people I met, and the knowledge that I did the right thing. I stood for who I am, what I believe, and there is no shame in that.

To this day, nearly ten years later, I keep in contact with the soldier who comforted me that night. He has visited me in New York on multiple occasions and I long to visit him again in Israel.

No regrets.

Scot's Story

San Francisco

Mark Bessen

IN 1981, A twenty-two-year-old Caucasian man staggered into the urgent care clinic at San Francisco General Hospital, clutching his side to control his coughing. Swollen purple lesions spotted his legs. He made it down the hall and into the exam room with the support of his lover under one arm and a nurse under the other. He died two days later, after being diagnosed with an anomalous case of Kaposi's sarcoma. The nurse and an oncologist looked on as the young man's lover knelt beside the hospital bed, his trembling forehead pressed into the crisp, white sheets.

Within the next month, more young men were admitted into urgent care, all suffering from similarly inexplicable conditions: atypical lymphomas, meningitis, tuberculosis, skin lesions, bodily wasting—all in what were previously healthy, active men.

Then the trickle of patients expanded into a deluge, filling emergency rooms and urgent care centers across San Francisco.

By 1983, frantic to contain the enigmatic epidemic, health and policy officials dedicated the entirety of Ward 86 at San Francisco General to patients with the symptoms characteristic of what we now call Acquired Immunodeficiency Syndrome (AIDS). The quarantine unit hung sixty feet in the air, giving patients a view of their now aching city. Extensive safety precautions were enforced, as studies on the transmissibility of the virus were inconclusive. The ward quickly devolved from a treatment center into a hospice, where doctors and nurses tried to comfort dying patients and their helpless loved ones.

Today the red bricks covering the exterior walls of Building 80 at San Francisco General are faded. Six floors above a concrete walkway, the windows of Ward 86 remain evenly spaced twenty feet apart to allow sunshine and warm breezes to drift inside when the Fog City weather obliges. At least, that's what they were designed for. Now the windows are shut, blinds drawn to prevent a glance into the past.

When I walked past the charge nurse's office at Ward 86 in the last week of April 2012, she glanced at me over half-moon glasses that rested obediently on the tip of her nose. Her face was tired—the skin under her eyes had settled into woeful parabolas; creases framed her thin lips after almost thirty years of bravely holding up the corners of her mouth. She had been part of the team that initially volunteered to staff the ward. The nurse moved slowly as she set down the pen that had been scribbling notes into a chart, and stood up with a creak of her chair before greeting us.

My college group and I were spending a week traveling around San Francisco to learn about the impact of HIV and AIDS in the city, and we were making a stop at the historic Ward 86.

The nurse reached out a wrinkled hand that I met with my own.

"Thank you for being a part of this effort," she said in a measured voice.

But what had I done? I'd watched some films, interviewed patients, and read a few articles on a cause to which she'd devoted her life. She had spent thirty years caring for HIV-positive patients. I wasn't born until more than a decade after that man died in 1981, his lover at his side. More importantly, I wasn't even born when another man was hospitalized in Ward 86—my uncle, Scot.

At family reunions—few and far between in a family of busy physicians—I've heard pieces of Scot's story. Fragments, misplaced subtleties; never anything concrete. It all happened before I was born. And I've been too timid to ask much more, after a seemingly benign comment from my mother chills the air at the dinner table into silence, or when merlot and the mention of his son fuel my grandfather's flaming temper. Whatever the truth, it's not my story. I don't even know whose it is, because no one will stake claim to it.

Family history is elusive when interaction feels like a business exchange. So I string together what I have, filling in holes.

Here's how the story, consistently, seems to play out:

The unit phone rang at a reception desk at a Los Angeles hospital. One of the doctors lay half-asleep on an exam table in an empty patient room down the hall. Decades of being on-call had made her hate that phone's shrill chirp, especially while taking advantage of a short break between back-to-back shifts. The doctor groaned slightly as she heard her receptionist's footsteps coming down the hall. She anticipated the light knock on the door.

"Doctor, a phone call for you."

"Who is it?" she replied, opening the door and removing the red flag that indicated the room had been occupied.

The receptionist shrugged.

The doctor picked up the phone and was greeted by a trembling voice on the other end, obviously trying hard to temper its emotion. The voice was unfamiliar, as was the rush of symptoms, dates, and numerical data. Just as the doctor was losing her patience, ready to hang up, the voice mentioned her son, Scot.

Scot was her fourth out of five children, all of whom were formulaically spaced out in two-year intervals. Like his three siblings before him, Scot had gone to medical school and become a physician. He eventually ended up working long hours at San Francisco General Hospital.

Scot's mother, my own grandmother, had been a textbook good mother while Scot was still living at home. She took him to his diving practices, found him a tutor when he got a low grade in chemistry, and signed his birthday cards "Love, Mom." But she and Scot were never close. Except for the obligatory Mother's Day bouquet and birthday phone call, once Scot left for college, he never looked back.

The two had been out of touch for years by the time my grandmother received that phone call in 1991. Perhaps that had been for the best. My grandfather's domineering position on family values had buried the concept of Scot's "variant" sexuality so deeply and darkly that the word "gay" has still yet to surface in their household. But I doubt that my grandmother would have been as brash. Once when I accidentally let slip that I thought an actor in the latest romantic comedy was attractive, she smiled from across the table; my grandfather went rigid.

Regardless, when the voice on the phone at the hospital that day finally gathered itself and became clear, the speaker chose to fabricate a story that Scot had become ill after being pricked by a needle while at work in the emergency room. And to this day, that is the story my grandmother tells when asked about her son's disease.

"Scot is very sick," said the voice. He then identified himself to my grandmother as one of Scot's colleagues. Much later, the man would truthfully identify himself as Scot's partner.

"You should come see him as soon as you can," he said.

Without further question, my grandmother obediently got on the next departing flight from Los Angeles to San Francisco. She took a cab over rain-slicked hills, driving directly from the airport to San Francisco General. When she arrived at the hospital's main entrance, a receptionist directed my grandmother across the grounds to Building 80, sixth floor: Ward 86. She was then fully aware that her son was dying of AIDS.

My grandmother made her way that night alone. Her coat was held tightly over her head, but water continued running down her face.

She dried off just inside the lobby, and a security guard directed her toward the elevator which announced its arrival with a ding and an orange light. The same light flickered undecidedly when I visited Ward 86, twenty-one years later. But that night, the elevator jerkily lifted my grandmother to the ward. She walked down the corridor, whose linoleum floors and sterile walls were perhaps too familiar. She found Scot's room; the door was ajar, and she nudged her way inside.

"Hello," Scot's on-call nurse greeted her, anxiously checking Scot's vitals. But my grandmother paid no attention. She could do nothing but stare into the blue eyes of the emaciated stranger lying in the hospital bed in front of her, tucked beneath crisp, white sheets.

My uncle died in 1991, one year before I was born and one year before antiretroviral combination therapy would have become available to him.

On my own visit to Ward 86, as I squeezed a nurse's hardened hand, I felt a connection to Scot that I had never experienced before. I imagined that this woman might have known about Scot's life better than any of the family members he couldn't relate to, and better than any secondhand fragments could tell me. I wondered if she might have known him, but I did not ask.

Allah and the Los Angeles Lakers

United States – the coasts

Haroon Moghul

ON JUNE 17, 2008, I turned twenty-eight years old. For my birthday, I got to watch the Boston Celtics spank my Los Angeles Lakers in Game 6 of the NBA Finals. The Lakers lost the game, the series, and the championship, by thirty-nine points. Nothing can more catastrophically wound a Lakers fan than to see his (my) team lose to the Celtics, let alone for the ninth time in the NBA finals, in Boston. It's not tremendously unlike watching Gollum hightail it out of Mount Doom with the Ring of Power, while Frodo and Sam's fellowship team bus gets attacked by Mordor's drunken citizens.

Perhaps the worst part of that day is that I watched the Lakers' humiliation while wearing my wife's birthday present to me—a Lakers warm-up jersey in their special home white. Fat lot of good that did. Don't even ask me when I next had the courage to wear it. (I still love you babe.)

Between them, the Celtics and Lakers have now met twelve times in basketball's greatest championship. The two have won more than half the NBA's titles: L.A. has won fifteen in thirty-one tries, the Celtics seventeen out of twenty-one. These teams are basketball royalty. My team even wears royal purple (sometimes they call it "forum blue") and gold. Have any other colors ever been more associated with power and glory?

Roman Emperors wore purple. When power shifted east to the city of Constantinople, the rulers kept purple. And when the Muslim Ottomans took that city and made it the seat of the Caliphate, they called themselves *Padishahan-e Rum*, the Emperors of Rome. But that Muslims once claimed to inherit the imperial mantle of Rome or the intellectual legacy of Greece, is little known. Certainly it would've surprised most everyone I grew up around, for whom Islam was entirely a mystery.

I was born in western Massachusetts, raised between there and rural Connecticut, and lived practically all my life in the American Northeast. When I travel to other places, even other parts of America, I cannot help but compare them to New England's modest communities, with their stoic manners and fierce commitment to a gentle, inclusive democracy. Growing up, I was ostensibly part of that liberal society, what the birthplace of America might have tolerated (it would be hard to say it "embraced"). I was academically successful, yet culturally alien, metaphysically tragic, and an individual outpost. I felt distant from my parents, weirdly unrelated to my friends, and left out of my local mosque since there were so few other children in my age group and I felt no durable connection to an elder generation that shared my faith but little else. My too-tanned skin color, my funny name, my incomprehensible religion, my taste for American food and grunge music—these were all sources of amusement, puzzlement, and at times harassment. Which is where the Lakers came in.

On June 15, 2010, the Lakers—2009's defending champions—turned in an impressive performance in a must-win match. It was Game 7, which the Lakers won in a nail-biting, terrifying, God-I-can't-watch fourth quarter, once again on my birthday. It is almost impossible to overestimate the importance of that one game to both of these teams, and to the Lakers' superstar Kobe Bryant, for his legacy, and even to the NBA, which must've thanked Allah (who is in fact the same God as God) that the Phoenix Suns did not meet the Orlando Magic in a Finals likely to have been welcomed like *Sex and the City 2*.

It's also amazing how important this game remains to me.

My very first NBA Finals memory was the 1987 match-up between the Lakers and—who else?—the Celtics. We won. For only the second time (against them) ever. It was Kareem Abdul-Jabbar who had teamed up with Earvin "Magic" Johnson to make the 1980s, the rejuvenation of the NBA, and the reign of the Los Angeles Lakers.

Kareem Abdul-Jabbar meant the (dream) world to me. Nor was it just me: If you visit the Muslim community of Western Massachusetts, you'll find that their children, some of us now scattered across America and other countries, feature an unlikely number of Lakers fans. We grew up in the 1980s with the Lakers and the Celtics representing two Americas, two great teams from opposite ends of the country battling it out. The Lakers won their first title of that era in 1980, the Celtics in 1981; the Celtics won their last title of that era in 1986, and the Lakers in 1988. They owned that period of NBA history between them. And it wasn't just Kareem who drew me in, not even all the excitement, the energy, the amazing talent. Forget red states and blue states. This was far more profound. This was about finding a home in America. An America that could be mine.

Because the Celtics were obviously white. They were an America we were too recently arrived in to be part of, to know how to, to want to, to understand or be understood by. How could my European-American classmates relate to my experiences, the way my parents were, the reasons for our being here—or why calling Iraqis "ragheads" during the Gulf War (1.0) hurt me personally?

Larry Bird, Kevin McHale, Danny Ainge. Boston was an Irish working-class town. My Lakers, on the other hand, were from the glamorous megacity that had room for everyone, and they were full of African American superstars. Magic Johnson, James Worthy, Byron Scott, Michael Cooper—need I go on? There was even another Muslim on the Lakers, Jamaal Wilkes.

Many people make much of how diverse sports teams, especially in international competition, help a majority population begin to really see its minorities. Players of Arab ethnicity on the French soccer team, or Turkish players on the German team, stick their talented feet in the door, perhaps making appreciation, tolerance, and then acceptance, possible. It works the other way around, too.

As a child of immigrants, I was torn between parents who didn't feel fully at home here—it's perhaps humanly impossible to let go of one place entirely in favor of another—and an America that I accepted in idea, but that did not always accept me in practice. An African American convert to Islam became my bridge.

I had friends who, even after years of knowing me, would casually refer to me as black. While part of me felt very cool, another part of me was horrified that these folks didn't know what African American was and who wasn't. I had another school acquaintance who couldn't understand why Muslims were neither Catholic nor Protestant. But through it all, I could always point to Kareem and say, *He's like me.*

For American Muslims who came of age in the '90s, I imagine that Hakeem Olajuwon played the same role as Kareem did for me and my peers (and Muhammad Ali well before both of them). They were bridges from immigrant attachments, to an America that had room for us. Because, you see, every idea in the world is contested. When some in the Muslim majority world call for Shari'ah, they mean very different things by the exact same word. It's sort of like when people endorse democracy, how it tells you nothing of their political proclivities— whether they are Tea Party agitators, welfare statists, humdrum centrists, or far-left socialist radicals. America has been different things to different people. But how does America become home?

Religion has often been the only support allowing many Muslims, from colonized traditional societies—and African Americans were, in a sense, the most horrifically colonized—to make the transition into a mobile and capitalist world order. (Some ten percent of slaves, it's estimated, were Muslims, though like much of their homeland heritage, Islam wasn't allowed to survive.) Islam isn't supposed to be a time period or a place, but a spiritual solace, a moral compass, a basket of practices, which assist and soothe and direct when you have to leave everything behind, or when you need to decide how best to move forward. I'm always amused when people allege that "we shouldn't tolerate mosques here because 'they' don't tolerate churches there." Many American Muslims are here precisely to get away from there (the Muslim-majority world frequently brings to mind a well-armed Clippers team, though their recent reversal of fortunes may suggest that there is hope after the Arab Spring). Other American Muslims are here because their ancestors were brought here from over there, in chains.

Kareem Abdul-Jabbar, and Muhammad Ali and Hakeem Olajuwon—they helped thousands of Muslims find a way to practice Islam in America, feeling rooted, authentic, and welcome. They helped us decide how to become a part of the place where destiny had brought us, whether on a plane or by sea, years back or centuries ago. All we had to do was watch. Everything else happened along the way.

Preparing for a Lesser-Known Journey

Drumheller, Alberta

Carys Cragg

DRUMHELLER, ALBERTA, IS a dry and uncompelling place. Its rolling beige hills, scattered with farmland, water towers, and bales of hay, brought a reflective tone as I entered its space. Drumheller is known for two things and I'm guessing two things only. When I was a little girl I visited the Royal Tyrrell Museum of paleontology, just as 400,000 people do each year, located in the badlands of Alberta where dinosaurs roamed millions of years ago. More recently, I visited Drumheller for its lesser-known institution, its prison. Situated just a few minutes drive out of town—on Institution Road, no less—perched up above the alternating layers of eroding sand and mudstone, coal, and shale, that seem to go on for eternity into the distance, the grounds contain both a medium and minimum security prison. Its medium security grounds looked as I had anticipated, perhaps some image formed in my mind from watching too many episodes of *CSI* and *Law & Order* over the years: massive gray block buildings with a chain-fence perimeter. The minimum-security prison grounds, however, surprised me given the lack of fencing and permanent buildings. Decorated one-story residential and administrative portable structures were scattered around, with a large greenhouse adjacent, open space abound. The child-size plastic patio chairs sitting in the friendly garden space in front of the administrative building, encircled by a white picket fence, captured my attention, perhaps because I counsel young people for a living.

"That's for family visits," I was informed as we parked in the gravel lot.

We entered the unspacious Boardroom 125, and I was surprised to see two windows and lots of light, albeit fluorescent. Jennifer and Dave, my guides, both restorative justice practitioners, had prepared me to expect a dull and oppressive atmosphere and to be impressed with any light. Jennifer, who I guessed was in her late thirties, was dressed plainly and exuded patient warmth. While I had met her formally only twelve hours before, she knew me well, having read my letters back and forth between me and the man I was about to meet. She always left kind notes on my faxes from him—*Just wanted to check in to see how Carys is doing with all of this* or *Please let Carys know that he writes about the crime in this letter*—so I knew she cared about me and was there to nurture the process I was about to embark on. Dave, an approaching retiree, longtime restorative justice practitioner, and leader in the field, started walking me through the entire journey that brought me here a year and a half ago, when I met him back home in beautiful British Columbia, 1,452 kilometers away.

They prepared me to expect the guards to be altogether unwelcoming and described the place to be quite dreary. I was impressed that I could walk right through the entrance, sign in, and go straight to our room. No guards checking pockets nor ID. This did not feel like a prison, not that I knew what that felt like. They had conducted these kinds of meetings before and their combined experience eased the questions I had but did not know how to articulate. I had no precedent to compare myself to, no guidebooks, no expectations. Perhaps that's a good thing. Really, there was nothing I could've done to prepare myself for the moment the person who murdered my father would walk into the room. The man who changed the course of my life in its entirety. The man who broke into my family's home in the middle of the night and violently took my father's life away from me twenty years ago, when I was just eleven years old. And all I could think about, waiting there at 8:30 in the morning, was where would the four of us sit?

Just weeks before leaving for Drumheller, I called upon a friend, a beautifully wise friend, who, having been critically educated in the spiritual side of life, was the perfect one to prepare me for this journey.

Over the years, we spoke about pain, how pain can be a source of learning, how understanding the depths of the world increases our understanding of people, of relationships, and encounters. I learned from pain, not wishing it upon myself, however, neither avoiding its presence.

I told him, "This day won't be just any day. The day that I visit him will be the day after my dad's death."

I had been thinking about this for a while and I decided there couldn't be any other day, as this day would be significant to me for the rest of my life. Healing after pain, I thought. Life after death, I reasoned. A new year, new beginnings. In this particular year, I learned, these two days fell on a holiday I was previously unaware of, but took great solace in: Rosh Hashanah, a day of remembrance and a day of judgment. How fitting. As a reluctant atheist, I regularly drew upon spiritual journeys from other faiths to guide meaning in my life.

I asked him to tell me about rituals, about ceremonies in general so that I may be able to treat this encounter with the respect that it deserved and elevate it from just a meeting. I would be traveling from the beautiful, lush scenery of the West Coast over the rugged terrain of the Rockies and into the rolling hills of the prairies. And I would be traveling from the safe and stable world that I had constructed over to a vulnerable encounter with someone who crashed into my life many years ago.

We decided to speak to the specifics.

"Instead of sitting across a table, conversations flow differently when not staring at one another. Do you know if you're able to go for a walk, be outside?" He continued his calm and thoughtful reflections. "You may want to think about food, sharing or offering food." We discussed sounds, food, lighting, etc.

I had no idea what I would be able to influence. Where *would* we sit? *Could* we bring food? *Could* we go for a walk on the grounds? As it turns out, I had very little control over administrative factors. I would have some influence over the process, however, and that was enough for me.

Instinctively sitting in the chair across from the door from which this man would enter, I decided I would sit across from him and the practitioners would sit in between us, around the end curve of the boardroom table that took up too much of the room's space. In that moment, there was something important to me about having a woman sit next to me, and so she would. Jennifer's warmth, despite having just met her but knowing she *knew* me, was a supportive factor in me being the most comfortable I could be. If I could be myself, I thought, then anything that may happen that day would be OK. And if anything happened that day and I was OK, that would mean I was present. Being present was my only hope of myself that day. If I were angry, I would be angry. If I were sad, then I would be sad. If I felt peaceful, then I would feel peace.

I decided to sit across from him not because I supported a conflictual stance but given the constraints of the boardroom—not a circle around the fire or a walk side-by-side in a park—I would sit *here* and he would sit *there*. These are the small yet significant constraints that were all part of that day. I sought control within the implicit and explicit constraints and always have. There are always constraints. Later that day, I learned the seats that I designated for them that morning were the two exact chairs that he and Jennifer sat in many times before when she would escort my letters to him. Knowing this made me feel at ease.

Jennifer and Dave spent time at the opposite end of the room setting up the video-recording equipment. Recording was required, I'm guessing for reasons of liability and recall, and I was relieved to know that it was not the property of Correctional Service of Canada. Rather, it was my property and his property to be housed in a fireproof safe until mutual consent determined otherwise. Despite it being the twenty-first century, the recording equipment was quite dated. Since this meeting could last anywhere from one minute to an entire day, they came prepared. Miniature one-hour videocassettes were stacked on the table, ready. I wondered how my attention would shift given this unfortunate distraction. I wondered about the underfunding of the restorative justice programs in Canada and thought they should be given some cash for a digital recording device. And then I laughed at myself for thinking about such things on this particular day and refocused my attention on what would be happening. I was silent while Jennifer and Dave chatted about something. I wasn't really paying attention to anything at all. No, I was sitting in a black, slightly comfortable office chair confirming my decision to sit here, and not in the other fifteen chairs surrounding the table. They came back to their newly assigned seats, and Jennifer informed me about the next twenty minutes of my life.

"When you're ready, Carys, Dave and I will exit the room, go to the guard station, and ask the guards to call him from his room."

I watched her silently but attentively.

"You'll hear his name being spoken over the intercom. Sometimes they'll say 'Offender' or 'Inmate.'" I scrunched my face. They really needed to be reminded of their status in prison? Jennifer nodded in implicit agreement with my reaction.

She continued. "He'll come from his room to the guard station just outside of this boardroom within a few minutes. I'll then introduce him to Dave. At that point, either Dave or I can come back to sit with you," she said, like a question.

"You." I replied instinctually.

"So, I'll come back to sit with you. And after a few minutes, Dave will come and knock lightly on the door to see if you're ready to have them both come in. If you're not, that's OK. He'll go back and wait."

"OK."

"I need to remind you, as I have said before, at any point we can take a break. There is no judgment here. You tell us what you need. People think they'll be stuck for what to say. But in our experience, the day can fill up quite quickly. We'll be here to guide you, but we know you and think you'll be just fine." I smiled. "If you want to end, just say you're done. You'll know when you're done. You'll just know."

She paused and said, "You just tell us when you're ready."

The room fell silent.

Ready? I had never considered this question before. How could I tell if I was ready? How do you make a decision like that when your entire life you've had things happening to you as opposed to inviting them in?

Of course, I trusted my intuition before. In uncertain situations I either knew I was OK or not OK. My radar for safety grew strong after this man broke into my home and shattered my world, leaving it to me to build a life again. Quite naturally, it would seem that my emotional and physical safety radar had increased. I tried to invite this knowledge into the room and it reminded me of the beginning of this part of my journey.

A year and a half ago, I sat across from a new friend having lunch. As with all new friends in my life, at some point they ask how my father died. They assume he died of a heart attack or something sudden and are surprised when I tell them the actual story: A twenty-one-year-old boy, high on drugs, entered my home intending to steal something, picking up a knife on his way. My father, attempting to protect the lives of his wife and four children in the home, confronted him. In an altercation the intruder stabbed my father multiple times and left him on the ground bleeding. He ran away, but was caught by the police hours later. When I told my friend this story, she of course paused in the tragedy of it all. I also paused, recounting the pain I had worked so hard to heal, the journey I had taken to make sure I was OK. Soon after though, unlike most people, she asked about the man who killed him. And so I told her.

"He's in prison and has been for twenty years. He received a twenty-five-to-life sentence, despite his second-degree murder conviction. If he were convicted here, in B.C., surely he would have only received ten years or so. But the community and the lawyers were mad because he blamed it on his friend and because my dad contributed so much to the community—he was a father, an orthopedic surgeon resident...a good man." I wondered how this comes across, *a good man*, what does that really mean? "He has five years left on his life sentence but he will always be watched, so to say, after leaving prison."

"A few years ago he had a parole hearing. I had a choice to go but decided against it. I realized that I wanted more control over a situation that is taken over by the legal system, the media, even the psychologists who try to tell you how to best live after trauma." We laughed a little, because we both counsel young people, speaking possibly to our collective resistance against the way our profession typically approaches them, as passive recipients rather than active participants in life. "I've been a 'registered victim' since that time," I say in quotation marks, rolling my eyes at the government's term for my status in this crime. "I realize that I have a chance over the next little while, to contact him in a way that I want to contact him, rather than be at the mercy of parole hearings, victim-impact statements, or whatever."

After that discussion, I spent the entire weekend researching all possible processes that may fit with what I wanted: to finally acknowledge this man's existence, and for me to introduce myself to him and invite him to be in contact with me, however that may look. Sitting across from my girlfriend that day, I realized that I could not *not* do this. I had a window of opportunity to take this journey under my influence, not Corrections Services, not the criminal justice system, not anyone's but mine.

Since that time thousands of words have been written between this man and me, sent back and forth across the Canadian Rockies, to be read in the presence, protection, and facilitation of these restorative justice practitioners. Intention. Identity. Family. Vocation. Privilege. Oppression. Interests. Pain. Government. Politics. Justice. Accountability. Rights. Responsibilities. Truth. This had all been discussed in the safety of letters. Pacing was everything to me.

I sat in that boardroom in silence, overwhelmed by what I had accomplished up to this point. I felt my body fill with intensity, acutely aware of the tingling in my legs, my stomach, and my arms. I was full of reflection, full of anticipation. I couldn't speak. I had been waiting for this moment for a long time and could not believe it was here, waiting for me to be *ready*. I held my breath and the pressure in my face rose. I couldn't stop the tears from streaming down my face.

I looked up at Jennifer, saying nothing for some time. She sat, patiently. I shrugged my shoulders, raised my eyebrows, and lifted my heavy palms up as if to silently say, "I don't know what's happening." I assured her I was OK.

At that time it hit me that I had a choice. I'd been intentionally engaging in this process and it had never occurred to me that I might not go through with it. I wondered if people traveled all this way, across this land, across minds, across emotions, across social divides, and then turned back. I could leave. I had a decision, if I wasn't ready, if it didn't feel right, then we could pack up camp and go home. And if I went home without going through with it, I may be understood or I may be judged. Had people come this far and turned around? I thought it best to wonder this in silence, not that they'd be disappointed. In fact, I was sure they'd tell me that leaving was one of my options. "This is your process. Anything you want we can do," they'd probably say.

As I came back to the present, I decided to trust my intuition, as I always have.

"Take your time. You tell us when you're ready." She sat there with no expectations, just ready for my instruction. I was surprised to be so reassured by these words.

How could I be ready to meet the man who came crashing into my life twenty years ago and drastically changed its trajectory? How could I be ready to meet the man who violently claimed my father's life? The man who invited me to wonder what was the point of life, what was the point of living? This man brought pain into my joyful world, so much pain it became familiar, so much pain, for life was ripped away. The joy in my life died alongside my father, only to have been reconstructed, put back together again anew but never the same. Death invites people to live.

I looked up at her and the tears came rolling down my cheeks again, falling into my lap. She didn't say a thing. She understood and let it be. She couldn't have offered more grace, just a foot away from me, both of us contemplating the complexity of life.

I thought of all of the people who were in support of me, waiting by their phones just in case I needed them. I thought of who was not in support of me, and who were neutral on the subject of me going on this journey. What would they think if I stayed? What if I were to go? I was so tired of their presence in my mind, attending to their needs and questions. I tried to let those thoughts go.

I thought back to the day before when I gathered with my family and my father's old friends. In a beautiful bay on British Columbia's coast, where we scattered his ashes many years ago, my mother let it slip to an old friend of my father's, "Carys, tell her what you're going to go do tomorrow." As soon as she said it, she knew she'd done something wrong. Perhaps it was the look I gave her. I had perfected this look over the years, a harsh stare, a thousands words rolled up into an expression. I looked at her, then her friend, then her again.

"Before the others come," I said, "I want you to know that I feel comfortable talking with people about what I am doing. I will tell her what I'm doing. But today is about dad. Today is about celebrating his life and the meaning it has in our lives today. Tomorrow is about what I've been doing, but today is about dad." I paused.

"OK," she responded, clearly receiving stern direction from her opinionated, headstrong daughter.

"Tomorrow, after a year and a half of writing letters back and forth with this man, I am going to visit him at Drumheller Institution." I said with a strange calm.

It was silent for a few moments and then she asked, "What are you expecting from doing this?"

I'd received this kind of question before as I disclosed my journey to others. The question, to me, always implies something, fully loaded in its intention. I always wonder, Is this, of all of the hundreds of thousands of possible things to say to me at this point in time, really what you want to say? They imagine I may be hurt, that I may want retribution, that I may expect an impossible healing where I will be no doubt disappointed.

So I took a deep breath and said, "to be honest," pausing for some time until I had secured their calmness too, "I don't expect anything. Nothing. I just need to do this." She nodded. My mother nodded. They seemed to get it.

Afterward, my mother informed me that they were satisfied with this response, thought it was mature of me to say. This of course made me mad. Why should it be up to them to have any satisfaction with what I am doing? Condescending, as though I need everyone's explicit permission to do this. I remained fully secure in my decision. But the experience itself reminded me of all of the apprehensive *ohs* and tentative *OKs* that came my way when I told certain people of my pursuit. Then the implicit looks of *Are you a masochist?* as though by participating in what I had constructed—acknowledging the presence of the man who changed the trajectory of my life—was somehow asking for more pain. What an odd assumption, or at least I thought, and then I also questioned my naivety in doing this. Was I naive or was I brave?

"It'll be overwhelming" was said on more than one occasion.

"It'll be painful," said others.

They are being protective, I told myself. It's one thing to have trauma struck upon you as a child, but to ask for it by participating in a conversation with someone who ruined your life, well that was just crazy, these looks informed me. It seemed as though experiencing anything intense was allowed if it happened to you but not OK if you invited the possibility into your own life.

And then I realized. None of these people—not my friends nor family—had done anything like this before, not one of them. They had no idea as to what to expect, what would happen, and how I would feel. Right then I knew I was learning, as I had learned many times before, that I had to trust myself, my well-being, and my values. With that, I was brought to the present again. It was just me here. There was no family and no friends. It was just me. *I'm here for me*, I thought. Then they all left my mind.

The lights fluttered.

Jennifer and Dave sat patiently next to me.

I breathed in and breathed out.

I held my heart in my hand and told myself I could do this.

I would pay attention to what I needed to pay attention to.

I would follow my intuition and do what I needed to do.

I would say what I needed to say.

I would feel what I needed to feel.

I would be myself.

When encountering a journey—a journey of restoration, of accountability, and of peace—taking a leap of faith seems a necessary part.

I raised my head to look into her eyes, straightened my back to sit with presence, wiped the tears off my face, and announced, "I am ready."

"Air Guitar is a Medium that Allows Me to Have a Voice"

United States and Finland

An interview with
Justin "Nordic Thunder" Howard, Air Guitar
World Champion 2012

AIR GUITAR HERO:

The very first time I left the United States was to go to Finland and compete in the Air Guitar World Championships. I went in 2011 and came in second place, and then I went back in 2012 and won the whole competition.

Since then I've had amazing opportunities that have allowed me to leave the country again, just to go do air guitar. I was invited back to Finland last April. I was there for two weeks and did a national tour, acting as a judge for Finland's national air guitar competition (which is not the same as the international competition). I also went to Germany and performed at a conference on "flow." Flow, is the psychological state that a person enters when performing a task, where they sort of check out and continue what they're doing without really thinking about it. So a college professor was lecturing at this conference and he tied air guitar into flow and how flow is related to air guitar. I got to perform for a bunch of German college professors and scientists. It was very bizarre and awesome at the same time. Also, I went to Poland early this summer to perform at a festival. There were just over 500,000 people there. Never in a million years would I have imagined that doing air guitar would give me such opportunities to travel the world.

WYOMING AND CHICAGO:

I grew up in Wyoming, hunting and fishing and camping and doing a lot of outdoorsy stuff. It's really cool growing up that way. It's not at all like here in Chicago. When I first moved here I lived in Lincoln Park. There are more people in that neighborhood alone than in the whole state of Wyoming—the least populated state in the U.S. Actually, there are more antelope in Wyoming than there are people. So yeah, moving to Chicago was quite a culture shock. It's weird though. I had a lot of friends growing up in high school who were like, "As soon as I graduate, I swear I'm getting out of here and I'm never coming back." But that wasn't what I wanted to do. I loved living there. My plans were to come to Chicago, go to film school, and then I wanted to move back to Wyoming and make nature documentaries. That's what I wanted to do. Obviously that's not what's happened. Interestingly, when I moved to Chicago, and I don't know how this happened, but I got more in touch with the way I lived in Wyoming. It's like I gained more of an appreciation for being able to walk out in my parent's backyard and see the mountains right there. You take that stuff for granted when you're so close. Now, I've just got this even larger sense of pride in coming from a blue-collar family and growing up working on ranches. It's kind of cool, knowing that I grew up that way and learned things that I did, that you would only learn or experience by living in the middle of nowhere in the country.

WHY HE LOVES AIR GUITAR:

So that first trip to Finland absolutely changed my life. The whole experience of going over there and playing air guitar, and meeting new people and leaving the country for the first time. To go somewhere else and see that like, *I'm so tiny and the world is just this huge place.* Coming back with a whole, fresh, and new outlook on the world, it was really great. And each time I've left the country to go do these other adventures playing air guitar, it's just amazing. I feel like I've found this new awesome thing in my life. Air guitar is a medium that allows me to have a voice, and to talk about the positivity that lies behind competitive air guitar.

THE MESSAGE:

I really believe that everyone, every person on this earth wants to be happy and that they deserve to be happy. But I think that it's difficult for people, and I know that it was for me for a long time. I think that I was searching for a form of happiness or a form of enlightenment. But again, I think that not everyone is as lucky as I am now, in the sense that they don't find that thing that they are just like, "Man, this is something I love more than anything else that I do." And I feel like everyone deserves that thing. I want people to find that thing. So it's given me that sort of outlook and also made me realize that it doesn't matter where you're from in the world, anyone in the world, we all have similarities, even if we don't speak the same language or have the same sort of cultural beliefs. It's just made me feel this strong connection to human beings that I want to explore more.

To me, a perfect world would be people having fun and doing things that they enjoy and supporting one another. Supporting someone in something that they're passionate about and care about that doesn't cause any sort of harm or disturbance to anyone else. Just wanting to actually be a good person and contribute something positive to the world, instead of just thinking about yourself all the time and sort of waking up and clocking in and going to work every day. Everyone would get along and have fun. I think that would be it.

THE INTERNATIONAL AIR GUITAR COMMUNITY:

With air guitar, people who are new to hearing about it maybe feel confused or don't understand it. Then they see a video, and then they get sucked in a little bit more, and then when they see it live, they're like, "Holy cow, this is amazing!" And that's just from an entertainment standpoint. But the stuff that happens for us backstage or off the stage, the time you're spending with the air guitarists who are the other performers, they're just the most amazing people I've ever met. These people couldn't be more supportive of one another in wanting to create a new, positive change in the world. That's what air guitarists do. At an air guitar competition, of course you want to win, but when you're in Finland at the World Finals, the competition almost takes a backseat to everything else that's there. The friendships and the relationships that we make, many of which you barely speak the same language, but you're communicating and you're sharing and you're all likeminded individuals chilling on the same brainwave. I feel that if the world acted in the way that air guitarists support each other, we would all be in a really good spot.

WHO ARE ALL THESE PEOPLE?:

The competitor from Russia is an attorney. And there are teachers and special education teachers, and musical therapists. Any time I find out an air guitarist's day job, I'm always like, "Wow. So crazy." The people that do it are very intelligent. Most of us are pretty big dorks. We're all kind of nerdy. We have that going for us and can relate. Before the finals, there's this "Airientation," and it starts on one of the first night's you're there. All the air guitarists that have come from all over the world, we'll all get together and meet in downtown Oulu, Finland. We all get on bicycles and ride out to the middle of nowhere and sit in a circle and introduce ourselves. You tell where you're from and everyone catches up on the year that's passed since we've all seen each other. You know that there's a competition, but every day thereafter we're all spending time together and just hanging out with each other. When you're with them, it feels like, wow, you got here an hour ago and you're picking back up on the conversation that started a year ago.

There's one night during the week where all the air guitarists go and we meet at this really cool old barn in the middle of the woods in Oulu. And you get there, and all the town's city council members and the politicians, they're all there. All these fancy people are there to welcome us. They thank everyone for coming. It's special because the air guitar competitions, when they happen here in the United States, it's not on that same level. So when you're in Oulu with these respectable people of the community and humanitarians, and other people who want to do good in their community, and they're listening and talking about air guitar, and I'm dressed silly and we all look weird. Just spending time with these people is really cool. It gives a weight to what it is that we're doing. During that time, air guitarists will stand up and some will give lectures and talk about air guitar and the history of air guitar, and they'll show videos and clips and tell personal stories about how air guitar has affected their lives. It really is wonderful.

THE BIG SHOW:

In 2011 I was the U.S.A. national air guitar champ, and my entire trip to Finland was paid for. I went out there and represented the United States. But the next year I didn't retain the national title. So I made a decision to go on my own and enter the Dark Horse competition, which is held the night before the finals. They take eighteen competitors in the Dark Horse, and then they allow the top five to have a spot on the big stage. I tied with a guy for fourth place, so it was essentially the last spot you could get and still move on to the finals. That night, it was intense. You're in the basement of a bar, and the stage is very small compared to the world stage. So what you would normally do, you tone it down a lot, even though you're still trying to pack as much energy into it as you can so you can win and go on to the world finals. I was nervous. Like, I almost didn't make it. But then once I made it, I felt more at ease, knowing that I was going to be on the big stage again. I felt like being able to have that experience again was going to be great.

At the final I performed early on, because the other disadvantage for the Dark Horses is that they're the first five people to compete on the big stage. In a competition like air guitar, the first several people that go up usually have very low scores, because the judges are just waiting for someone to come out and really blow their minds. So, the deck was not stacked in my favor. I was nervous, because I did want to win. But I knew that whatever was going to happen was just going to happen. So I went out and did my thing. After the first round, the whole nerves and anxiety just kind of left me. I felt OK, and like I did the best that I could do. So I just wanted to have some fun and watch the other competitors and be supportive of everyone. Then I performed the second round and came backstage. I was watching the scores, because they stream the scores on a screen back there. And I said, "Oh my god. I legitimately have a chance of winning this." When I won—I notice now when I watch the video or see pictures of myself immediately after—it was one of the happiest moments of my life so far and my biggest accomplishment.

I received a guitar as a trophy. It's a beautiful guitar, handmade by this guy in Finland. He makes one every year for the competition's winner. But the coolest thing about this guitar is that earlier in the year while I was on the two-week tour, I'd been to his studio space and met this guy, who really has spent his whole life making guitars with his hands. I went through his studio and met his daughter and saw some of the projects he was working on. And actually, I took pictures of the guy's hands because they were sort of rough, calloused, working man's hands. I just thought it was the most amazing thing. When I won, and he was on the stage, and he handed me this guitar that he made, I felt more than just a response like, "Cool, I got a free guitar." It was like, "Man, this guy's blood and sweat went into making this, and it's something that he cares about." It just made it that much cooler.

CHANGING THE WORLD:

A couple of years ago I met this guy who had just moved to Chicago and had responded to a Craigslist ad that a friend of mine posted. He'd moved here from Juárez, Mexico. When we met, he told me why he'd come to Chicago: he wanted to do comedy. I thought it was the coolest thing ever and I was so inspired. I started to tag along and take classes with him. There was one night early on, when I barely even knew him, that he told me he wanted to "revolutionize comedy" and "to change the world" through comedy. And when he told me that, I responded like, "Who the heck are you? What are you talking about? You're crazy!" I just thought it was weird that someone would say that and be saying it stone cold sober and very serious. But over the past few years I've changed in how I think.

Since winning the U.S. and world titles and going abroad, I've begun to see air guitar as a blessing. I've found myself thinking, truly and honestly, about the next thing I want to do with air guitar. I've won the world title, so now I don't have anything else to prove as far as competitions are concerned. But I really, honestly, want to do good in the world. I've been thinking recently about how I was taken aback when he said that. But now, I have that feeling too. I can understand. I want to continue to have some sort of role in air guitar and use it, like I said earlier, as a medium to get people's attention.

Climbing in Venezuela

Venezuela

Andrew Bisharat

WHEN I MET Jose Miranda at a local bouldering zone near Carbondale, I thought he might be homeless. In the climbing world, that's not an insult—but that is how I meant it. Like he might be a crazy, jabbering vagabond. It's just Jose's look. Unkempt. Earthy. The missing incisor tooth. The oppressive beard of black barbs swallowing his face and neck. Jose looked like a young Osama, or rather King Leonidas from the movie *300*, only he wore Crocs.

Real homeless people have no walls, no personal sanctuary, to cordon off their crustier edges. So they build up different walls. But Jose was as open as a wild field. He carried his daughter, Paz, in his arms, while his son, Kawak, tugged at his flowered board shorts. He absorbed their anxieties the way acoustic foam dampens noise.

Last year, Jose sold his house and his solar-panel business, and moved his family from Colorado to his native Venezuela. Before leaving town, he showed me some pictures on his iPod of the climbing. He told me that I should visit. I told him that I definitely would.

But that's not what I meant.

Venezuela wasn't a place one would just go—especially not a working climber with limited free time and the option to easily visit somewhere better vetted. Like France's Céüse or the Verdon gorge.

Venezuela is a country of corrupt bureaucratic chaos that makes visiting it enormously challenging for Americans. This story feigns nothing different.

The reality is you may never know how deeply religious it feels to be at the entrance to La Puerta—a 600-foot-tall canyon of paper-white limestone sprouting an unreal tufa garden.[1]

You may go your whole life without ever knowing the true succulence of the ubiquitous guavas, papayas, pineapples, and mangos that grow in the coastal Andes, or the delicious air that circulates the mountains of El Caripe.

You may never feel the quickened pulse caused by being sixty feet above the sea on an insecure deep-water solo, or know what it means to tranquilize the visceral pounding out of urgent necessity.

You might not get to experience any of this. Unless you know Jose.

Frantic at 5 a.m. the Houston red-eye touched down in Caracas. Boone Speed, Jill Daniels, Emily Harrington, and Sam Elias were rolling with *me*. I was the one who had confidently assured them that Jose would be there to greet us and that we wouldn't be stranded.

In truth, I had no idea whether Jose would be there or not. I had made Facebook plans with him weeks ago, but never confirmed anything. I just assumed everything would work out. Why not? It usually does.

A gentle breeze moved the warm dawn. Sixty seconds of wordless disquiet passed. Jose rounded the corner. We hugged. He apologized for being "late." Everyone squirmed into a box-shaped car. The adventure took off.

---

1 Tufas are basically stalactites; typically, a tufa is attached to the rock wall, while a stalactite hangs free from a cave's roof.

The topography of Venezuela is arresting. Verdant peaks of the uplifted Cordillera plow directly into the blue and green Caribbean. Everything is just so green, except for sporadic russet-colored scars that look like a giant cat once clawed through the frangipani. These are the geographical relics of the 1999 mudslides, when a whack of torrential rains revealed just how unsound the steep earth was. In the course of two days, tens of thousands of people died, thousands of homes were destroyed and the state's infrastructure completely collapsed.

The road into Caracas takes you through oxygen-starved tunnels and over deep chasms. The overhead power lines appear to be strewn with gray moss, only it's not moss. It's the weathered carcasses of a thousand runaway kites that escaped the slums upwind.

The tyranny of a mountain range that goes from zero to 15,000 feet controls so much about how all things here work. At 3,000 feet elevation, you pass by the outskirts of Caracas, the capital city of a very rough three to five million.

Over half of the population lives in the barrios, a kaleidoscope of shanties built on top of each other. The barrios absolutely dominate the modern Spanish-Colonial panorama. This is all squatter land, at once owned by no one and everyone—lawless, frightening, beautiful, heartbreaking. The degree of self-organization and inventiveness that coalesced to create these architectures is nothing short of amazing.

Life has many layers here. Saying the city is stacked is the best way to describe it. A thousand feet of terrain separates the lowest and highest structures. No matter where you are, someone is living above and below you. Extreme wealth that could rival anything in Hollywood nestles beside outrageous poverty and rampant crime. Caracas has in recent years become a murder capital of the world with an average of more than fifty murders per day.

But these superficial observations belie the warm, spirited, happy and generous culture of most Caraceños, and Venezuelans in general. Keep your nose clean, don't go where you're not supposed to, always carry USD $40 in case you need to pay off the police, and there's a good chance you'll be OK. The better part of the human spectacle involves people enjoying outdoor cafés and drinking shots of espresso from locally grown beans and fresh juice. The scent of pulled roast lingers near *areperias*. *Arepas* are the Venezuelan staple: a cornmeal biscuit stuffed with either sweet or savory delicacies. Men play dominoes, snack on peanuts and tamarinds, and watch baseball in bars. Meanwhile, their nearby young daughters dance sweetly (if suggestively) to punchy brass music blaring out of trucks.

Hundreds of years of sundry genealogical fusions—Spanish, Italian, Portuguese, German, Lebanese, other Arab, African, indigenous— have created a diverse and handsome society. Only 5 percent of the population is indigenous. The people wear all shades of skin, eye, and hair color.

The women are stunning, famously so. Female beauty is cherished in Venezuela, though perhaps not by the standards of American feminism. Men whistle at the majority of women who strut around in the latest vogue. In Venezuela an ample and enticing bosom is the centerpiece of the feminine character. Even the store clothing mannequins are *stacked*. It's not uncommon for girls turning fifteen to get enlargement surgeries for their *quinceañeras*. Venezuela has produced more Miss Universe winners than any other country. There is even a beauty-pageant academy in Caracas that includes plastic surgeons among its faculty and where girls go to train in hopes of one day realizing this national dream.

Jose grew up in Caracas and was introduced to climbing at the city's excellent urban crag, La Cueva del Indios, fondly called La Guairita (pronounced *why-ri-ta*) by climbers. When Jose, now thirty-three, was cutting his teeth here over a decade ago, not many other Venezuelans were climbing. He'd boulder along the cliff's base to its end, a figurative mile away. Then he'd reverse and go back the other way. Through this experimental game, Jose fell in love with the sport.

Climbing La Travesia became a morning ritual that always ended with a trip to the Coco Frio stand to get a tall glass of *cocada*, a refreshing blend of iced coconut milk dusted with nutmeg.

La Guairita is a long and complex limestone bluff. Some of it is brilliant—white and orange tufas, deep pockets, incut edges. Some of it is mangy, vine-choked choss. Everything is here: trad, sport, and bouldering of all grades and styles; about a hundred routes up to 5.14a. The Venezuelan climbing community is growing, and now climbers frequent La Guairita daily—a testament to the increasing popularity of this resonant sport.

The Traverse begins in a steep cave, which smells like yerba maté tea, on V4 jugs. Jose insisted we do it first. It was a screeching warm-up, and after reaching the first rest point, I hung on with one hand and squirmed out of my shirt because I was sweating like a pig in a monkey suit. Sam, then Emily, then Jose crawled out of the grotto and we were off.

I don't know if you've ever climbed for "a mile," but it takes forever. Coming from 6,500 feet and 0 percent humidity to a jungle near the equator had apparently traumatized my internal thermometer, because I've *never* sweated like that before. Covered in white paste from a gluttonous chalking habit, I dripped like a wilting ice-cream cone.

I had arrived in Venezuela at the end of a particularly cruel and unhappy winter in the U.S. I had compounded general work stresses with the brutal anxiety of my own side project: writing my first book. This was a massive undertaking that I had underestimated. Subsequently, I suffocated.

These compulsions, however, are nothing new. I find very little satisfaction in the past. I always seem to be thrashing toward a vaguely silhouetted future, where my prospective successes finally equate to some inner peace. *If only I could climb 5.15, write something great, change the world...then...what?*

I'm cynical enough to find my ambitions pointless, but too zealous and insufferable not to blindly pursue them. I often wonder if this feeling dwindles with age as a person realizes that he may never stand on top of his personal mountains, and if that reconciliation is awful or not.

A thousand moves and a thousand feet of rightward climbing later, I grabbed a deep vertical handlebar. Its texture was crisp and coarse, which was odd to find in a limestone wall this polished and slick. I loved that hold, and held on to it for a moment. I continued to the next hold, and became fascinated by its distinct shape and texture as well. The Traverse had suddenly enchanted me, and under its spell I found myself moving without any thought of the past or the future. Each hold appeared, and then it was gone, like seconds on a clock. Like time itself, the Traverse seemed as if it would never end.

I then began thinking about sport climbing and how painstaking it can be. Sport climbing is pure science.

Reductionism. You dissect something so complex into its fussiest elements. The right-hand pinch. The left-toe smear. The pocket that must be taken with the middle two fingers in just the right way. You make recipes out of routes to the point that the actual climbing becomes uninspired, a peremptory process of combining ingredients. This disconnects you from your sensibilities. The more sport climbing consumes you, the more you lose the power to see a climb for its exquisite emotional and aesthetic totality.

The Traverse seemed silly—hardly worth traveling 3,097 miles for. Or, maybe not. Maybe this greasy V4 was exactly the reason to travel to go climbing in the first place. When you feel as though you've been typing with heavy hands and climbing with a ten-pound rack for as long as you can remember, then it's time to get out of the house.

The Traverse was also purgative. It was the sweat. A half-year of stress poured out, and in the cleansed space I felt a tingle. My senses and sensibilities returned from a distant, cold hibernation.

The wall had finally begun to peter out, but Jose explained that a single crux remained. What if we fell? We joked that if we wanted to *send*, then we'd have to start all over from the beginning, a mile away.

We all laughed at this ridiculous stupidity...but mine was an uncomfortable laugh. A seriously obnoxious part of me knew that it was true.

I slotted a gaston mono and gave it everything. But I fell.

Jose's parents' house is in the hills outside of Caracas, far, far down a dirt road cut through a thick forest of araguaney trees. The single-story home is cozy with character. Hand-painted bathroom tiles showed a cartoon of a guy peeing on a flower, and a handwritten note of daily to-do's taped to the refrigerator included "snuggling." Glass doors open up to a rolling green vista.

Jose's wife, Kami, gave us strong, welcoming hugs. Kami is American, thirty, tall, dark-haired, and freckled. Her shrewd and cynical edges are tempered with a warm and hopeful spirit. She's a healer, a massage therapist with an innate gift for detecting imbalances in back muscles and relationships alike. Serenity composes the space surrounding her, a tender equipoise to Jose's prickly gusto.

Kawak, age six, ripped around the corner, and Paz, three, chased after him. Today Paz was covered in body paint. Kawak had painted headphones onto his sister's ears, with wires leading down to an iPod drawn on her waist. Jose picked Paz up and held her upside-down by her ankles. Her dress fell over her head and revealed two eyes and a "smile" painted onto her butt cheeks.

Kami had spent the day preparing Venezuelan *pabellón*: slow-cooked pulled roast, plump black beans, rice, fresh white cheese, and fried plantains. There were also *arepas*, a flavorful and herbaceous *chupe*, and avocados, which in Venezuela are the size of small melons and creamier than butter.

We stayed up until the inky evening air surrounded us and our bottle of strong, dark rum was gone.

"There are three different trips you can take to Venezuela," Jose explained, Paz nestled in his lap. "You can take a trip to the East. You can take a trip to the West. And you can take a trip to the South. Doing them all at once would be too difficult."

To the west lie the 15,000-foot peaks of the Andes, which have ice climbs and classic mountaineering routes. The crown of the range is Pico Bolívar (16,335 feet). Granite bouldering, trad, and sport climbing can be found around the town of Mérida. Lake Maracaibo, also in the region, is a popular area for recreation, not to mention the hub for the country's booming oil industry.

Venezuela is the fifth-largest exporter of oil in the world, and supplies 15 percent of the U.S.'s reserve. As part of his socialist agenda, former president Hugo Chávez gave gasoline to the country's people for about forty cents a gallon—a price that hadn't changed in almost two decades. And despite Chávez's harsh rhetoric toward America (remember he called Dubya a "devil"), we remain economically tied. Halliburton trucks dot the highways among a million other cars.

The circumstantial fortune here is how focused the development and infrastructure is around the oil-rich parts of the country, leaving most of Venezuela relatively pristine and uncontaminated, in both an environmental and cultural sense.

To the southeast lie the Amazon and the lost world of the tepuis: tabletop mountains buttressed by 2,000-foot walls of Roraima sandstone. Tepui rock is the oldest in the world—the first to rise out of the primordial gook over 3.6 billion years ago. It is so hard that climbers say you can easily go through a drill bit in one hole. You don't find much steel on the handful of big-wall climbs currently being established by the Venezuelan climber Ivan Calderon and the late German climber Kurt Albert, the father of sport climbing, who had in recent years taken on a Kurtz-like obsession with the tepuis.

The southeast is also where you'll find Angel Falls, a 3,200-foot waterfall that holds the title of the world's tallest. Getting to the Amazon is a complex nightmare. It can take as long as ten days, involving a nineteen-hour drive, a bush plane, and paying off the right locals, just to reach even the most accessible of tepuis. As with all travel within this country, though especially so in the Amazon, you cannot have an agenda. Getting around Venezuela demands going with the flow. Understanding that you will get there when you get there is a vital concept to imbibe as a tourist. Pull off on the side of the road, *pana*, and have a green-bottle beer.

We went east. East is where there is deep-water soloing, and La Puerta, perhaps the country's best sport crag.[2] East is also where Jose's land is. He and Kami recently purchased thirty acres, covered in citrus trees and flowers, in the mountains outside of a very cool village called El Caripe. Tangerines, oranges, lemons, pineapples, and mangos grow everywhere. A natural spring exists on either side of the acreage.

When all is said and done, this wild spot will become an organic farm and climbing/wellness center that Kami and Jose are calling Lolokal—the local word for "local." They are currently building their own house, shelter for their animals, and tree houses for their guests. They will farm and live sustainably off the grid—running on hydro and solar power. Lolokal will house adventurous rock climbers, kayakers, and families alike. People will be able to go climbing while their children enjoy a high-ropes course, trampolines, horses, mountain biking, a pool, and an arts center.

They are eager to realize this new chapter of their lives. But in Venezuela, being in a rush gets you nowhere.
The starboard diesel cut. We rocked in a gentle swell under a ruthless sun. A phantom fleet of bonefish ripped through the emerald tide. Emily fearlessly climbed to the top of her first deep-water solo, but

---

2 Deep-water soloing is the climbing discipline of scaling seaside cliffs with only the water below to protect a fall.

fell at the blind last move. She dropped like an angry cannonball and splashed through the brine.

We were in the Islas Borrachas, the spiny archipelagoes that comprise Mochima National Park. Obviously, this is where one finds deep-water soloing.

The climbing is ten miles offshore from the happening beach town of Puerta La Cruz. At night the boulevard comes alive with art vendors and dancing. People sit at outdoor Arabic restaurants and pick off platters of hummus, dolmades, and lamb. They socialize and flirt around the truck with the loudest music. Tin shacks occupy million-dollar beachfront real estate where fishermen have lived for generations.

Somehow, our group had become a dozen strong—half American, half Venezuelan. Jorge Rivas and Lawrence Dugarte G showed up from the western climbing town of Mérida. Ramiro Ortiz, Briand Oaks, and Paul Robinson had arrived from Portland, Oregon. We had picked up Gabriela Aveiro in Caracas and were staying at her father's house in Puerta La Cruz.

It's needlessly complicated to explain how we all came together, and to be honest, I still don't quite understand how these connections conspired. It didn't matter. We were eclectic, electric, and there. The more the merrier, bring it on, and so forth.

A few teenage fishermen agreed, for a decent wage, to sail us around the Islas for two days. The climbing—most of it unexplored and undeveloped—is found on various walls, but the best wall, where we spent most of our time, is a gently overhanging face of jugs and popcorn tufas that is tucked away in a little turquoise alcove.

I was interested in what the young fishermen thought of what we were doing: climbing up big cliffs, dropping into the water, etc. So I asked them.

They thought it was dumb.

Fair enough. But why? I have a hard time understanding what people don't get about deep-water soloing. Perhaps it's like dogs and raw red meat—you don't know what you're missing until you've had some of it. I had tasted the flesh eighteen months earlier in Mallorca and had felt a little hungry ever since.

The memory of the last time I was hopelessly exposed without a rope in the middle of an outrageous sea bluff coursed within me. I knew what I was doing this time. Your climbing experience is always compounding like this, even if you don't know it. Occasionally, you stumble upon a way to look inside and see just how far you've come. It only happens every so often, on special climbs, in special places.

Venezuela is not Mallorca, though. The actual climbing ranged from good to amazing, but it lacked the infrastructure that makes Mallorca matchless. Boat access was mandatory to reach the climbing, meaning the boat would sail up to the wall, let one person pull on, and then back away. We all went to different walls, or routes, together. It was akin to a Hueco tour, where the communist mechanisms of the group quash individual whims. Of course, you'll find much camaraderie in this style of ascent, too.

The most critical difference was that, unlike in Mallorca, when completing a climb means reaching the cliff top and walking away, here you *have* to jump off to get back down to the boat. At first, this aspect sucked— because the idea of falling thirty, forty, or even sixty feet made me anxious. But the mandatory jumps ended up making us all better soloists because we logged so much airtime. I hadn't anticipated this effect, but once I got comfortable being in flight, the climbing got substantially easier.

Man-o'-war birds fluttered over distant mangroves. Sam and I dried off in the hot boat. I bit through a soft apple guava. The climbing was in a happy afternoon lull.

"Do you miss your life at home?" Sam asked.

"I guess so," I said. "I miss my girlfriend. I like my life at home. I obviously love this, too."

"I don't think about home," Sam said. "I feel like I could do this forever."

That's the dream. Yet experience has shown it to be an unsustainable one. You come to Venezuela for an escape, but without a sense of home, traveling loses its capacity to affect.

You travel to feel like a kid again. The newness of your position in that rare spot, wherever it may be, instills you with the curiosity you felt at ten when you climbed trees just because you'd never been up one before. But as life goes on, our vision narrows and our interests become more discriminating. The inquisitive space around us diminishes. We become who we are because we figure out what we *don't* like. This is why traveling is really just a vacation from growing older. Your eyes open and your senses grow sharper in ways that they cannot at home.

The fishermen had become bored, and decided to go climbing—no chalk, no technique, bare feet. They threw themselves at the easiest route on the cliff. Our listless posse stirred and cheered. This was just a joke to the fishermen. You could tell. But then something changed. They started swapping beta, and got serious about topping out. Part of them, I suspect, had a desire to show us "real" climbers up. Yet I couldn't help but hope that they were just inspired to climb for all the usual reasons.

The oldest fisherman, who was probably only eighteen or so, was the one who had told me earlier that he thought deep-water soloing was dumb. But he was getting the highest, and it looked like he might actually make it. He instinctively shook out on a deep handle and prepared himself for the crux. He grabbed the next hold, then the next and we all screamed crazily.

But he fell.

Every time we traveled to a new crag or area, we hit the road at 5 a.m., or 4:30 a.m. New York time. This will require some explanation.

One of the many—some say pointless—changes to come with Chávez's socio-political movement, called the Bolívarian Revolution after the nineteenth-century South American liberator Simón Bolívar, was setting the clocks half an hour ahead of New York. Jose interpreted this as a show of power—as if to say, "See? I control even time."

It's not just time that is off; the currency situation is a mess, too. As of 2008, the country uses bolívar fuertes, a "stronger" currency than the traditional bolívar. The official exchange rate is about two bolívar fuertes to every dollar. However, the black market exchanges at roughly *five to one*, an illegal statistic to print in Venezuela.

Time, money, and laws: they're all subject to the whims of the Venezuelan free-for-all. Some sources estimate that as much as 70 percent of the oil revenues are off the books. The police are completely corrupt. In one sour encounter, a fat cop pocketed Boone's Blackberry as we were all being patted down against the car. We had to bribe him with $40 to get the phone back. Nothing "works," it just moves.

This may provide a glimpse into why it was necessary for us to wake up at 5 a.m. to do a three-hour drive. You never know what you're going to get into, and you may not reach your destination for another twelve hours. This also explains why it's sometimes necessary to take a swig of Ron Selecto before the rooster has finished crowing.

Ron Selecto, aside from being an amazing porn name, is one of Venezuela's finest rums, produced by the Santa Teresa distillery, a sugar-cane plantation in the *llanos* that lie west of Caracas. Due to preferences in oak, and industry standards in aging, Venezuelan rum is more akin to sweet Kentucky bourbon than the froufrou stuff served to the girls who are with the guys in Tommy Bahama shirts in Las Vegas. Gustavo Vollmer, the grandfather of the Santa Teresa distillery, is one of the all-time wealthiest Venezuelans. The pediatrician who attended to Vollmer's children was Jose's grandfather Francisco Miranda.

After Jose turned eighteen, he began two years of veterinary school in Maracay, but soon realized that completing his education would take ten years due to the constant student and teacher strikes. Jose's grandfather suggested talking to Vollmer to see if he had any suggestions for a young man interested in agriculture and animals. Vollmer liked Jose, and offered him an opportunity to work on his ranch in Billings, Montana.

After working a couple of years on the ranch, Jose told Vollmer that he was interested in going to Montana State University, in Bozeman, to complete a program in animal science and ranch management. Vollmer paid for his education and said that if Jose ever showed up at his door to pay him back, he'd pretend he didn't know him.

One summer Jose worked as one of two climbing instructors at a summer camp in Virginia; the other instructor was Kami, from Wisconsin. After their summer fling, Kami declined Jose's invitation to move back to Montana with him, and he left without her. Two weeks later, Jose called Kami from a bus station all the way in South Dakota to ask if she could pick him up and drive him the rest of the way home. "How could I say no?" Kami joked, recounting the tale. When they reached Montana, Kami was surprised to find that Jose had already rented them an apartment.

"I always try to buy Ron Selecto," Jose said. We had left the plush luxuries of Puerta La Cruz and were now camping on the Lolokal property in the mountains of El Caripe. The air was clean and smelled of flowers. Miles downwind, the faint orange glow of an oil fire burned in the twilight. This was the only clue that civilization still existed.

Jose laid a domino tile on the concrete floor of his future home. He picked up the rum bottle, and turned its bottom toward the zenith. A few jiggers disappeared into the center of the thick black beard. "The Vollmers are a good family," he said. "They take care of others."

Though Jose's story seems extraordinary, this type of hospitality also seems to be quite common in Venezuela. Complete strangers opened their home to the dozen of us climbers, and even cooked us delicious meals so long as we supplied the food. I don't know whether this is a warm byproduct of a socialist society, or just basic human decency, the kind that we Americans have abandoned out of paranoia and fear.

Kawak carried a machete down into the forest to pick some tangerines. Jose helped. He plucked the ripest fruits from the branches and threw them so they gently struck his son on the head. Kawak laughed. Kawak and Paz are being home-schooled by their parents. Jose proudly boasts that Kawak has already attained a degree in farm-animal care.

Seeing this interaction was a little heartbreaking for Boone, who hates being away from his eight-year-old son, Nic. Boone had proudly explained that Nic recently received an A+ on a report he wrote on three-toed sloths. "Their heart beats once a minute, and they can only move thirty feet in an hour," Boone recited. In Venezuela, sloths grow on trees, literally and figuratively. "If I could get a picture of a sloth to give to Nic, it would be *everything*."

That night Sam, Emily, and I lay shoulder to shoulder, "like an Oreo cookie," as Sam observed. We looked up at the black fathomless canvas pocked with untold tiny white lights. Emily had never seen fireflies before. We watched the insects go about their peculiar business. Politics, money, and laws, which often intrude so painfully in quotidian life, felt absent out in the wild mountains of El Caripe. People are forced to exist awkwardly somewhere in the space created by these two irreconcilable worlds—just another one of the lame jokes played on humankind.

During the trip, we had stopped at a few less-than-inspiring crags. By that, I mean low-angle sun-baked choss that is guarded by nefarious insects of exaggerated stature and banded together in extreme numbers. One day ants the size of quarters bit me and I broke out into hives the size of dinner plates.

There was also a black "bee" that lived on many cliffs. The bees burrow into your hair—just your hair, for some reason—and go to work secreting glue to embed themselves there. On various occasions I was forced to climb dirty runout terrain with the maddening sensation of buzzing insects crawling on my scalp. When that happened, I promptly lowered and demanded that my partner pick the bugs out, like we were monkeys.

Toward the end of the trip, we reached the quiet village of Miraflores, the entrance to La Puerta, the best sport-climbing area in Venezuela.

From the Lolokal property, it's less than a two-hour drive to Miraflores. This town is a precious and happy anachronism. There is no cell-phone reception, no grocery store, and no campground or hostel. There is a tiny *tienda*, really just a local woman's kitchen, which sold beer, chips, eggs, and basic supplies. Next to the *tienda* is a natural spring, freshly filtered by the dark, rich soil.

The people of Miraflores wake up at 3 a.m. when the rooster crows and ride their horses or donkeys up into the hills to work their lands. We stayed with an old rancher named Cheymo. Our three days spent here offered a rare glimpse of what a true community looks like. Everyone knows, works with, and helps each other. And everyone is peaceful and content.

From town, the climbing area is one mile up a flat, paved path that crosses through the river three times. After the third crossing, the forest abruptly ends and 600-foot walls appear. Coming upon this anomaly is a truly arresting and visceral experience that sets your chest on fire. It feels as though you are about to enter a portal that leads to a mysterious and benevolent place. You feel small in front of these immense white walls. The stiff breeze cools your hot face.

We noted an astounding compilation of rare aspects. Because the walls are so tall, the climbing is always in the shade. The consistent stiff breeze keeps the conditions in legitimately good form. The approach is only twenty minutes. It is spiritually restorative to be in a place like Miraflores, where the people are so nice and life is so simple. And the routes are just fantastic.

We climbed one anonymous route that we all agreed was the single best 5.11 any of us had ever done. It miraculously linked the most deliciously juggy tufas for a full one hundred feet of climbing. You'd climb one tufa feature until you were standing on top of it, looking at the hold-less white wall, only to reach up and grab the tip of the next hanging stalactite.

La Puerta was a place of blank beauty. The essentially grade-less and nameless lines forced us to reconnect with our most creative instincts as climbers. These are the reasons to travel, and they are experiences you can have anywhere, I think, as long as the setting is powerful and you are with people you love and love to be around.

One of the most enticing lines at La Puerta is a sustained hundred-foot route that I later found out is called Nueva Era. Sam spent an hour onsighting it, then Emily flashed it, and then it was my turn. Jose hooked the rope through the belay device, and I jumped headlong up this white shield of complex sequences through intermittent features.

When you are onsighting or flashing, a necessary element of true spontaneity ends up either working for, or against, you. And you're never quite sure which way it's going to go.

In a wild stem against a giant twenty-foot fin of rock, no more than ten inches thick, I mulled over the crazy paradox of being happy with where you are and being driven to change your situation. Routes can become microcosms for life in this way. If I just stayed at the rest, I'd never get to the top. But leaving the rest also invites the opportunity to fail.

I left my stem and made some intimate moves around the fin to regain the steep face. I climbed up and then back down, sapped myself and made the mistake of resting too long. Realistically I was doomed. But I'd begun to learn how to climb through the pump. It's simple, actually. If you're still on the wall, you keep going. The commitment to *keep going* places you in the moment, into a vacuum of all anxiety—that you might fall or that you might succeed. There's no thought, no cynical self-absorption or analysis, about whether what you're doing is right or not. This is a place where nothing matters and everything matters all at once.

I did a *Rose* move under my arm, and two blind fingertips caught a pocket.[3] I kept going, and, as it turned out this time, I didn't fall.

---

3 This distinctive move is named after a route in France called *Le Rose et le Vampire.* You do a famous move in which you duck your head under your arm and cross your other arm to a pocket.

ASSAULT RIFLES IN THE RUINS

CIUDAD PERDIDA, COLOMBIA

FRANK IZAGUIRRE

WE WALKED SIDEWAYS and used our hands for balance over hundreds of stone steps so thin and slippery that, as Wilson, our trip leader, had warned us, hikers sometimes fell from them and required air evacuation. When I reached the top of the flight and took a breath, I saw several more tiered stories of ruins.

We'd arrived at Ciudad Perdida, the Lost City, an abandoned stone citadel deep in Colombia's Sierra Nevada de Santa Marta mountain range. Built by an indigenous group known as the Tairona, the site was uncovered by archaeologists in 1972. An ancient metropolis never conquered by the Spaniards, the Tairona had simply abandoned it, moving farther into the tropical mountains.

For three days we'd hiked through forests filled with birds such as jacamars, antshrikes, and manakins. There were honeycreepers and piculets, bush tanagers and dozens of different flycatchers. At every stream crossing, a black phoebe skipped across the gray rocks that broke the water's surface. Since Colombia has more avian species than anywhere else in the world, I'd wanted to do more birding along the way, but Wilson had insisted we keep pushing forward so we would arrive at the city with enough time to spend a day among the ruins.

Anthony, a friend, sat on a bench of stones for a quick break. I sat beside him. We passed around a water bottle, and after a long sip I looked up into the layers of stacked greenery and could see an area of camouflage netting atop the highest level.

A thin rain began to fall as I climbed up the final flight of stony slabs. I peered up and saw the soldiers watching us from their encampment. There were about ten of them huddled beneath a rusted tin roof. The rain intensified.

I reached the top, with Anthony right behind me, and said a hesitant "hello" in Spanish from ten feet away, trying to explain the reason why I'd come so high, intentionally to see them. But the men were already waving for us to join them, looking at us as if we were crazy for staying out in the rain. Inside there were few belongings besides assault rifles, camouflage clothing, and leather boots. In a corner, water started to boil on a tiny stove. Being Colombians, they ranged in complexion from very light to very dark. Smiling and shaking their hands, I could see in their faces how young they were. They were boys.

I pulled out my headlamp from inside my jacket pocket, ready to offer a trade. All at once they stood up and began rifling through their packs. Within seconds I was sampling a barrage of different shirts, undershirts, and other items with military insignia.

One of the soldiers, who reminded me of a geeky friend of mine from high school, held a bandana. One side was pixilated camouflage, faded from so much use, while the other was black with an embroidered white dog, with thick, menacing fangs and a red beret slouched over its grinning face. The soldier told me the dog's name was Woofy, their company mascot.

We agreed on a trade and shook hands. I handed him my headlamp and piled six spare batteries into his palm. He stood behind me and tied the bandana to my head. Anthony knocked me forward with a hard pat on the back and everyone laughed. Neither party wanted the encounter to be over.

"Where are you from?" came the first question from the group.

"United States," I answered, and they all nodded and grinned. They especially liked that I knew Spanish.

Another guy spoke up, asking me what he could say to a beautiful blonde American woman so she'd fall in love with him. I never wished so badly that I knew the secret to women.

"Wait," came another voice, "you do have a blonde girlfriend, right?"

Some smacked their foreheads and burst out laughing when I said no, while others solemnly shook their heads. Anthony stood in the back of the shelter, smiling as he picked out what Spanish he could. I asked them what it was like living as soldiers in the forest. I learned they'd been assigned to the Lost City for six months, after which they would receive a two-week leave and be reassigned somewhere else.

The soldiers sat around me, some cleaning their rifles, others chatting. I asked another question, and they explained that in Colombia, up to two years of military enlistment has been mandatory for men once they're eighteen. I'd just turned twenty-three. At their age, I'd been deciding which bed sheets to take to college. But these guys were conscripts, the next set of recruits in a civil war that's become generational. I wondered if some would die.

"Do FARC come here?" I asked.

"Yes," one answered, and he went on to explain that their most recent firefight with the decades-old guerrilla army had happened just three months ago.

"Don't worry," he said grinning, "We killed more of them than they killed of us." Many nodded, proudly.

The dimming forest light made Anthony remind me we needed to return to our group. I asked him to take a picture of me with these men. Several gathered around me and snarled while they lifted up the sleeves of their green undershirts to flex their muscles. We waved to them and walked back down the ancient steps.

In another part of the Lost City was a wooden shelter where we were staying. When we arrived, the others looked up from their card game and asked what I'd traded for. I showed them the bandana.

Wilson gathered us the next afternoon, our only full day in the Lost City, for a hike around the ruins. The forest had reclaimed large sections of the place, and we followed him through tunnels of vegetation. Because we were at such a high altitude, the trees didn't grow much further than our heads, turning the path into a narrow corridor. As we ventured in, several of the group members talked to one another. There were no sounds in the forest other than their voices.

I hung back, but even after I could no longer see them, I still heard their chattering. Once it finally grew silent, two wrens appeared within seconds just to my right off the trail. The pair hopped and tumbled through the low vegetation as they chirped at each other and bumbled past me. More birdsong seeped in through the emerald walls, and a purple hummingbird whirred past my head. I didn't even see the guan, big as a turkey, a few feet beside me until it began leaping through the tangled bunches of vines.

The morning of the first day of our return hike to Santa Marta, I woke up earlier than anyone. The birds of the high montane forest amazed me, and I deeply regretted not having bought the field guide to Colombian birds before leaving the States. I'd figured I could pick it up while traveling, but it turned out that even in a big city like Cartagena, the bookstores don't carry dozens of bird guides like they do back home. They didn't even have one.

I couldn't identify the birds to exact species, but watching the bustling life amid the stony ruins was enough. One common tanager with a muddy brown cap, bright green wings, and an aquamarine breast seemed to pop up almost everywhere. Several different species of woodcreepers scaled the barks lining the narrow trails. Two gorgeous green toucanets I'd never seen before perched atop a thinly leaved tree. Then they all flew away at the sound of an approaching Black Hawk helicopter. From a higher tier of the city, I watched the canopy of the forest sway and flatten as the giant machine descended onto a landing pad in the center of the ruins, surrounded by tropical greenery. A half dozen soldiers jumped out with guns held up, the long barrels of their rifles aimed at the forest all around them.

NOTEBOOK

ISLA PROVIDENCIA, COLOMBIA

PRIA ANAND

I spent the summer of 2011 on Isla Providencia, Colombia, seven square miles of lush mountain jutting out of the Caribbean and ringed by one of the largest barrier reefs in the Americas. For centuries, the island was isolated from the outside world, and from this isolation, Providencia's high rate of congenital deafness was born. By 1953, 12.5 out of every 1,000 children—between 12.5 and 25 times the worldwide rate—were born deaf. As a medical student, I was there to document the island's deaf community through narrative journalism, but in the evenings, when rain often tethered me to my porch, I kept a journal of events from the day that had stayed with me.

June 18, 2011

On the mainland, someone tells me that Providencia islanders are like crabs: "You are walking around and you feel that there are eyes on you, but you can't see them." I won't understand this until I arrive in Providencia and hear the real crabs scuttling through the grass or clattering over tiles, peering at me from behind flowerpots. It takes me a full day to realize that they're crabs, not cats or turtles or any other creature. At night, I think there are rats in the walls, until I realize the sound isn't just rodent claws scrabbling against the wood—it's something hard, ungainly, long-legged.

June 22, 2011

Santa Isabel, Providencia

The air conditioner is broken, and the front keeps falling off onto the bed with a crack and a thud. I've learned that the chirruping in the kitchen is from lizards, not birds, and that the worst bites I get are from little black flies that raise white welts the size and shape of a small country before fading into little red hillocks.

In town, I see a lamppost with a light bulb in one side and a bird's nest in the empty space in the other, a funnel, with straw and stray down, and at home, I feel the soft bulk of the little orange kitten at my feet. He pleads, but I know he is fierce. Last night he ran in my neighbor's front door, open because of the heat, and ran out with a mouse.

July 8, 2011

Lazy Hill, Providencia

Today, my neighbor shows me the beach behind his house. Before we leave, he grabs his machete from the porch—"I never go anywhere without my machete." In the back he's growing melon and sweetsop and soursop. The ground is littered with ripe plums, bright red. It's overgrown, and he hacks a path with his machete in one hand, swinging it loosely to clear vines.

We slide under one barbed-wire fence and step over another, walk down a path to the edge of a low cliff over the water. There's coral below. It's low tide, and we can see it protruding from the water. He points at the dark spots on the coral—sea eggs, with a spine that can break off in your foot. This is a good place to snorkel, he says. The actual beach, with sand, is towards Aguadulce from here. It's tiny and flat, and he calls it White Man's Beach. He says it was named for a man who was up on the cliff, much higher, taking pictures, and fell to his death. People say that he was pushed.

On the way back, he points out medicinal plants. I learn that guinea hen is actually a plant, with a potent smell when you peel its roots to the white core. When I ask him to name plants, he says, "If I came to California, to your home, and I brought back some fruit that doesn't grow on the island, people will call that my fruit. So we got Bertha's vine, Bertha's flower," He points at a tiny purple flowering grass. That's Bertha's flower, named for another neighbor's late sister. She brought it back from Caiman to treat her diabetes.

July 9, 2011
San Felipe and Manchineel, Providencia

It's difficult to explain the ways in which Providencia is insular. Everyone knows my face now, has seen me at the school or on my moto. In the center of town, a friend of a friend yells, "Pria?" from the bed of a pickup truck, even though she's never seen me before, because I look the way someone named Pria ought to look.

July 13, 2011
Santa Isabel, Providencia

Here's what I learn from my friend in town: In the old days, when everyone gave birth at home, the midwife would have them blow into a conch to help them push through the pain. They'd do the same if the woman had trouble delivering the placenta.

My friend says they'd lock up the new mother without light or air for nine days, and that she couldn't leave the house for another thirty. On the last day of the mother's confinement, the midwife would give her a green bath with leaves from the bush, and she would be free.

Sometimes babies were born on boats, and the captain and sailors had to take care of them. Our friend was born on a boat lost at sea on the way to Panama.

When a baby was born on land, they'd bury the placenta under a tree, and when the navel string dropped off, they'd bury that too.

July 16, 2011

Aguadulce, Providencia

I go out to scuba dive in the reef that rings the island. When we get underwater, I panic. I want to breathe, but I can feel the water pressing my temples and I can't help but hold my breath. When my vest flattens and I drop down, I start to breathe, and after ten minutes, I stop trying to use my nose.

Sometimes, the reef is still, schools of tiny silver fish that manage not to move at all. It has gamete clouds so thick and tiny that they seem like fleas, and it has heavy fish a foot long.

There are little fairy basslet, with royal purple heads and golden tails, and one black-and-white fish with stripes on its body and spots on its lacy fins—the spotted drum. There are anemones that look like thick, tan worms, but when I look closer, they're covered in little florets that open and close and curl their fine petals.

The reef is royal colors, dark purple and gold, and when it dies, it becomes white and smooth. On a cloudy day, the colors of the reef aren't startling, except where it's dead, sickly and hard and ostentatious.

July 17, 2011

Aguamanza, Providencia

By the gate, there's a steer skull and a sign that says they sell honey from bees here. I'd like to buy some honey. The house is ringed by flowerpots and plants, and on the patio, there's a tiny, low table with a blue mosaic top. There's a well-kept dog, and their water cistern is painted with a sun and a rainbow.

The bees they keep were wild here, something Italian. They travel up to three kilometers from the hives, in Aguamansa and Rocky Point, up the peak, and they mostly feed on wild flowers. There's a black wooden box in the yard like the hive, but the beekeeper says that's where they keep old frames so the wax will melt in the sun and they can mold it into things like candles. He brings me a nugget of wax, smooth and pliable, and then shows me an old frame, the wax black and the hexagonal cells still perfectly intact. They haven't started to sell the wax yet, but his daughter molds vases for flowers out of clay with tiny wooden tools, and she works the wax into the clay.

The beekeeper walks me across the street to show me the rest of his hives. They're in the woods, on the other side of a barbed wire fence and a sign that shows a man and bee—keep away. There's a clearing here, in the middle of the woods, and thirty hives backed by a flaming tree.

There's a tank of water swimming with tiny minnows, and the beekeeper says it's biocontrol. The water is for the bees to drink, especially in the winter, when it's dry—it's crawling with bees then— and the minnows eat the algae in the water.

In the woods, he shows his daughter and me a grave. His daughter asks if there was a cemetery there. No, he says. People used to bury their dead by their home to keep them close.

July 22, 2011
Pueblo Viejo, Providencia

In Old Town, I visit a woman who spends an hour looking for a book of stories that she collected about the island in one of the soft-cover graph paper notebooks that she used for school assignments, the ones with stylized drawings of flowers or photos of blonde girls and puppies on the covers. She even had a title: "Disasters of the Island." The book was about a shipwreck, about a plane crash, about an uncle who came to Providence to buy land and, on his way back to San Andres by boat disappeared, never arriving at the other end.

She wrote about the hurricanes, 1940, 1961, and 2005, that leveled Providence. She says that when Hurricane Bertha came in 2005, the old people thought it was just a breeze—nothing like the others they'd lived through. Providence is at the mercy of the water. It's a place of shipwrecks and hurricanes and epic rains. It's a place of uncertainty—unforeseen potholes and stolen gas and a plane that just drops out of the sky and an uncle on a boat who never arrives at his destination.

July 12, 2011
Lazy Hill, Providencia

When I get to the house up in the bush, my friend is finishing up his dinner—fish in a bowl—and sitting on the back porch. He scrapes the leftovers over the railing for the cats—two black and white kittens, one orange and big. There are chickens all over his yard, some fat and glossy, a few adolescents, still scruffy, and some tiny white and yellow chicks, one with no down on his dark wings. We can hear the chicks peeping throughout the interview, tiny, light voices, and some clucking from the two fat golden hens settling on the edge of the porch. "Have a lot of chickens," he says.

He's lived in this house for ninety two years. The yard is overgrown now, but up above the bush, I can see a mango tree and an orange tree. On the porch, he has a potted plant and two hanging planters in the shapes of birds, green tendrils curling out from their backs.

When I mention flowers, he gets excited. "Flowers? Oh, she used to have a lot of flowers there! She used to plant flowers, ooh, everybody come and get flowers. Bertha's flowers, they come and get it and plant. Everybody come and get. We still have flowers here from them days," he says. "From them days, we have a lot of flowers. She used to plant those flowers like these," he points at the planters and pot on the porch. "See? Down there, she used to plant. We have one down here from Bertha's days that she plant."

He points out into the overgrown green where his sister Bertha once gardened. I see bananas and trees and long grass, but only one flower, a tiny one, growing like a weed by the shed.

WHEN NOWHERE ELSE WILL HAVE YOU

PARAGUAY

NICK DALL

THE NATION OF Paraguay doesn't seem to have much going for it. It's land-locked, often confused with Uruguay, and over the centuries it has lost hundreds of thousands of square miles of territory from fighting wars with its bigger neighbors, Argentina, Brazil, and Bolivia. Add this to the fact that Paraguay's most noteworthy tourist attraction—the Jesuit mission ruins of Trinidad and Jesús—can be visited in a day trip from Argentina, and you have a black hole on the map.

I've come to think of Paraguay as a landlocked Sargasso Sea. A place where people who have been abandoned by the rest of the world, wash up. The group known as The Moonies has bought huge tracts of land there. Similarly, the Mennonites own half of Paraguay's Chaco region, personally given to them by a former president. Even Nazis, on the run after World War II, were welcomed into Paraguay.

The Paraguayan government asks few questions of potential immigrants, and it gets few answers in return. This makes it a fascinating place to visit. It's so far off the tourist map that I went two weeks in the Chaco without seeing a single traveler. Locals were fascinated by me and I by them. Everywhere I went I spoke to people—in buses, on ferries, and even on the back of a donkey cart taxi—and they spoke to me. I met lots of people who had lived in Paraguay all their lives, but I also met some who had ended up there, victims of fate.

La Gringa

The rainy season makes Bahía Negra, Paraguay, inaccessible by land for half the year. Most people, clearly, take the hint. I was one of the first outsiders to visit in months, arriving as I did after a few days of travel on a cargo boat from Brazil.

Bahía Negra sits strung out over a few hundred yards along the banks of the Rio Paraguay, the watery spine of the nation. The town may only go two or three streets back but its houses are neither outlandish nor overly rustic. Every house seems to serve double-duty as a shop, each one stocking a small selection of items bought from the *Aquidabán*, the region's weekly passenger boat (which itself doubles as an incredible floating market).

The main street of Bahía Negra consists of compacted mud. When it rains, this mud comes back to life—so much so that I actually lost a shoe in the magma one afternoon. When the sun shines, the ground hardens again; becoming tacky after three hours of Paraguayan heat, and rock-hard after six. This road maintains, in serrated cameo, all the footprints and tire tracks, and peaks and troughs, inflicted on it during a downpour.

"La Gringa! La Gringa!" Everyone I met in Bahía Negra talked about La Gringa. I was directed to her house, and introduced to this small, dark-haired Afrikaner, who spoke better Spanish than English. Her family had lived as sharecroppers in the Highveld of South Africa. Always short of money, even when privileged by apartheid, they left in 1994 when democracy came into that country, my country. Paraguay was willing to give residency to the family, as well as the promise that in three years they could be full citizens.

La Gringa had not started out in Bahía Negra, but she'd moved to this town from the regional capital of Concepción after her husband took a Paraguayan lover. She might not have had much, but La Gringa certainly knew how to move on in life.

In Bahía Negra she'd invested in a freezer, something which most of the other shops did not have. This was her family's livelihood. While I drank *tereré* with La Gringa in her once-white living room, her ten- and twelve-year-old sons sold bags of ice and frozen chicken to the neighbors who waited outside. She told me that the boys spoke, in order of fluency, Afrikaans, Guarani, Spanish, and English.

As a South African myself, I knew that whites had left in '94, but I'd imagined that they'd gone to places like Canada and Australia. That they had gotten jobs as accountants or construction managers. La Gringa, the disenfranchised Afrikaner, was not really a stereotype that existed in my homeland. I had to go all the way to Bahía Negra to find her.

The Moonies

Days later, I did finally board the *Aquidabán*, jostling amongst livestock, carburetors, and motorbikes, to find a place to rest on the deck. The ship chugged dutifully down the river, stopping every few hours at some or other settlement which was even smaller than, and not as appealing as, Bahía Negra.

Local people poured onto the boat to buy provisions—week-old lettuces and slightly funky sausage. Local gas stations siphoned directly from the *Aquidabán's* tank to buy their fuel.

And then we stopped somewhere different. A place called Puerto Leda. We did not supply them with fuel, instead we refueled from the town's supply. In Puerto Leda, the buildings—all prefabricated shells— were hospital-white and shimmering. There was a row of gleaming new equipment: ploughs and tractors, dinghies and boats, even a combine harvester. The community had come out to greet us. All of them, to a man, wore pastel colors and floppy hats. That's when the penny dropped. "They're Asian," I said to myself.

I asked a fellow passenger (a guy whose chickens had shat on my bag during the night) about this place. He didn't have many details, but he was able to get the basics across: "*Japonés. Reverendo Moon.*"

I wanted more, but chicken man didn't have it.

Later I found a manifesto on the Internet: Japanese Moonies had settled in Puerto Leda more than a decade ago. The site had been chosen for its remoteness and the hardships it would bear upon the missionaries. I read about jaguars and mosquitoes, thick brush and rudimentary toilets, and floods and undrinkable well water. This was all as it should be: Reverend Moon had charged the people with "protecting the nature that God created, and cultivating the land so that humans can live, without repeating the past developmental mistakes of destroying creation."

Unlike the now-deceased reverend, those outside the church see Puerto Leda differently. Rumors of money laundering and drug manufacture at Leda are rife. Unfortunately I didn't get to stay and investigate—and I'm not sure I would have been allowed to if I'd tried.

The Mennonites

Unlike my chance encounters with La Gringa and at Puerto Leda, I'd expected to meet Mennonites in Paraguay—in fact I'd actively sought them out. They are, after all, the poster boys for Paraguay's "ask no questions, tell no lies" immigration policy.

The Mennonites, a conservative Anabaptist Christian group, were forced out of various parts of Europe in the late-nineteenth and early-twentieth century. Many of the early departures went to Canada, but the Canadian government insisted that English be spoken in the Mennonite schools and that they pay taxes. Neither of these caveats went down well with the more conservative Mennonites.

Later departures, notably those kicked out of Eastern Europe, headed toward South America. The story goes that a group of Mennonites heading for Argentina happened to be on the same ship as the Paraguayan president. They got to talking, and the president offered them citizenship and huge swathes of land in the country's Chaco region. He also gave them the right to speak their own language, Plautdietsch, instead of Spanish, and the power to administer their own finances and hospitals, and an exemption from military service.

This all suited the Mennonites just fine, but there was something in it for the Paraguayan government as well. The Chaco—one of the last remaining frontiers of the twentieth century—was largely unpopulated and utterly uncultivated. It was rumored to harbor oil reserves, which neighboring Bolivia and Argentina were keen to get their hands on. The Chaco War with Bolivia had left Paraguay with a very tenuous hold on this region which constituted over half of its entire territory.

The Chaco needed to be populated and tamed, preferably by hardworking farmers. The Mennonites were perfect.

When I visited Filadelfia, the center of the Fernheim Mennonite Colony, I was amazed by how exceptionally dull it seemed. Obviously I had expected the men to be dressed in checked shirts and jeans and the women to be in drab frocks, as they were. But I had also envisioned quaint architecture, picturesque churches, and character-filled stores.

What I found was a town constructed almost entirely of yellow-face brick; and a hotel (possibly the most boring place I have ever stayed) of boxy rooms and bedside Bibles.

The colony's cooperative supermarket was interesting, but only because of its location. It was an American-style supermarket in the middle of nowhere. Locally made cheeses and yogurts, and locally butchered cold meats were sold in vacuum-packed portions, while imported cereals and cookies lined the neatly stacked shelves. Blonde, blue-eyed cleaning staff mopped the aisles endlessly, and the cashier spoke to me in Plautdietsch, not Spanish.

The Jakob Unger Museum was one exception to the yellow-face brick rule. The museum, a two-story wooden building, housed a huge collection of taxidermy made by one of the founding fathers of the colony, as well as relics from the Chaco war, and antiquated farming equipment. The curator spoke English as his family had come to Fernheim from Canada.

This man told me about the early years of the colony. Hundreds were lost to typhoid, and that was not the only danger. The settlers had dealt with insects, scorpions, snakes, and pumas; a lack of water in the dry season, and a ridiculous overabundance in the wet; and a heat which never let up. But the Mennonites had God on their side, the curator told me, and so the people did more than merely survive—they flourished. Today the Mennonite colonies play a major role in the Paraguayan economy, and their cheeses and meats can be bought throughout the country. Many Paraguayans have relocated to Mennonite colonies to find work. There are even some Mennonite members of government.

Interestingly, the museum curator did have concerns about his community and the future generation. His kids were teenagers, and when they finished school they would go to Paraguay's capital city of Asunción to study at university. There they would be exposed to twenty-first century vices and perhaps wouldn't come back to Filadelfia. He'd seen it happen to friends' children.

"Obviously I'd like them to remain Mennonites," he said, "and I think *my* kids will. But if they don't, it is their decision. And their loss."

After a few days in Filadelfia, I traveled to Asunción myself. Five hours in an air-conditioned minivan was all it took. An asphalt highway had recently been built, and there are future plans to extend the highway beyond Filadelfia to the Bolivian border. The Chaco is no longer in danger of being taken away from Paraguay. There are still no signs of the supposed oil deposits, but the government has found a far more valuable raw material in the Mennonites: perseverance.

Good-bye Paraguay

The last thing I did in Paraguay was visit the Jesuit ruins on the Argentine border. I saw a few tourists, but not nearly as many as I did at the ruins on the Argentine side. There were no curio shops and very few hotels. The gatekeeper there turned a blind eye to me pitching my tent inside the ruins.

Late at night, under a full moon, I climbed the ramparts of what was once the main church with a bottle of bootlegged whisky. As I drank from the bottle, wincing as the ethanol bored into my throat, I thought about how I would miss Paraguay—a place where anything is possible.

IT STARTED
WITH A BANG

RIO DE JANEIRO, BRAZIL

ALISON MEDINA

I'M LYING IN the bottom bunk of my bed in the largest favela in South America. It's 8:30 a.m. and there are fireworks going off that sound a little too close to home.

I recognize a bunch of short pops followed by two big booms and it becomes obvious that this is the known warning signal for people out on the street to duck into the nearest house and stay low to the ground. This community, Rocinha, with its history of conflict between local drug factions and police, has grown eerily accustomed to recognizing such instructions and sounds.

With a brain still foggy from a night out, I head into my roommates' room when more gunshots start firing. The signal had already woken them up and we trade surprised looks at how alarmingly close the shots now sound.

The morning noises that I usually hear from inside this house's front door have been silenced. No plastic flip-flops slap the ground, and no early neighbors on the street shout a good morning, *"Bom dia!"* This silence unnerves my ears almost more than the gunshots. Inside, we all try to stay low and away from the windows. Val, the oldest daughter of the family who lives here in the house, runs down from the top floor, wide-eyed after seeing my empty bed. At first, she'd assumed the worst, thinking I hadn't made it home last night.

Everyone inside is still unsure of why we're hearing a shootout so early; the assumption is that the Pacification has come, when government forces move through the favela to "rid it" of street organizations and drug dealers. This push to pacify the favelas has been spurred on by the close approaching World Cup and Olympic games, both to be hosted in Rio.

Even living here for as short as two weeks, I can see that this plan is slightly askew. While Pacification in theory seems a sound idea, all residents suffer; some from stray bullets and daily inconveniences; others because of the cousins, sons, nephews, fathers, and brothers of this community for whom the police are about to decide their fate. Many men will be killed, some will go to jail, and others will go into hiding or flee.

Their tension radiates and touches us all.

After what seems like hours—probably only fifteen minutes have passed—the firing dies down and I hear a slowly emergent bustle beyond our door. Someone clicks on the television to find out what happened. The news reports that ten *bandidos* have taken guests hostage at the local Intercontinental Hotel, but the situation is now "under control" and nobody has been hurt. The bandidos have been arrested and their mug shots are being dramatically splashed across the screen. That explains the loud exchange of gunfire, as the Intercontinental is a five-minute walk down the hill from our house.

Over the next few days, those of us inside Rocinha came to learn more than the news reported: The group of bandidos had been escorting the *dono* (drug lord of this territory) home from a party when they unexpectedly had a run-in with a group of cops. The chase led to the hotel, where holding anybody hostage was probably the last thing on the bandidos minds. The encounter with the police ended with jail time for the men, and a "score" for the police as the government sets out to increase public support for the idea that a quick Pacification is necessary.

On a typical morning walk to the neighborhood's Instituto Dois Irmãos, where I teach English, Spanish, and art, I pass at least fifteen bandidos, each armed with a variety of AK-47s, grenade belts, and backpacks of ammunition, always ready for battle should the moment arise. Walking alone and being a girl with dark hair, I don't usually draw too much attention. But after this morning, I am with another volunteer, James, who is helping me get the morning round of coffee for all the teachers. As volunteers, bandidos don't have a reason to mess with us. The institute is well known and has been around for more than eleven years.

But this morning a bandido walks up to my friend and grumbles the words, *"Te mato."* I will kill you.

James rolls his eyes, grabs the coffee, and we walk back to the institute.

"What was that about?" I ask.

"They think I look like a cop," he tells me, clearly showing that this is not the first time. Apparently he specifically looks like one of the cops that came in a few weeks ago and murdered some of the bandidos' friends. Even though the bandidos should know by now that James is a volunteer, his strikingly similar appearance pisses them off.

The battle on the streets of Rio over territory and the drug business is ongoing. Shootouts and operations by killing squads are real here and not just scenes from a movie. Permanent and visiting residents in these communities are often silent observers to these battles, feeling they will lose no matter who is in power.

By 10 a.m. the morning's gunshots have died down, but I can still hear the helicopter circling overhead.

BIRTH IN PACHAJ

PACHAJ, GUATEMALA

LIZ QUINN

THE TOWN OF Pachaj is, in some ways, easily accessible. By bus or pick-up, it's no more than five minutes off the Pan-American Highway. With any luck, it's under an hour to Quetzaltenango, Guatemala's second largest city, and only forty-five minutes to the nearest public hospital. It's a mere fifteen minutes to San Francisco el Alto, the biggest market town in the Western Highlands. Cable TV connections arrived right around when I did, and the children love *Batman* and *Teletubbies*. Nearly everyone in Pachaj has at least one family member living in the United States, and most households receive frequent international calls on their pay-as-you-go cellphones. There is an express mail service near the bus stop, making it easy to receive money and packages from loved ones abroad.

In other, maybe more important ways, Pachaj seems remote. Quiché, a Mayan language, is universal. Spanish is not. Running water arrived in 2002, but when I first visited, in 2005, it appeared only between 6 and 8 a.m. every second or third day. I was warned repeatedly about the unaccompanied *gringa* who had, a few months before, mysteriously appeared in town. Scared she would steal the children, the townspeople locked her in the school and summoned the National Police. The first time I myself entered Pachaj unaccompanied, the fare-collector on the bus interrogated me extensively before a fellow passenger confirmed my suspicious story about staying with a midwife in the center of town.

During the rainy season flooding can make the road to the highway impassable. Even on the driest days, the rest of Guatemala—with its formal Spanish and its flushing toilets and its polite respect for tourists—can seem very far away. It was dry on the July morning that Juana gave birth. The short stretch of stone and dirt that connected us to the highway was clear, open for travel. Doña Martina, the town's busiest midwife and my host, could have borrowed her brother-in-law's pick-up truck, which was parked just a few doors up the hill from the bare kitchen in which Juana labored. But no one—myself included—suggested bringing Juana or her newborn daughter to the hospital. We never considered leaving Pachaj.

The town itself—with its few steep dirt roads, its mountain views, its perpetually closed but very dignified white stone church—is profoundly, humbly beautiful. Somehow, despite all the cooking fires burning kindling of unimaginable variety (wood, cloth, weeds, Styrofoam cups, and plastic packaging), the air smells good in Pachaj. The few square miles of the town's center are bare of trees, just low cement and mud buildings nestled among the fields of corn, all built onto a significant incline, so that from any home in the center, all other homes are visible. This aspect of Pachaj's charming landscape never failed to embarrass me, as it meant my frequent trips from house to latrine could be observed by everyone in town.

I first visited Pachaj in May of 2005, month five of my Guatemalan year. I was twenty-three. I had come to Guatemala to learn about traditional Mayan *comadronas*, the midwives who attend most births in the country. I was a new college graduate, an English major, with no medical or midwifery training. It would be another two years before I began medical school. But I was fascinated by childbirth and by the Maya. I began my year volunteering for an organization that offered comadronas biomedical training, but I quickly grew frustrated with editing grant applications and designing fundraising materials. Eventually I convinced Ana, one of my Guatemalan colleagues, to play matchmaker, and she paired me with Doña Martina, who had been a star student in the training course. Martina was literate and had aced the course's tests on taking blood pressures and listening to babies' heart tones. She'd been a midwife for decades, since the births of her own children, and attended five or six births each month. With Ana as my go-between, we arranged for me to stay in an empty room of Doña Martina's home and to follow her when she visited patients or attended births. I bought a new wooden and straw bed at the market in San Francisco El Alto. For a small fee Martina's brother-in-law drove it back to her house in his pick-up. The first time I came to stay, Martina and Ana and I had a long and awkward conversation about money. Martina insisted that I was an honored guest in her home; I insisted on contributing *something*. In the end we arranged that each time I visited I paid 25 Quetzal per day (a little more than three dollars) to cover the cost of feeding me.

I have no idea how my three daily dollars compared to any of Martina's other forms of income. There are no jobs in Pachaj, and the town is located within Totonicapán, one of Guatemala's poorest states. Martina's husband lived most of the week in Guatemala City, where he sold cheap polyester pants to other poor rural emigrants who have flocked to the city looking for work. Martina's son lived in Los Angeles, where he worked in factories run by Korean entrepreneurs. The small improvements Martina has made to her home, including the construction of the half-finished cement room I slept in, have been funded by her son's remittances. Martina herself does not earn any money: attending births is a sacred calling, not a commercial enterprise. Always, for Martina's family and for everyone in Pachaj, there was a tremendous amount of work to do: walking miles into the surrounding forest to collect the twigs and branches needed for cooking fires, dressing and changing and feeding the children, hand washing clothes using water saved in big plastic tubs, grinding the corn needed to make tamales, the steamed cornmeal staple. And, of course, all the work needed to grow and process the corn: tilling the earth, sowing the seeds, eventually harvesting the white or yellow ears and putting them out to dry.

There is a lot of corn in Pachaj. Depending on the season, there are ears of corn drying on every roof in town, or hanging from the rafters in kitchens and bedrooms. There may be young corn, still low to the ground and neon green, planted in neat rows up and down the mountains, defying gravity with its angles. Or, towards the end of the dry season, in April or May, there will be tall stalks of tawny, dry leftovers. Miguel Angel Asturias, Guatemala's Nobel Laureate, titled his epic novel *Hombres de Maiz—Men of Corn—*for a reason. Still, malnutrition is epidemic throughout the Western Highlands, visible on the faces and bellies of children and in the sunken eyes and rotted teeth of their mothers. Many of Martina's patients are so chronically malnourished that the women lose teeth with each pregnancy. Periodically, the World Food Program delivers giant bags of dried corn to the town. It is temporarily housed in the small elementary school until a committee of zealous women can organize its disbursement. Delivering sacks of corn to a corn field always struck me as absurd, even a little tragic, but I had no way of assessing its impact on the health of Pachaj's inhabitants, and Martina told me the bags were appreciated. Once, at a party, a child asked me how we grew our corn in the U.S. The donated corn used for that day's tamales was tasteless compared to Pachaj's own kernels.

It was at parties that I was introduced to Pachaj's residents, and I was quite the novelty item. Despite my ignorance of Quiché, it was not hard to know I was being discussed: there is no Quiché translation for "gringa," "*los Estados Unidos,*" or most other words that relate to post-conquest life. At first, I feigned polite ignorance, but I soon realized that Miss Manners' etiquette had no place in Pachaj. I learned to delight roomfuls by responding in Spanish to questions they'd been puzzling over among themselves in Quiché. How many cars did I have? How many buses did I take to get to Guatemala? How much did it cost me to fly to Guatemala? Why did I wear pants? Where was my husband? Did I have a boyfriend? Did he send me money? Did he send me clothes? Did I like to dance? (This was a strangely ubiquitous question; I think someone must own the *Dirty Dancing* video.) Are there dinosaurs in *los Estados*? Do I know how to speak English? Do I have *"papeles"* to go to Los Angeles? Why didn't I stay in *los Estados* where life is so much easier? Am I cold? Have I felt cold before? Do I know any Koreans?

With the exception of the dinosaur question, which Doña Martina herself asked me after we watched *Jurassic Park II*, I fielded all of these questions regularly. *Los Estados* Unidos were a revered fantasy-land, known through a few movies and the stories the Pachaj men told when they called from Los Angeles, where so many of them lived. For many of these women and children, whose husbands, sons, and fathers almost all worked in factories run by Koreans, the idea of anyone being actually *from* the U.S. was as incomprehensible as a 23-year-old woman without a toddler to nurse. My explanation that I don't *need* papers to go to Los Angeles was met with puzzlement. As was the information that my hometown is often colder than Pachaj (where it is, in fact, quite cold; I slept under wool and dreamt of heavy down). Life in *los Estados*, the thinking goes, is better: how could better be colder? That it cost me $300 and took about six hours to fly to Guatemala is astonishing: their men pay several thousands of dollars to a "coyote" to spend perilous weeks illegally tramping through the desert to the U.S. The mothers and grandmothers were only sort of joking when they offered (and they all offered) to gift me their infants. The American Dream never felt more potent to me than it did in the low-roofed adobe homes of Pachaj.

On my first morning in Pachaj, Martina announced that we would go to her brother-in-law's house to bathe his wife, Susana. That is, she hastily added, if I wanted to go. We would walk to Susana's home, she explained. Perhaps I would prefer to rest? It took me several moments to realize that she meant a ritual post-partum bath. I'd read about this custom, a common one among Mayan comadronas. Of course I wanted to go! But Martina's deference made me uncomfortable. Was she hinting that she didn't *want* me to go? Why did she always think I needed to rest? From our earliest moments together, she treated me gently, as if she expected me to break, but I'd vowed not to be a prima donna in Pachaj. There was no reason why I couldn't live as Martina did. Certainly, I could walk across town with her.

A few hours later, I trotted behind Martina as we crossed the dense corn fields. She walks quickly, and I struggled to keep pace, regretting that the hike didn't leave nearly enough time for all the explanations I sought. I knew that Susana had given birth eight days earlier and that Martina had already come to the house twice to bathe mother and baby. Today would be the third and last bath. Was the third bath always at eight days? Why? Did Martina follow up with her patients other than at the baths? What if Martina was worried about a patient, would she administer more than three baths? What kind of care did she provide before a delivery? Had Susana's birth been peaceful or difficult? But Martina didn't say much as we hurried through the corn fields. Most of my questions were barely formed and went unanswered.

Susana's patio was just a dirt clearing in the fields. When we arrived, there were a few women and children gathered there, preparing a fire, and Martina greeted them warmly. I hoped to be introduced, and I watched carefully as Martina waved to or embraced each of the adults, but she didn't acknowledge my presence before we made our way into the long, low adobe building. Inside it was dark and cool. There were double beds in three of the four corners, and Susanna lay under heavy covers on one of them. Martina spoke to Susanna in Quiche, then instructed me, in Spanish, to sit on the foot of the bed before walking off to another part of the room. I understood that I was to stay put, but I didn't know where Martina was going or what she was doing. I felt at sea. I smiled shyly at Susana, wondering what Martina had told her about me. I tried not to resent Martina for leaving me behind with a woman I'd never met. I wondered where she had gone and who of the gathering women lived in this house. Susana and I smiled at each other. A few younger girls—I took them to be teenaged relatives—were milling about, staring at me, whispering in Quiche and giggling. I hesitated, not knowing how to dissipate this awkwardness. Finally I decided I would address Susana. I might as well start the conversation.

"Is this your first child?"

To my relief, she spoke Spanish, and she seemed happy to talk to me. This baby was actually her fourth. All had been delivered, she told me proudly, by *"La Martina."* Her second child, a boy, had been breech and had died just after birth, an event that Martina had predicted during labor. That loss had been very sad, Susana confirmed, but she had delivered two healthy children since then and she had been in good hands always. *"La Martina sabe,"* Susana told me, "The Martina knows…"

I saw this for myself when Martina returned and the baths began. I peered over her shoulder as she examined the newborn. Her brown hands held the baby firmly and moved over its small body with efficient confidence. She rubbed the baby's fontanel, the soft spot in her skull, and then held her toward me so that I could do the same. She examined her belly button and wiped away the few flecks of dried blood where her umbilical cord had been. Once satisfied with her exam, she swaddled the infant tightly in a series of blankets, some fleece, some woven, and passed her to eager waiting hands. The gathered women took turns rocking the baby while Martina turned her attention to Susana.

I stayed out of the way while Martina directed several of the women to fill a metal tub with the water they'd heated on the fire outside.

They did so methodically, bucketful by bucketful. I wasn't worried for the baby's modesty, but Susana, I thought, might not want a stranger inspecting her naked body too minutely. But she was not bashful removing her *huipil* and bra. Martina wrapped her lower half with a thin sheet, a sort of bathing skirt, and she wore that as she immersed herself in the circular metal tub. Martina added fragrant leaves to the hot water, and the scent of mint began to compete with the smell of wood smoke. She began her work, massaging each of Susana's breasts with heavy downward strokes that looked painful, but Susana didn't wince. Moments later, Martina reached her arms into the bath water and massaged Susana's belly with her fists. Susana leaned against the metal edge of the tub, her eyes closed.

When Martina's ministrations were through, Susana's husband brought a sphere of greasy brown soap and Susana seemed to wake from a trance and vigorously soap her arms and belly. Her skin was smooth and unblemished. The pale outline of her huipil was plainly visible on her body, the sun-darkened reddish brown of her face and arms giving way to paler beige at her collar bones and elbows. Her black hair was tied back and up with a bandana, revealing her thin neck. The skin of her cheeks was darkened, freckles combining over the bridge of her nose to form the mask of pregnancy, melasma, a beautiful word for the darkening of pigment that is common in pregnant women. I thought she was very beautiful, heavy breasts and belly hanging from her small thin frame. I had turned twenty-three a few weeks earlier. Like many of my friends, I didn't plan to bear children for nearly a decade. But that morning I envied Susana's maternal form. In Pachaj, surrounded by nursing mothers younger than I was, I felt my breasts to be conspicuously small, inert and useless.

And I was not the only one concerned with my somehow less-than-fully-female form. As the days and weeks went by, the little old ladies who sat around talking shop during these baths began a running joke about getting me into the tub. Seeing the gringa naked, they seemed to think, would prove illuminating. I was, after all, a confusing figure: white, unmarried, educated, childless, wearing jeans. Anytime Martina brought me to a prenatal patient's home, she would introduce me first to the man of the house, and we would talk briefly of worldly matters before he would invite me in to see his pregnant wife. *El Bush Chiquito* (the Little Bush) was in power in the U.S., and Pachaj's men still held out hope for immigration reform. More than once, these men expressed their condolences for the terrible events of *Nueve Once* (Nine-Eleven). Women, including Martina, did not speak during these conversations but waited patiently for their completion. When the men stepped out, and Martina began her prenatal ministrations, I felt myself being ushered back into the fecund world of women. I knew the women had been listening and watching as I spoke to the men, and sometimes, much later, once I'd been re-established as one of them, they would ask me about the details of our conversations. Who was *Bush Chiquito*? What, exactly, had happened on *Nueve Once*?

On the morning of Susana's bath, I was still so new that no one had dared speak to me after my first halting conversation with Susana. And no one had explained to me that the third bath doubles as a celebration. Moments after Susana emerged from the tub and dressed, the guests began to trickle in, carrying plates of food and cans of beer. Susana's female relatives had cooked a feast and her male relatives had bought cold Guatemalan beer, Gallo and Brahva. Eventually I learned that Martina's "payment" takes the form of this feast and its leftovers. This custom was hard on me. As the midwife's sidekick, and as a guest, I too was given large cans of Gallo and Brahva, piles of tamales, and the largest available bowl of a soup that usually involved chunks of very tough beef. I've never been much of a morning drinker, nor much of a beef-eater, but I was determined to prove that suburban gringas are substantively the same as rural Guatemalans, at least physiologically. If toothless children could swallow the beef, if elderly ladies half my size could handle the beer, certainly, I reasoned, I could too. "*Todos somos humanos.*" We are all human. I said it aloud when Martina's friends and family wondered how I could possibly withstand the difficulties of their daily life. Can a gringa even eat tamales? Or wash her clothes in the outdoor sink? Can a gringa carry buckets of water for a hot bath? More often, I repeated it to myself when I was feeling lonely or desperate, or on nights when my fifth trip to the fly-infested latrine seemed too much to endure. *Todos somos humanos.* It was my mantra, the insistent refrain of my willful denial.

Doña Martina is, in some ways, a cosmopolitan woman, a modern and modernizing midwife. This, in fact, had been Ana's reason for selecting her to be my host. Weeks before I first arrived in Pachaj, when I began planning what I then called "my apprenticeship," I had considered asking a different comadrona, a woman who lived in Momostenango, to host me. I had interviewed her for one of the NGO's fundraising projects and had liked her. Now, many years later, I'm willing to admit that I was mainly attracted to her hairdo. *Momostecas,* the women of Momos, wear colorful ribbons woven into their braids, a traditional style I particularly admired. Ana, ever-pragmatic, dissuaded me, explaining that the Momos midwife was not a very good student and didn't attend many births each month. And there was something else. Ana didn't say so until years later, but she feared that the cultural divide would be too great. She had worried about me, her naïve gringa friend. That is why she'd volunteered to find me a more suitable match.

Martina does not wear her hair braided into ribbons. And I've never seen her use woven cloth as a decorative crown, even on the most formal occasions. Always she keeps her long hair in a single braid that hangs neatly down the center of her back. Her huipiles are machine-woven of synthetic material, colorful flowers over white polyester. For some, a machine-made huipil would suggest abject poverty—hand weaving is laborious and expensive, a status symbol—but Martina's dress always struck me as pragmatic, even cosmopolitan. On that first day, when I met her at *Cuatro Caminos*, the busy junction where the road from Xela meets the Pan-American Highway, she looked not quite of that place. I spotted her from across the highway, picked her out of the crowd of indigenous women waiting at the edge of the dusty road. She held herself quietly, regally midst the dirt and the squawking chickens and the bus drivers' shouting. Her prominent cheekbones and narrow, almost Castilian nose contributed to the impression that she might have been visiting from somewhere else. And Martina *had* traveled: she'd studied in the capital, and she'd attended trainings throughout Guatemala offered by foreign NGOs.

Shadowing Martina at prenatal visits, births, and postpartum baths I saw that she had incorporated many medical ideas into her practice. She is rightly proud of her stainless steel equipment, and is careful to boil it all before and after each birth. She steers clear of traditional Mayan sweat baths, worrying about dehydration, and when she told me about a patient whose family is rife with troubling birth defects, she thought it probably had something to do with genetics. She not only speaks but also reads and writes Spanish, a fact that distinguishes her from most of her patients, her barely literate husband, and the four other local midwives, who are illiterate and speak Spanish less than fluently. She loves to get out of the house. If an NGO offers a training of any kind at all, that's anywhere vaguely near Pachaj, she's there. She once told me that when her children were young and she couldn't get out much, she grew depressed.

But in other, perhaps more important ways, she is a traditional Quiche woman, a comadrona called to her vocation by a higher power and instructed in cryptic dreams. Even on that first day meeting her at *Cuatro Caminos*, the way she hurried for the bus, and haggled with the fare collector, and pronounced her Spanish words with the wide vowels of Quiche marked her as a native of the Highlands, an indigenous woman very much of that place. Fellow passengers greeted her by name as we boarded the bus. She had been born in Sololá—just a few hours to the east, near the famous Lake Atitlan, and had moved to Pachaj as a teenager, when she'd married.

Martina had been a midwife for more than twenty-five years and still attended five or six births per month when I first knew her. In addition to the births, she also made prenatal visits and administered the postpartum baths. The baths were always scheduled for one, four, and eight days following delivery, but the prenatal care was more haphazard. If her patients gave her enough warning, and their husbands said it was OK, and it didn't rain at the wrong times, then Martina would visit them a few times before delivery. Sometimes she checked a blood pressure or listened for the fetal heart, but this wasn't routine. If she had any, the women in her care also got pre-natal vitamins and perhaps a vitamin B shot. Martina attended births in her patients' homes day and night, helping to prepare a birthing area—usually a tarp or straw mat on dirt floors—and staying with the mother throughout labor. The two births I attended were remarkably modest events, with Doña Martina casting only rare glances under her patients' skirts until the last possible moment. Though Martina's wisdom is much respected, she is by no means viewed as the final authority; her patients' mothers and mother-in-laws attend the birth as well, offering sometimes stern advice. I knew that she had aced her tests on blood pressure measurement and fetal heart tone auscultation, but I didn't see her practice either of these exams during the two deliveries I observed. Everything about that training course felt very far away on the July morning that Juana delivered her baby, as inapt as those sacks of tasteless U.S. corn.

In 2005, when I met Doña Martina, I had no medical or midwifery training. Years before, as part of an internship, I'd taken part in ten births at a clinic in Mexico, but I'd acted as a labor support person or observer; not as an actual birth attendant. I'd read about labor and delivery, Mayan cultural practices related to pregnancy and childbirth, and the history of midwifery and obstetrics, but I knew next to nothing about *caring for* a laboring woman or her infant, especially in the event of an emergency. My role as Martina's observer came easily to me. I was her guest and sometimes assistant and deferred to her authority on any number of topics. Even when I knew that something was wrong, I was certainly not capable of personally improving on Doña Martina's care. I didn't know how or when to listen for fetal heart tones. I didn't know how to properly resuscitate an infant who wouldn't breathe its first breath. Now, as a physician, I realize that my ignorance was liberating. It made it possible for me to observe Martina without interfering. Once, when I returned to Pachaj for a visit, Doña Martina reminisced about our time together and hoped that one day I would again accompany her at births. Years have gone by since she suggested this, and still, sometimes, I am kept awake at night wondering about the ethical impasse that would create.

Martina's daughter Estela woke me at four on the morning of Juana's delivery. By that time, I'd attended dozens of pre-natal and post-partum visits with Martina, but I'd only witnessed one birth, the precipitous and peaceful delivery of Martina's next door neighbor. We both had missed several recent deliveries, the babies arriving more quickly than we could, and I was growing impatient. When Estela told me that her mother had gone to a birth hours before but hadn't wanted to disturb me, I was annoyed. *Disturb me?* I wondered as I hastily changed clothes, removing the tall woolen socks that protected my ankles from fleas. *Isn't this "disturbance" the reason I'm here?* Estela stood in the doorway and pointed down the hill into the darkness.

"You can see it from here," she assured me, "the door on the left."

In the years since, I've tried to recall the events leading up to Juana's delivery, believing that if I could identify a single pivotal moment, perhaps I could deduce what we might have done differently. I remember arriving at the bottom of that dark hill and not knowing which door to knock. I remember my relief when the door cracked open and Martina called out my name. Her grinning at me as she introduced me to Juana and her mother. My sitting in that spare kitchen clutching a hot cup of sugar water between my chilled hands, jealously eying the warm blanket under which Martina and Juana were snuggled. Later, as Juana's labor progressed, what I remember, in vivid stills, is my uncertainty. I recall looking at my watch, thinking that Juana had been pushing for a long time, but how long was too long? She labored kneeling with her arms and head resting on a rickety wooden chair. Martina told me that many of her patients delivered in that position, but eventually Juana grew tired and lay on the cool cement floor, her head in her mother-in-law's lap. I recall that the upbeat chatter among the three women gave way to long silences and tremulous queries. At some point Martina stopped translating their conversation from Quiche to Spanish. I know I deliberated for a long while before finally asking, "How do we know the baby is OK?" I remember moving from my low stool to kneel on the floor closer to Juana's side, wanting to do something, to intervene, but not knowing how.

When the baby's head emerged I was sitting by Juana's hips. The umbilical cord was taut and wrapped twice around the infant's neck, embedded under her jaw. Martina scanned the floor for her scissors. She made one cut, to the outermost loop of cord, at a spot near the child's ear. I winced when the dark red blood spurted toward me, but the baby didn't budge. Perhaps it wasn't the cord but the infant's shoulders that blocked her passage? Martina made a second cut, and the untethered infant burst forth into her hands. Martina looked up at me, wide-eyed. We both saw that the baby was lifeless and that Juana was bleeding heavily. "Maybe if we rub her..." I said it aloud in English before I realized my mistake, but Martina passed the baby into my arms anyway. I realize now that she must have been birthing the placenta, massaging Juana's uterus, praying for her to stop bleeding, but in the moment I didn't know why it had fallen to me to squeeze life into Juana's little girl. Unlike many of her patients, Martina never assumed that my being a gringa imparted magical powers. If anything, she treated me delicately. I was her pale and fragile guest. That morning she handed me the baby simply because mine were the nearest arms. I have no idea how much time passed while I rubbed and squeezed and prayed. Eventually, the baby gasped once and mewed a weak cry. I remember well my relief, the grateful realization that she was alive and that I could not be held responsible for her death. But I can't begin to estimate for how long she'd gone without breathing.

Over a year went by before I learned that Juana's daughter was severely disabled. Martina told me the sorrowful news while we sat on her patio catching up. I'd moved back to *los Estados* by then but had returned to Pachaj to visit. She was quick about it, eager to talk of other things, and I could only wonder about her feelings. Much is lost in translation from Quiche to Spanish to English and back again. Often I have misunderstood Martina. Knowing this, I have asked her about Juana's daughter at every subsequent visit to Pachaj, hoping that the answer will be different, that I had misunderstood what she'd told me years before. Instead the facts have remained the same: Juana's daughter has never walked or talked. She is blind and extremely weak on one side. I have not seen Juana or her daughter since the day of the birth. Martina has never offered to escort me, and I've been too afraid to ask. The little girl's disability feels unreal to me, perhaps unacceptable. So each time I visit Martina, for years now, I ask about her, and each time Martina tells me the same thing, and I am newly disappointed, newly invested in remembering the details of that morning, though they become less vivid with the passing years. Juana still carries her daughter—who is now more than seven-years-old—as she would an infant, in a cloth tied to her back, but as the little girl grows heavier they both leave the house less and less. I wonder what Juana thinks of her daughter's disability. Does she accept it as a God-given condition? Does she blame God? Does she blame Martina or me?

For a long time after Juana's delivery, I rarely spoke of it. It wasn't something I chatted about on my phone calls back to the States. Years later, when I talked of my time in Pachaj, I'd mention it obliquely, blandly, just: "a birth that went wrong." In the States, as I went about my life—buying a car, studying medicine, falling in and out of love—many months could go by without my thinking about Juana or her daughter. When I did remember them, the memory produced a dull, hard-to-identify feeling: sadness, yes, and a little guilt, but mostly confusion, that same uncertainty I felt kneeling on the cool kitchen floor, unsure of my role or of what my reaction should be. Now, when I tell people of that delivery, their reactions are predictable: "She gave YOU the baby?" they wonder incredulously. Hadn't I been terrified, horrified, angry? Where is my anguish? Sometimes I wonder that myself. In Pachaj, I often didn't know what to think or feel, and I learned to follow Martina's lead. My reaction to Juana's delivery was matter-of-fact because Martina's reaction was matter-of-fact. She catches babies in a place where mothers and infants sometimes—and not rarely—die during childbirth. Maternal mortality is one hundred times higher in Totonicapán than it is in my home state of Massachusetts. Infant mortality is fourteen times higher. A devastating birth injury is a tragedy no matter where it takes place, but it feels different in Pachaj than it does in Boston.

We are all human. But in Pachaj, after Juana's delivery, that mantra felt hollow, inane. It's a true statement, but it hides vast inequity. When the little old ladies used to joke about seeing me naked, I was always tempted to take them up on it. In my imagined scenario, I would defiantly reveal to them my breasts and hips, so similar to their own, and they would have been forced to see how much we shared. They thought I was some alien being, and I was certain that my body would prove them wrong. After Juana's delivery I realized how wrong I had been: my body itself is marked by my rights, my wealth, and the place of my upbringing. Growing up in the antiseptic United States, my intestines never developed the flora that would have given them a fighting chance against Pachaj bacteria that didn't bother Martina or her family. Decades of healthy food, fluoridated water, and dutiful brushing have left my smile intact, while Pachaj's malnourished mothers are gap-toothed in their twenties. If and when I choose to bear children I will do so in Massachusetts, where mortality rates are as low as any country on earth. The world and all its options are as open to me as they are closed to the women of Pachaj. How dare I pretend that we are more the same than we are different.

Martina and I have never spoken frankly about Juana's daughter. Whenever I timidly bring her up, she is vaguely regretful. *"Que pena,"* she says, "What a shame." She never says anything more than this, and I imagine she thinks me morbid or naïve for continuing to speak of it. Often she changes the subject, and talks instead of a neighbor's new pick-up, her grandson's success in school, her recent decision to pave the patio or to paint the house hot pink. We have never itemized what-might-have-been. But I know that Martina has wondered what-might-have-been because I remember what she said to me barely an hour after Juana's delivery.

After I had clumsily resuscitated the baby and passed her to her grandmother, and after Martina had somehow stanched Juana's bleeding, and after four of us had awkwardly carried Juana into a bedroom and put her infant to her breast, I returned to the kitchen to find Martina. Re-entering the room I appreciated the foul metallic smell of birth and saw for the first time the streaks of drying brown blood on the white-washed walls. Martina was kneeling by one of the bloodied blankets on which Juana had lay. The placenta sat in a metal bowl next to her. Uncharacteristically, Martina was still; she seemed to be thinking. She held a beer in her hand but was not drinking it. She gestured me back to my stool, where another beer sat. Someone had opened the slats of the one window in the room, and I saw with surprise that the sun was up. Outside this kitchen, the day was well on its way.

We didn't yet know that the baby was permanently disabled, though we both thought she should eventually see a doctor. I thought it might be wise sooner rather than later, but no one else seemed to share my worry. We both took tentative sips of our cold Brahva, and Martina turned her head to look at me. Her usually placid face was lined. Black strands of hair had fallen loose from her long braid, and she pushed them away from her eyes with the back of her hand.

"A birth like that...? In *los Estados* it would have happened in a hospital, right?"

I remember my uncertain feelings dissolving into sadness. I was sad because Martina's question reminded me of all the others I'd fielded about my wondrous homeland. Yes, we had washing machines (and dryers!). Yes, my parents had a computer, from which they sent me emails. And they had two cars, one for each of them. But no, we didn't have dinosaurs. It pained me that a safe birth was among the foreign marvels available to gringas like me but not *guatemaltecas* like Juana. And I was sad because Martina's imagined alternative for her patient was a hospital in the United States, not the public hospital just forty-five minutes from where we were sitting. There are a multitude of reasons why Martina and her neighbors rarely travel to that hospital. The unfortunate reality is that the staff at most Guatemalan hospitals speak only Spanish, often treat their patients—especially poor, indigenous, women—with astonishing disrespect, usually don't let family members or midwives anywhere near the delivery room, always strip their patients naked from the waist down, and often cut them wide open. Certainly, I was not surprised when one of Doña Martina's most loyal patients told me that a "good midwife is one that makes sure you never have to go to the hospital." In Pachaj, birth takes place at home with a midwife. That's how it's done; usually it works out fine, and in a place where life can be unremittingly and senselessly difficult, not so great an emphasis is placed on evading seemingly inevitable hardship.

I don't remember how I answered Martina. I didn't say much. I didn't tell her all I was thinking about the differences between us. We were both tired. In a few moments we would bring the placenta outside and bury it near the patio. But for now we sat quietly, the bloodied room between us, drinking our beers. After my first tentative sips, I began to drink in gulps. I realized with surprise that I'd acquired an appreciation for post-partum beer. It was barely 9 a.m., but I couldn't believe how good my cold Brahva tasted.

ANTARCTICA
AND OUTER SPACE

UNITED STATES, CANADA, AND ANTARCTICA

AN INTERVIEW WITH
LAURA DRUDI, ASPIRING AEROSPACE PHYSICIAN

THE FACE OF SPACE MEDICINE:

A flight surgeon (that's the military term for an aerospace physician) is essentially the person who provides medical care to a flight crew. So in space medicine, medical care is provided to the astronauts. Something new is that we now have the growing commercial space flight industry and the general population may soon be going to space. It's an exciting time and a paradigm shift happening in aerospace medicine, knowing that we will likely be taking care of the commercial space-flight participants.

THIRD TIME'S A CHARM:

The thing that inspired me to go into the space industry was the astronaut corps. Being a Canadian, it's very difficult to realize such a dream because the selections are much rarer and there are fewer participants compared to NASA. I've applied to two selections so far. Once in 1992 when I was five (obviously they didn't take me seriously), and another time when I was just twenty one, in 2009. And I'll be applying again in the next selection. The chances are infinitely small but I'll give it a try.

WHERE TO START:

The space industry is so small and aerospace medicine is even smaller. My first exposure to this world happened in 2008 when I learned that a conference in aerospace medicine was going to be held in Boston. Being from Montreal, it was really just a drive away. So I encouraged my parents to take a family vacation to Boston. They could enjoy themselves while I went to the conference. So that's what we did, and that's where I met all my mentors. They know how difficult it is to start doing research in aerospace medicine, because it is so small and there are such limited research opportunities. I started with literature reviews, doing small projects from Montreal remotely. Then I expanded to going to NASA and doing research with leaders in the field. It's been a crazy ride, and I have all my mentors to thank for that. I wouldn't have been able to do it by myself for sure.

MAY I BORROW $14,000?:

Antarctica is a wonderful environment for space research. When I first heard about the Antarctic expedition, in 2009, I wanted to participate. However it's very expensive to go, about $14,000. I didn't have the funds, so I asked my parents, "Would you be able to loan me $14,000 to go to Antarctica?" Obviously, they rejected my proposal. But I told them it was something that I certainly wanted to do. It would be an expedition of a lifetime and an opportunity for me to grow and meet people from all over the world, all in this remote environment.

It took me two years to raise the funds for the trip. I raised $14,000, with help from family donations, friends helping out, and from companies mostly in and around Montreal. I approached the Canadian Space Agency as well, because I knew that they were sponsoring students from the previous years. Unfortunately they, like all other space agencies, are going through huge budget cuts. But they encouraged me to go into this wonderful experience. And then everything sort of came together. So yes, I really did raise that much money. When I realized that I needed some big sponsors to get me to that $10,000 mark at least, I was really approaching big companies. Fortunately, everyone in business speaks to each other. You know one person, and then you're in. But it's still a big push. A month before the Antarctica expedition, I was still trying to get the last few thousand dollars, and finally, some sponsors came in last-minute, before I knew it, I was on a plane heading to Antarctica.

SPACE ON EARTH:

All I really knew about Antarctica before taking off on the trip is that it is a remote and hostile environment on our planet that people rarely go to. There are research bases on Antarctica, and, yes, a lot of research focused on remote and rural medicine, where people are isolated from full communities and an urban lifestyle. A lot of the research going on there is related to the psychological and physical constraints of the elements as well, as Antarctica is such a perfect platform for that. It all led into my involvement with the space industry. To be truly secluded from humanity, it's such a unique thing to learn how to survive in such an environment. That's why many space agencies are pursuing research on the Antarctic continent. When you're in Antarctica, it's really hard to leave, especially if you're there over an Antarctic winter. I was there during an Antarctic summer, which pretty much is like a Canadian winter.

During an Antarctic winter you're secluded in your research base and wouldn't be able to go outside.

AN EPIC JOURNEY:

I left Montreal and I flew to Florida, and from Florida I connected to a flight in Buenos Aires. And then in Buenos Aires I changed flights and I flew deeper into Argentina, to a small city called Ushuaia. From there, we spent a few days just meeting everyone else that was going to be participating on the Antarctic expedition and literally coming from all over the world.

From that point, we got on the ship and set sail going through the Drake Passage. If you know a little bit about the Drake Passage, it's one of the most treacherous waters on our planet. I just remember, we were two days into this Drake Passage, and the boat was tipping forty-five degrees to one side and forty-five degrees to the other. So if you were seasick, you were definitely not a happy camper for two days. Panic attacks broke out, obviously. A lot of people thought we were going to tip. Some people were vomiting throughout the entire two days, or couldn't eat because they were nauseous. However there were physicians on board and they were giving anti-nausea medications. Sometimes it worked, and sometimes it didn't. But the Drake Passage was sort of like a mini psychological experiment in itself, because two days, forty-eight hours on these horrible waters, really tests your limits.

THE IMPORTANCE OF COMMUNITY:

We were allowed to go anywhere on the ship. Going through the Drake Passage we were told to stay inside, so I spent a lot of time in the main cabin area. There were couches and there was a bar where you could have food and snacks. And then there was the cafeteria area where everyone came together. What I really liked actually, and I think that this sort of parallels a lot of the experiences that astronauts have on the space shuttle or the International Space Station, is that there's a specific time for lunch and dinner where everyone sort of stops what they're doing and comes together. Everyone sits down and talks about their day and just enjoys the meal. There's a community feeling that's unparalleled by anything that I've experienced.

STILLNESS:

Seeing the Antarctic continent for the first time, I was overwhelmed and enthusiastic. My emotions were going up and down throughout the entire expedition. The Antarctic environment can take a person by surprise. It's a beautiful place. It's a place that should be cherished and treasured. But Antarctica can be very unforgiving, and that's part of what stays in my mind. There were beautiful moments though, on our small boats, the little Zodiacs, when you could just go off on your own and explore. I remember getting to this one particular area, called Paradise Bay. The boat (the motor wasn't on) slowly moved over the water. No one was talking. There was no sound. It was just complete stillness and you couldn't even hear any signs of life. I think I recognized at that time, where I truly was. I appreciated how fragile our environment really is, because Antarctica is one area where humanity has not touched and has not destroyed the environment through urbanization. It's really a treasure on our planet.

TAKING MEASURES FOR THE ENVIRONMENT:

The pristine beauty of Antarctica really puts you into perspective, looking back on the city or town you've come from, and trying to tackle some of the largest challenges we have in terms of the environment. There were different working groups on my expedition, from marine biology to geology, and oceanography and more. One of the major projects was going out on the Zodiacs and recording temperatures and salinity in the different regions of the Antarctic Peninsula. We had a device we lowered from our boats to many feet below the surface, and we recorded the temperatures at different depths of the ocean. And we did this at many different areas, and they were all tabulated and put into a database that belongs to a professor who's been there on many occasions, to trend variations in temperatures and salinity.

So yes, ideas of environmentalism and conservation really permeated throughout our entire two-week experience. "We only leave footsteps in Antarctica," is what our trip leader said. I really appreciated that comment by the end of the trip. We truly did only leave footprints there and we did not stain the environment. It's something that I really cherish, looking back.

Antarctica and the Southern Ocean, the Old-Fashioned Way

Antarctica and the Southern Ocean

Colin Souness

1. Approaching a Frozen Coast

When you spend a lot of time at sea you get used to seeing things in a slightly different way. Stars burn brighter and the occasional meteorite burns red, visibly breaking apart as it falls. The water around you sometimes fluoresces and lights up your wake, like the tail of a comet. Waves become mountains and their troughs become valleys. Every so often, when the moon rises at night, it looks like the world is ending on the horizon, and unless you move faster, it will rush up and consume you.

Stranger still is the sensation of waiting for the appearance of land. Generally it's oddly disappointing, as the first thing you see is a thin and unremarkable line of dull grey which you often spend many long minutes finally deciding that it is land, not just a line of bad weather coming in. This grey line then slowly grows into the coastline you were expecting.

My first sight of Antarctica, however, broke all of my preconceptions, and was anything but usual or unremarkable.

We had started off from Ushuaia, Argentina, in a fifteen-metre sailing boat with a crew of eight and berths for six. From there we had passed south through the group of Chilean islands that make up Cape Horn and, with the failing light of mid-December, had set our sail into the wind and started in the direction of the distant ice, a number of Magellanic penguins swimming alongside. From there, the South Shetland Islands of the Antarctic Peninsula were a mere 442 nautical miles distant.

I remember standing on my first watch and seeing the grey outline of South America's southernmost extremity slowly fading into the murk behind us. It was a strange and somewhat sinister feeling, with wind filling the sails and only ocean and time standing between us and Antarctica—the bottom of the world. I was only twenty-two years old, and in this moment felt a strange sensation of falling. I really had no idea of what to expect, and standing alone on the deck of our tiny sailing boat, pushing through the rising swell into the Southern Ocean, filled me with a brand new kind of excitement. But was it excitement? How much of it was simply fear? Regardless, I knew I was in the right place.

The next week of that crossing exists as a bit of a blur in my memory. The things I do remember include the strange grey tone that came over the water when we crossed the Antarctic convergence where the warmer Atlantic and Pacific Oceans meet the cold polar currents that perpetually circle the southern continent. I remember that the wind never once seemed to be behind us, and my stomach still recalls the deep, sideways tip of the boat, as we fought into the austral gales. I clearly remember not being able to use the onboard toilet because every available space had been taken up by mountaineering equipment (this, in anything over a Force 7 wind, made life a little more interesting). I remember an e-mail I much later sent to my mother back in Scotland describing the recipe for a crossing of the Drake Passage under sail:

Take one long steel tube, fill it with unwitting mountaineers, add a couple extra for good measure and then pour in a generous quantity of salt water. Seal the tube and shake well for approximately eight days. Check with a blunt knife, and when all hope is gone your crossing is probably almost ready to eat.

I also remember sighting my first Antarctic iceberg, which was massive and the size of an island. Before I left home Antarctica's Larsen B Ice Shelf had collapsed, and I'd seen a satellite image of the main Larsen B iceberg drifting towards the island of South Georgia. The berg and South Georgia had been almost the same size.

The one I saw now was considerably smaller—perhaps only a couple of kilometers long—but my heart rate quickened at the sight of it nonetheless.

We came no closer than four miles from the berg, but it still stood out clearly in the distance. It seemed quite unreal—very unlike the classic "fairytale castle" icebergs I'd also seen in the arctic. It looked somehow more business-like and menacing, as if it was sailing to a specific bearing with a destination in mind. In fact, at first I'd mistaken it for a far-distant supertanker, so long, flat-topped, and linear it was. We would see a couple more of these mega-bergs.

Empty seas, seemingly inhabited only by petrels and albatross (or giant sea turkeys, as I came to call them), persisted for a while. Sometime later however, in between fitful bursts of broken sleep, I became aware that firstly, the weather seemed to be improving, and secondly, that it appeared to be the day after Christmas. Boxing Day, at the bottom of the planet.

I extracted myself from my now very salty sleeping bag, put on my even saltier thermal wellies, and, keeping at least three points of contact between myself and the boat at all times to deal with "sailing gravity," went up above to enjoy the fact that the deck had gone from trying to be a wall to being more of a floor. Andy, one of my crewmates, was on watch. Straddling the tiller and shielding his eyes from the brightness, he nodded towards the southeast and said, "Look! We're almost there!"

I peered in the direction he had indicated, around the port edge of the dodger, and searched for the thin, dull grey line of approaching land and rain that he seemed to be implying ought to be there. I saw nothing—just the seamless white of low clouds that I was used to seeing ahead during day watches.

"I don't see anything mate. Where is it?" I asked.

"No no. Not down there." Andy took his eyes off the compass for a moment and pointed above the horizon. "Up there!"

I looked a few degrees above the horizon and almost stopped breathing. Mountains! Just remembering the sight now sends a shiver up my back. I could barely believe it. I was looking at Antarctica. For most of my adult life I had dreamed of getting to the southern continent, and, at that very instant of looking a little up instead of straight ahead, my ambition had realised itself. It was absolutely electrifying.

2. A Quick Turnaround

Without stating the obvious, Antarctica isn't like other places. The ice goes all the way down to the sea almost everywhere. There are few spots in the world where you can stand high on a glacier or icy mountaintop, with the spindrift stinging your face, and still hear the crash of waves and the shriek of seabirds below you. Antarctica is one of them. It doesn't have many beaches or cliffs or rocky shorelines. Mostly, it has calving glaciers and sea-swept snow banks. It is a white coast that, from the eyes of a sailor, merges with the southern horizon until its remote and defiant peaks inch slowly above the sea mist. I was now looking up at the summits of Smith Island, one of the most southerly of the South Shetland Islands. I will never forget the sight as long as I breathe.

What may have been twenty-four hours later, we were moored up in a cove amongst a small group of islands called the Melchiors. Four ropes on four boulders on opposing sides of a narrow inlet held us steady (the fjords in Antarctica are usually too deep and the seabed too clear of sand or gravel for an anchor to be of much use) and we rested and enjoyed a belated Christmas dinner. The lamb carcass that had been strung up in the rigging, absorbing the salt of the stormy Southern Ocean, ended its voyage amidst watery bread sauce, oily potatoes, and a wee dab of rum.

Unfortunately, Christmas was cut short by a sudden gale that threatened to blow us off our moorings and onto the rocks. Needless to say that in the face of Antarctic winds, driving sleet, the apparently imminent possibility of being wrecked on the rocks, and the unspoken understanding that help was very, very far away, all traces of that well-travelled rum evaporated rather quickly. After much shouting, one cut rope, and a lot of hauling later, we had managed to pull the boat around into the wind and were moving once again, under engine this time. There had been one man, on an inflatable kayak, who single-handedly braved the chop to release those mooring lines. I've never seen anyone fall into the water and then jump out of it again as quickly in my life (a better case for dry suits over the traditional sailing fowlies than any other I've ever seen or heard).

My next memory is of being on watch with my friend "the Highlander." It was probably only seven or eight hours after Christmas had been so rudely cancelled, and it was the middle of the night. The wind had dropped off again suddenly, the sky was silver and the water was pale blue-grey. Snow was falling thickly as we motored southwards through the De Gerlache Strait, flanked all the while now by barren, icy mountains. To our port side was the Antarctic mainland, and to our starboard side Brabant and Anvers Islands. It was cold. We had been cold for days on board, but now it was a different kind of cold. It was a drier, straight from the horse's mouth kind of cold.

The snow fell and gathered on both the boat and the sea, unable to melt in the frigid Antarctic waters. After a short time we were plowing not through water anymore, it seemed, but through a thin layer of slush, leaving an open trail of inky darkness in our wake. I still remember the sound of the bow cutting through the sloppy ice, like a Slush Puppy machine stirring its neon payload.

Our object on this course was to drop off five men, the bulk of the equipment on board, and several months' worth of supplies at a small cabin known as Damoy Hut on Weinkie Island. And what a spot for a holiday house it was. Nestled in a small cove in the shadow of serrated polar peaks and within sniffing distance of a colony of (noisy) Gentoo penguins, it was, at that point, the most beautiful place I'd been in all my life. By the time we had arrived and deployed the mooring lines, it was the next day, and the sun was out, clouds drifting on light winds. To the west lay Anvers Island, the peaks of its so-called Trojan Range protruding fiercely into the clean and unspoiled blue sky. I was tired. I was tired of living in a cramped boat, tired of being constantly battered by southern storms, and tired of being constantly salty and wet. I wanted nothing more than some space and a bed that didn't move.

As it turned out, I got it, but only for a night. The skipper told me that I was to stay aboard and sail immediately for the Falkland Islands, where our yacht was to pick up a British military mountaineering team and deliver them to the Antarctic Peninsula, the most northern part of the mainland. This was a change: the original plan was for me to stay in Antarctica with the climbing party. But, these things happen, and so I resolved to make the most of my fourteen hours of shore leave. I kayaked ashore in the little inflatable (that had already proven itself so admirably in the Melchiors) and got some rest.

I paddled over "the long way," dossing around in the bay for a good half hour, soaking in the silence, floating on the tranquillity, bashing at iceberglets with my paddle and enjoying the way they moved. It was a sublimely relaxed and satisfying moment, made all the more so by the knowledge that on the following day I'd be heading back into the clutches of the Drake Passage with almost eight hundred nautical miles (about fourteen hundred kilometers) of open-ocean sailing ahead of me. That night I slept strangely. I woke up in the hut at about 1 a.m. It was almost broad daylight, and the plywood platform bunk was moving under me. Weeks of choppy yachting had acclimatised me to a wholly different kind of gravity arrangement, and this night of stability had obviously surprised my system. I felt ever so slightly ill and very disoriented. Now everyone has mornings when it takes a moment or two to remember where you are. But on this occasion I wasn't round a mate's place, or at my girlfriend's, or at anyone else's place. I appeared to be in Antarctica!

3. Shuttle Run to the Falklands, Anyone?

Exhaustion prevailed, and I quickly fell back asleep, but in what seemed like almost no time at all I was back on the boat, hauling the anchor and waving a somewhat forlorn cheerio to the shore party. As they were breaking out the oranges and fine china, I was slipping back into my well-salted foul-weather gear. Back once more unto the Drake!

The weather, it transpired, had not improved since our last crossing. We were really pushed hard, and it took us eleven days to reach the Falkland Islands. With only three crew aboard this time we did solo watches, meaning that everything was twice as much work and generally had to be done twice as quickly in order to get back on the helm before the wind vane auto-helm (which was regularly overpowered by the weather) dropped the boat either off the wind or straight into it. On more than one occasion I was caught out by the weather conditions whilst working on the foredeck dealing with one calamity or another.

Sometimes, in particularly massive seas, you don't just get soaked, you get completely submerged. It's the white-headed waves that you really have to look out for. When they begin to break, they become loaded with air pockets and their density decreases, so instead of riding over them, a boat will just sink into them.

Once, I hadn't clipped my safety line in yet when just such a wave took us broadside. I had undone the line so I could climb up the frighteningly tilted deck and get a better position from which to tie down some apparatus that was threatening to liberate itself. Having wedged myself between two low lashing points, I was reaching for the business end of my lifeline when the ocean came at me from behind. The sensation was a lot like falling on your back from a high place. The impact was immense, and I tensed up in my precarious little nook and closed my eyes as everything went dark and wet around me. Water shot into every available breach in my clothing. It surged up the cuffs and trouser legs of my fowlies, and I was completely underwater for what can't have been longer than a second, but for what felt like an age. I believe to this day that I came to within a hair's breadth of losing my grip and going over the side. As it happened, though, the moment passed. I opened my eyes, accepted that I was still on the boat, did the job I'd come forward to do, and crept very carefully back to the relative safety of the dodger.

"Did that get you?" came a shout from the skipper's berth.

"Yes," was all I could muster in reply.

The days passed slowly as the weather kept us working and kept us wet. I don't remember eating much that week. Each of us spent almost every off-watch moment in our berths in a bid to shorten the crossing through sleep. The top wind speed we recorded fell upwards of sixty-five knots. That's almost seventy-five miles per hour. If nothing else, I can say that all of us built a lot of character during the course of that sail. Soon enough, though, we moved on to Burdwood Bank, a large shallow shelf to the south of the Falklands, and from that point onwards the weather was less fierce. Instead, we met sudden squalls and bizarre misty patches that would roll in, seemingly from nowhere, and obscure everything. Sometimes they lasted for only a few minutes, but other times they persisted for hours, and we would become worried about shipping in this far busier part of the ocean. Fortunately, the only other occupant of the seas that we came close to was a whale. A blue whale!

4. Boot-Camp Holiday

Our arrival in Antarctica had been a surprise, but I smelt the Falklands a mile away. After the best part of a month at sea, and with only a short stay amongst the rocks and ice of the world's least smelly continent, my nose had been starved of any action (other than the niffs that leaked from beneath my own clothing, all of which was now quite ripe it's fair to say). So, when the now warm northerly winds swept over us, I could almost taste the grassy flavours and peaty musk of the Falklands. It was beautiful. Soon we were motoring towards the coast, indulging what were fast becoming very black senses of humour at the place names on the chart (Low Island and Bleaker Island stick in my memory) and worrying about the engine, which was working overtime driving the propeller through some very thick kelp forests that thrive in the shallow coastal waters.

We headed into Lively Sound, bound for Mare Harbour, which serves the Falkland's main military installation, Mount Pleasant Airbase (MPA). I went off watch and fell very quickly asleep, lulled by the sound of the engine's humming and the flatness of the seas.

The next thing I remember is waking up with an unfamiliar face looking down at me.

"Sausage or bacon, mate?" It said.

"Uuuhhhh…what was that?" I mustered in reply.

"Steve Ayers. Sergeant. Good to meet you. Sounds like you've had quite a week or so! What kind of butty would you like mate? Sausage or bacon?"

I can tell you, it was like I'd died and gone to heaven. I can't even recall which way I opted.

We stayed on MPA for more than a week, and I loved every second. The base was only a ten-minute truck ride from the harbour where we were incongruously moored up alongside large grey destroyers and supply ships. We were billeted up in the Sergeants Mess which had dry and stable beds, showers the like of which I'd thought I'd never see again, a very pleasant bar and, get in, baked beans! I hadn't seen baked beans in months, and, as my mother will testify, I love my beans.

The two feelings I remember most clearly from MPA were, firstly, how much the whole complex reminded me of a large spacecraft. (I watched a lot of sci-fi in my teens, and the large corridors of MPA connected nearly all the different buildings and could easily have been a set from *Alien*.) Secondly, I realized how windy the Falklands were. It was mid-to-late summer there but still the winds howled most days. This held us up a while, delaying our return to Antarctica, but I enjoyed those days. I could lie in bed listening to the air racing and howling past the window, knowing that it no longer ruled my life. I didn't have to race up on deck and reef any sails. I was back in the world of floors, walls, and roofs, at least for a while. Bliss.

Soon enough, though, and we were back on the water, tacking to and fro into the wind in an effort to escape back down Lively Sound and southwards. This proved to be a false start, as an engine component, just replaced in MPA, shrunk in the cold water and worked its way loose. We limped back to Mare Harbour, quickly arranged another replacement, and were away again.

All I remember of the sail back to Antarctica is people's faces. The military team, six strong, were all brilliant company. There were four lads from the army (including the expedition leader, Major Dick) and two from the navy. There was an infantry lieutenant who excelled at cooking, even in the fiercest weather; an army doctor who had once run an art-house cinema in London; a Royal Navy reservist who skippered luxury yachts in the Mediterranean as a civilian and who spent the whole time on our boat seasick; and Sergeant Ayers, the team's troop sergeant, who's positive attitude kept everything in proportion.

My favourite memory of this little chapter is of being on a day watch with the doctor. It was as "choppy" as ever, and we were sitting on opposite sides of the dodger chatting about films and stuff, as you do. Now, the military lads had brought their own lifejackets, all of which were auto-inflation jobs that would set themselves off upon submersion. This is a good safety feature, for it means that if you go overboard unconscious (as is very possible on a sailing yacht, what with booms and things flying backward and forward across the deck) you should still float. The rest of us—that is, the resident crew—had removed the auto-inflation switches from our jackets, and I soon discovered why. The doctor and I were chatting away, constantly looking over each other's shoulders to warn of coming waves. And then one hit, and for a good few seconds we were both submerged as the icy waters once again swept over our little floating world. In a moment I opened my eyes again only to be met with an unexpected sight: I now seemed to be sharing my watch not with a man but with a massive yellow balloon. The doctor's jacket had gone off, framing his perplexed-looking bearded face in a large, Day-Glo vinyl tire. He looked like a margarine salesperson or something. The sunflower man.

5. Back to the Cooler

A week or so later, we had just dropped the military party off on the peninsula from which they were going to mount an attempt on the "forbidden plateau." Once more there were only three of us aboard—

me, the skipper, and the Highlander too. We were motoring down the De Gerlache Straits again, heading back to our base camp at Damoy. The wind, fickle as ever, ebbed away to nothing, and the black, frigid waters became still. It was so calm that even the slightest disturbance was obvious from a distance. It was amazing, floating in the midst of such a massive, perspective-defying landscape and yet hearing not a sound other than that of the boat itself. After many long weeks of crewing in some of the most inclement conditions I have ever experienced, the tranquillity softened my brain like a warm bath softens your body.

As I watched from the helm I started to notice large patches on the surface where the water seemed to be alive. Something was moving, almost imperceptibly, just beneath the skin of the sea. It was like the water itself had goosebumps from the cold, and those goosebumps were moving around in a bid to stay warm.

At first I wasn't sure what was happening, but then I saw a line of bubbles breaking through from below. They led around the disturbed patch in a wide arc, almost like someone was using a bubble cannon to cut a circle out of the sea. I steered the boat clear of this commotion just in case, and I'm glad I did, for a few moments later the bubble cutter was revealed. As I watched, the water suddenly betrayed the faintest apparition of white just below the surface, and then all hell broke loose. The water parted, and upwards thrust the colossal open maw of a humpback whale. With its jaws parted wide and its gullet swollen with tons of water and krill that it had trapped, it looked every bit the kraken of the deep. I felt like a character from an ancient Greek legend, sailing a sea beset with monsters that swallow ships whole. (For anyone who has ever seen David Lynch's screen adaptation of *Dune*, recall the image of a giant Sand Worm breaking the desert surface and you will have an idea of what it was like.)

And then we appeared to be surrounded with hungry mouths bursting out of the inky waters. Sometimes two or three mouths rose simultaneously. The krill death toll must have been monumental, but

I'm sorry to say I wasn't really thinking much about them at that precise moment. I was more concerned with not driving straight into *a whale!* Fortunately they were making no attempt to hide themselves, and their sheer size and proximity made them impossible not to spot. Still, they regularly came so close that it seemed they thought we were one of them.

Eventually, we returned to Damoy, and there we would stay for more than a month before finally setting sail for the final gruelling crossing of the Drake Passage. I left Antarctica and the Southern Ocean behind, but neither of them ever really left me.

Living in and ultimately leaving places is a strange thing. Living in Antarctica like that—sometimes on a boat, sometimes in a hut, and other times in a tent—I really discovered for the first time in my life that you don't need sci-fi or your imagination in order to live in other worlds. You need imagination to make things happen and to get there, but those "other worlds" are right here on Earth. The oceans are one of those worlds. Antarctica is another. Since that expedition I have made it a life objective to live in as many "worlds" as possible. I even joined the armed forces for a time (possibly drawn in by the ready supply of baked beans), which is another world in itself. And I have lived and loved every one of those worlds in a different way. Every place you live in changes you, and those changed parts never go away.

Major Dick said to me on the boat once, "Antarctica is one of those places you visit once and then spend the rest of your life trying to get back to." I think he was right. Different people find their Antarctica experiences in different ways, and when we leave we sometimes miss living out the parts of ourselves that came alive while we were there.

I've rarely felt as alive as I did whilst sailing in Antarctica. I will go back.

Fading Memories

Athens, Greece

Theopi Skarlatos

I AM STANDING in Agios Panteleimonas square, reminiscing about the Greece I knew as a six-year-old girl. I remember playing in a similar *plateia* (square) next to a decorated church, buying chocolates from the *periptero* (kiosk), and skipping with my friends, while old *giagiades* (grandmothers) looked on. Somehow back then, the breeze carried, along with the summer pollen, an intense notion that you lived in the best place on earth. The scent of jasmine and honeysuckle together with the smell of cooling marble instantly brings back memories.

But now, off Acharnon Street, migrant children play ball games on a ground scrawled with graffiti that says "Greece is for Greeks."

On the corner, plain-clothes police officers arrest and handcuff Somali men without papers, and a one-legged man struggles by on crutches, begging for money.

The stone walls beneath the church are stained with the words *"Chrisi Avgi"* for the right-wing extremist party Golden Dawn.

A mile up the road, more graffiti reads "Down with the fascists."

Here, the Greece of my childhood is nowhere to be seen.

Greece is in its fifth year of recession. There are no ideas for reconstruction or production. Mistrust of members of the Parliament is rife.

This has left a gaping hole in society and the extreme right is slowly starting to fill it. They have to, they say, claiming the government has no real plan or a positive vision for the future—only a sea of endless debt. Golden Dawn's popularity is increasing dramatically, in a world where wages are being cut and cut and cut again.

Taxes are increasing. Young adults' unemployment is at more than 50 percent. There's been an increase in drug use, depression, and prostitution. People have been filmed foraging for food in bins after dark, and schoolchildren are reported to have collapsed from malnutrition.

Hope does not reside here anymore.

What does exist now evokes an image far different from the pretty pictures displayed on dusty postcards at stalls beneath the Acropolis or even the all-welcoming Greece captured in my family holiday photos all those years ago.

Many Golden Dawn members see it as their right to take law and order into their own hands. They beat up and stab immigrants and minorities and wreck their market stalls, and have also been reported to strip and humiliate women.

But the party now has eighteen seats in parliament and claims it wants to create a new glowing picture of Greece and how it "used to be" in ancient times, both prosperous and at the forefront of science and philosophy. They want no more orders from Germany's "Frau Merkel," they say. They would expel all of the immigrants, or "invaders," as they like to call them.

Golden Dawn is preparing, it says, for "civil war." A civil war with "everybody."

When the Golden Dawn is out, anti-fascists here take to their motorbikes to protest in opposition. It makes the entire situation feel like a Shakespearean play with two opposing political families fighting. A battle to rule the streets of Athens.

But with figures suggesting that 50 percent of the police force supports Golden Dawn, the anti-fascists gain little ground.

Some demonstrators claim they've been imprisoned and tortured by police, who talk unashamedly in front of them about their far-right idols; that they openly praise Stalin and Hitler and make sure their strip-searched captives leave with the thought in their minds that things have changed in Greece—that it's not as it used to be.

Recently Golden Dawn picked a battle with the cast of the controversial play *Corpus Christi* because it reimagines Jesus and the apostles as gay men. Their political representatives, their members, and other supporters managed to shut down the theater before the show even started. They glued the locks of the entrance door shut, threw rocks at ticket holders, and have continued to threaten the theater director ever since.

The actors must now deliver their performances shrouded in secrecy and to a small audience. The director's parents have been told on numerous occasions that their son will be "delivered to them in little pieces" someday soon.

Many Greeks have left the scene's battleground. Gone abroad or to the countryside to bury their heads in village soil where the grass is greener and life is cheaper.

But on this trip, I now feel like the Greece I once knew is disappearing before my eyes.

The land that gave birth to democracy is now struggling to show that it's still in possession of it. The Acropolis, once proud and towering above its city, appears solemn and looks on as citizens fly from tear gas, throw firebombs, and scream at police: "You are just Golden Dawn dressed up in uniform. Open the roads and let us through so we can make our voices heard."

Parliament is barely visible for all the smoke.

As my return flight to the United Kingdom awaits, I no longer feel sad to be leaving a country that has, in the past, managed to keep a hold on my heart every time I visit.

This time I am sad about the past I have left behind. I am skeptical about whether I will ever see that Greece again. That Greece, which my six-year-old self, playing in the *plateia*, has managed to keep alive in my memory for so long.

BORN IN THE WRONG TIME

FRANCE

MARI AMEND

I'VE NEVER BEEN able to name it: the fleeting shiver of excitement while waiting for the train on an autumn day in the in-between time, just after afternoon and just before evening, glimpsing the light through the colorful trees beyond the last visible stretch of train track. I breathe the sharp air into my nostrils. I've never been able to name it: the feeling is gone and all that's left is the disappointment at its loss.

Johannes Hofer would call the feeling a "disorder of the imagination." In 1688, the term nostalgia was created by the young doctor Hofer to define the deadly psychological disorder afflicting Swiss mercenary soldiers.[1] They dreamt themselves ill thinking of home, the place and the people that were missing to them. As I define it, nostalgia is the fleeting feeling of an unknown excitement. It is the feeling that magic is real. The feeling that some idealized place and time for one second simultaneously passes through you in the present and back into the past. That the impossible, unattainable, already disappeared exists in the present moment for a moment and then it's gone.

---

1 "Irony, Nostalgia, and the Postmodern," by Linda Hutcheon

Growing up in Los Angeles, I've felt nostalgic for a past that I have never experienced, a home that is not my own, a magic that has always been missing from my life. In a smoggy landscape composed of low stucco buildings and never-ending asphalt roads, I have always longed for the history, the presence of the past and the romantic setting that I imagined to abound in Europe. Sitting in my cement city, scrambling to finish my French homework, I used to daydream myself traipsing through lavender fields, living in ancient cottages, milking goats. It was my inner search for magic and my outer desire to research French stories that landed me on a plane, on a train, in a car careening away from society and towards *la* France *profonde*: deep France.

Deep France is crisscrossed by the Loire and Allier rivers. Deep France is the department of the Haute-Loire. Its green landscape rolls with rocky hills dotted by medieval architecture and Romanesque ruins. Historically the area was always hard to access, and even today it is difficult to navigate, especially without a car. There are very few places in France where the custom of meeting and greeting another is to give more than two kisses. Here they give three. Tell a Parisian about your travels to the Haute-Loire and they will ask, "Where?" Repeat the name of the towns and they will ask "Why?" I answer the first question by holding up my hand as though it's a map of France and pointing to my palm somewhere south of the two horizontal creases and just east of the center. I answer the second question with some variation of "I am researching the local folklore." If I am lucky, they don't repeat the second question again.

When I set out for the place and the magic that I had longed for in my imagination, my project was to collect folktales. I had two months to study over seven hundred years of stories. I wanted to talk to the locals, host interviews and record any tales that were still shared between people in the Haute-Loire at home and through the towns. I was willing to loosen my definition of folklore, to make sure I could find something to satisfy my research questions. Any stories, tales native to the area, family histories, general French lore, would do. But the inner part of me, the part that sought the magic, hoped that people still shared the folklore I had been reading for months. I wanted to sit in a circle around a fire and listen to the old French stories as they passed through wrinkled lips and mixed with the heat of the flames.

If this were a different kind of essay, I would tell you about the quaint, native peoples who live in the remote countryside of deep France. First, I would describe the little houses and cottages they inhabit, then I would write about their petticoats and buckled shoes. Next I would devote an entire paragraph to the native women and their customs in the home and kitchen. I might even throw in a photograph or two, with analysis of course, of small children playing traditional games in the gardens and local squares. But this is not that kind of essay. When I boarded the stuffy bus in the ugliest French city I have ever seen, I became less hopeful that I would find that unidentifiable feeling in this place. The bus bumped and jostled me through picturesque river valleys broken up by harsh metal super stores. This is an essay about a quest for a place and a feeling that no longer, and perhaps never did, exist.

The bus left me at a molding train station in the middle of downtown Retournac. A group of dreadlocked kids kicked a trashcan as I nervously awaited the car of someone I did not know from the farm where I would be working for a month. The barefoot, slightly unraveled farmer, Renée-Jo, arrived and we wound over the river and to her farm. I thought I might yet hope again, as the pipes of the last factory faded in the rear view mirror. Chickens and dogs mingled with a motley, bohemian crew of farmers and we ate grainy bread in the late afternoon light. The chimes tingled, the wind blew. There might be magic here. There might be.

In this remote historic landscape filled with contemporary people I discovered the Musée de Croyances Populaires en Velay (Museum of

Popular Beliefs in Velay), which is housed in a sixteenth century city structure, and displays original artwork based on locally collected tales. I sought out Patrice Rey, the unassuming, thoughtful artist, who creates the colorful and creepy clay sculptures based on folktales and popular beliefs. In the 1980s, Patrice collected folklore, songs and popular beliefs from his grandparents and their friends in a small mountainous town in the Haute-Loire. The beliefs in his collection range from stories about white-faced ladies met on foggy roadsides on late, lost nights, to cures for warts. All tales, remedies and legends are from the town where he grew up. An artist by trade and a folklorist by interest, Patrice decided to combine the visual and the oral in order to create a museum that both told the folk stories and did not bore its goers. It seemed to me, Patrice and I shared the love of old tales and the knowledge that not everybody loved them. No one wants to read at a museum, Patrice told me, they will stop after the first paragraph and then the audience is lost. Not so in the Musée de Croyances Populaires. Patrice's small, clay-sculpted scenes are brightly colored, drawing the viewer in, and then keeping the viewer hooked with the creepy action, exciting and detailed, until they want to read Patrice's condensed version of the accompanying belief, tale or superstition.

I wandered the ancient building, alongside the old and young museum goers, listening to the folkloric songs playing on the speaker. I was drawn to a scene in which there are two gray, warty grandparents and their two young, knobby kneed grandchildren. The miniature room is older looking, with traditional furniture and the grandparents blend well with the appearance of the house, the grandfather wearing a sweater vest, and grimacing to show his missing teeth, the grandmother's head swathed in scarves and growing giant, hairy moles. In the left foreground, the two children scream, the boy sporting a *Harry Potter* T-shirt and kicking his leg over a Bart Simpson doll at his crying kid sister. The blatant juxtaposition of the two generations is comedic. I asked Patrice about his choice to make the scene a mixture of contemporary pop culture and traditional Velay culture. He laughed and said that it was realistic. For a century, these shifts have been occurring. Two generations ago the stories shared were real to the people who told them. They were events that had happened to them and what we call superstitions were their explanations for the world around them. Then, for his grandparents, the stories were still real, but they happened to someone else, a while ago. "To my grandmother, these were not popular beliefs, these tales and stories were real, they were explanations for the things that had occurred." To kids today, these stories are in books, they not only happened to someone else, but their veracity is doubtful. I wondered what had gotten lost between the generations to cause this change. Patrice talked about the shift from reality to belief in the context of the shift from tale-telling to TV watching. "It is neither good nor bad. It just is. We live in a world where this is the reality and it is up to us to decide what to do with it." The past is past whether we like it or not, but it's up to us to choose how we relate to it.

After a few weeks of milking goats, making bread and several interviews with local taletellers I finally translated the quizzical raise of the eyebrows I received in reaction to my use of the word folklore. The French definition of the word folklore is synonymous with the past. Folklore is a collection of stories written down in a book, recorded many years ago, and accessible in the library. It is fixed. To me, folklore is the word for the stories we share today. It is flexible. It is the legend about the origin of a lake and the story my grandma tells me about her childhood. Was what I was looking for already gone from deep France, locked in the pages of a dusty book somewhere in the Haute-Loire?

There is a French tale that was collected by a folklorist, Victor Smith, in the Haute-Loire in the 1800s about a not so average stepmother. Wife dies, man with two small children remarries, stepmother is about as wicked as they come. Not particularly happy to inherit two measly, ragamuffin children, the stepmother hatches a plan to reduce her burden by at least one. The stepmother promises whichever child can run to the edge of the forest and back the quickest a small lump of butter. Apparently the greasy prize is enough motivation and the children scamper off, the boy returning in record time. Only, when he goes to the pantry for his prize, his stepmother shuts the door on his head, severing it from his body. She makes small boy soup, serves it to his father and crafts a bird with the bones that remain. All is well for the stepmother, in spite of her weird plan and abusive ways, except that this is a story and in this story, the bird made of little boy bones starts to sing the tale of his death and the whole plan is unraveled to all who hear.

During the first month of my project, on a goat farm in an old tent in the middle of deep France, the two farmers who were hosting me were also trained to host abused or abusive children. They were part of a French program that placed children with family or abuse problems in safe, comfortable homes for a week at a time. The kids would move around so that they would be secure and would not learn the household rules in time to break them. Even in my escape to read stories and find magic, the problems of the world persisted. And yet, it made me wonder about the idea of folklore as being a thing of the past. I imagined the wicked stepmother on the page to be the parent from whom these kids were seeking refuge; these farmers were tending to the lost children in the tales I was reading.

The first professional taleteller in France, Jean Pierre Chabrol, worked with the new shifts in technology to bring his past into the present through storytelling. Jean Pierre Armand, the crusty taleteller who makes his living telling stories to children in Puy-en-Velay told me how it all started with Jean Pierre Chabrol. As a child, Chabrol was raised by goatherds. People would share stories and songs while they worked and at home to pass the long, dark, winter evening hours. With the invention of the radio and its arrival to the rural areas of France in the 1960s, people stopped gathering to tell stories and instead gathered to listen to the radio. The radio had replaced the traditional role of the taleteller. As an adult, Chabrol started a radio show in which he told the stories that he grew up hearing. The radio that replaced the taleteller became the taleteller again and Chabrol's shows were heard in living rooms across France. I imagine Chabrol's radio shows as his own self-sacrifice to keep the past alive. I can picture him recording stories alone in a studio somewhere so that families across France could gather together around his voice as it curled out of the metal speakers, mingling with the smoke from the hearth. Today there are thousands of professional taletellers and as many amateur ones. Too many according to crusty Jean Pierre Armand. There are also thousands of television sets. The television was at the center of the living room in both of the homes where I stayed, on and off and on again during the long, dark evening hours. Jean Pierre Chabrol is dead.

Maybe I was born at the wrong time. In the 1800s and early 1900s, the Haute-Loire was studied up and down by folklore collectors. Henri Pourrat, Victor Smith, Ulysse Rouchon. These names fill the library shelves in any Haute-Loire town. These collectors were obsessed with preservation. Convinced that the folk were changing and folk culture would be lost, they traversed the countryside recording tales told by nuns and old women, farmers and blacksmiths. A religious man, Henri Hugon, born in the Haute-Loire in 1869 wrote in a preface to his collection of tales, "The memories of my young years, the stories, the legends, told by the old during the dead of winter remain engraved in my memory....Today we do not repeat the old stories and legends of the past and as the years pass, the youth become ignorant of all that was....This is why, before I disappear I need to report well those tales and legends..."[2] Hugon was fearing the gradual loss of his native region's traditions, the lessening importance of the past to the present day people. He felt the need to write down and record what was left in order to preserve the memories he held dear for the future of his hometown. And yet, even with these fears and desires to preserve what remained, there was also a certain aura of mystique that surrounded this area and its legends. Pourrat, another local who sought to preserve the tales of the region, wrote that the events of his recorded legends are "not useful to talk about...to those who are not from here...these things remain a mystery. It would be too long, too complicated to explain...the feelings are too old to imagine."[3] Already, as he recorded the legends he collected, Pourrat felt that it was inaccessible to people, untranslatable to the contemporary French imagination, much less that of foreigners. Maybe I was born in the wrong time and the wrong place.

Before I moved to a new farm and started the second month of my quest, I snapped a picture of Dédé, the farmer who taught me how to milk a goat, knead bread, feed the pigs. He crinkled his eyes asking if I would caption the photo "the *autotochtone*." I nodded, smiling without knowing. "You know? The native? The indigenous person?" He laughed his stubbornly hearty laugh at me. I followed the lines of his face. I imagine Dédé's birth was more of a plucking. Someone somewhere planted a seed and he grew out of the ground. Just as Dédé was poking through the soil, the sun and the spring rain tending the fine hairs on his head, the sand and rocks grinding the lines across his face, someone picked him. Each root was ripped out of the ground, toe by toe, his long, yellow, cracked nails the only shriveled reminder of his life as a plant. In reality he was a city boy, raised further north without an inkling of his future farm. But everything about him breathed that he was native to this farm, straight out of a collection of tales I rented at the library. A man of the earth, of this earth.

---

2 *Legendes du Velay*, by Abbé Henri Hugon, translated
3 *Histoire Fidèle de la Bête en Gévaudan*, by Henri Pourrat, translated

Some places are passing through places. Towns are constructed along highways and roads so that you can look at them through the car window. Other places are destination places. For thousands of years people have traveled from high and low to these places. They have passed through miles of passing through places just to arrive at their destination. After selling bread at the market, Dédé stopped the car to share his own, secret destination place at the top of his stretch of the mountains with me. From the vista I could see the silver stretch of the Loire as it wound through this small valley towards the small stretch of land that I knew here. I saw the world as he saw it. Green and moist, old and quiet. There were empty-looking places full of farm life and there were buildups of rock where the town centers grew out of the green ground. This was a place. This was a place as it existed in the past and persisted into the present. It belonged to Dédé and he belonged to it. But where did I fit into this scene? Perhaps a few miles down the Loire River a new farm was the answer, and so, a week later I passed on to a new place.

The dulcet tones of Justin Bieber's voice were what greeted me when I arrived at the second farm. Out of the iPod speakers perched in the window of the chateau built in the 1300s flowed yet another reminder that no matter how deep I got, my nostalgia for a pure and historical place filled with a people dedicated to the folkloric traditions, was still a mere "disorder of the imagination." I wanted to believe that there remained a place in contemporary France where Internet and supermarkets had not yet taken hold, but this was not so in deep France. The teenagers in the chateau didn't care about Victor Smith and his collection of tales. They didn't care that they lived in a house that was seven hundred years old. They cared about getting their braces off. They cared about whether or not they would get the shoes to wear to the dance and whether or not they would dance at the dance with that person that they've been dreaming about ever since they crossed paths in the hallway two weeks ago. And I had no right to judge them for it.

As the second month in France passed, I tended sheep at the chateau and tried to talk to as many taletellers as I could. Just before I headed home, I fit in my last interview. I was sure that I reeked of my own foreignness as I waited with my giant baggage at the train station for the taleteller. Farzaneh Valaï arrived at the train station in her postal truck turned traveling caravan and lured me in with her warm spirit and exotic eye makeup. She is the head of a troupe of performers, "The Flying Rug," and like me, was foreign to this place. She lived in Iran until she attended university in France where, training to become a lawyer, she became enamored of puppet making and acting. Though she had lived in the Haute-Loire for fifteen or more years, she still felt her identity was tied up in being Iranian. And in fact, the contemporary array of stories told by Farzaneh Valaï and the professional taletellers in the Haute-Loire has a wider world scope. Folkloric events range from the International Folklore Festival which features exotic dances from faraway islands to the performances by taletellers who prefer to read Spanish, Moroccan, Chinese, you name it tales. In fact, of the taletellers I interviewed, not one was interested in the folklore from the Haute-Loire that can be read in the library. Farzaneh's favorite story is by an Iranian writer. She has adapted it to her own style and she tells the tale of a small black fish that is lost from its parents. "No, it's not Nemo from that Disney movie..." she rolls her eyes, laughing lowly. I smiled, understanding the sentiment more than she knew.

From the same Victor Smith collection I read another tale about three goats, cuddled up in my tent, during my first month, working on the goat cheese farm in deep France. Two are happy, healthy goats and one has a hole in its neck. The hole is just large enough that most of the food the goat eats falls out, but just small enough that the goat does not die. The man who owns the goats sends out his daughter to tend them and when she comes back, he asks the goats if they have eaten well. The first two reply that yes, they have eaten well and are full of milk. The hole-y goat states that she has not eaten well, she is still hungry and she has no milk.

The man beats his daughter to death.

The next day he sends his son to much the same ending and after that his wife, until he decides to go out with the goats himself. He feeds the goat the choicest leaves on silver platters and still gets the same answer from her at the end of the day. That's when he blames the goat for all of his troubles, skins it and sends it off to its death. Once again, I was struck by the story's relevance to the goat farm where I was living. Just as in the story, the goats on this small Haute-Loire farm were dying. One by two by three their bodies stopped absorbing the nutrients from the food that they continued to eat. An unknown disease caused their food to dribble down their tails, and crust onto their back legs. From a herd of seventy-two goats, all that remained were seven. Here were the goats, here were the fields and the farms. I was living the tales I studied. But where was the magic?

I have a photograph. No, I have twenty-nine photographs of the old tent I slept in during that first month. I spent a lot of time photographing that tent. At different angles, in different lighting. During the sunrise, the sunset, the heat of the middle of the day. I wanted the perfect picture. The perfect memory. In my favorite of the twenty-nine photos, I can almost see the air as it pours over the old mountains, mountains that have persisted these hundreds of years. The air and the light and the clouds roll through the wheat and past my tent. On my first night in this tent, I wrote, "Finally...I found it. The magic of France."

On the next page I wrote, "The magic includes a giant roach!"

Like the hole-y goat, I had everything I wanted and more served to me on a silver platter. I was in the midst of the magic of France, on a farm, living the tale, but it was not and would never be the same as that fleeting shiver, that disappeared, disordered feeling. Even now as I think back to Dédé's ridge that overlooks the river valley, I know that I was standing where I had never stood before and where I would never stand again. I was foreign. This valley had thrived and grown before me and it would flourish and wear away without me. I was small. I could imagine the stories told in past times, rising up with the smoke of a fire into the valley air and disappearing, never to be heard by me.

But all I could do was imagine.

SIX MONTHS
WITHOUT A MAP

CANADA, SCOTLAND, ICELAND, AND TURKEY

LISA HSIA

IN REYKJAVIK IN August 2012, I came across a headline in the city's English-language newspaper, *The Grapevine*, which read "Woman Takes Part in Search for Herself."

The rest of story went like this: A woman described as "Asian, 160 centimeters tall, wearing dark clothing, speaks English well," was reported missing from her bus tour in south Iceland. The woman in question, not recognizing herself in the description, shared in the general concern, and even joined in the search. A few days later it occurred to her that she might be the "missing" woman, and it was found to be so. Apparently the bus driver had made a mistake in the head count, and since the woman changed her clothing and hairstyle during a break in the bus tour, her fellow travelers hadn't recognized her upon her reappearance.

At that point we had been in Iceland for three weeks. As a fellow Asian woman, I felt a weird kinship with the woman in the story. Who was she? What went through her mind as she joined the search, and did she do so out of pure compassion, or was she moved by the plight of another Asian woman, lost in the wilderness? Were there other Asian women on the tour, or did she not notice she was the only one? Had the truth dawned on her suddenly, or had she been experiencing niggling doubts all along? Maybe they got her height wrong; maybe she was actually 165 centimeters tall (5'4"), like me. Maybe she didn't think a blue jacket qualified as "dark clothing." Maybe she didn't actually speak English well, which would explain a lot.

More than anything, this woman's predicament made me wonder how much of an impression a traveler can expect to leave upon her new surroundings. And how can she know how she is seen by the people with whom she mingles?

Four months prior to the *Grapevine* story, my husband, Erik, and I left the San Francisco Bay Area to travel the world. We had no itinerary and no end date, just portable careers and a desire to change scenery. I had not been much of a foreign traveler until that point. I'd spent my entire life in California, and all in the Bay Area, except for five years in Los Angeles as a grad student. Until a weeklong trip in Hong Kong at age twenty-eight, I hadn't even known if I would like international travel; I saw it as risky and frightening, and I didn't know where to start. But I'd loved Hong Kong, and Taiwan the year after, so when Erik suggested we take our lives on the road, I hesitated only a moment before saying yes. Less than half a year after we made the decision, we had given up our lease, our possessions were in storage or with family and friends, and that spring we were on our way.

We started in Toronto because it seemed easy; linguistically, culturally, and geographically close to home. We had family friends there, with whom I was eager to reconnect, and we spent the first week of our trip at their home in Mississauga.

It could not have been a more comfortable start. But even so, after arrival, my habitual self-consciousness made itself felt. Could everyone tell I was new? In Toronto, the architecture looked different. The chain stores were different. I fumbled with unfamiliar one- and two-dollar coins. I dressed carefully in the clothes I liked at home, but out in the heart of the city, upon catching sight of my reflection in store windows or restroom mirrors, I felt dismay at my dowdiness. At home in the East Bay and South Bay, fashion, though intriguing, seemed a thing I could ignore. But in the crush of young people waiting for the crosswalk at the hip corner of Bloor and Bathurst Streets, or in the packed Toronto Transit underground trains, and most especially in the weekend shopping hordes along Queen Street West, I felt prematurely aged: a nerdy, round-bodied woman in a knee-length skirt and dark opaque tights, out among the cool young men and slim girls in colorful skinnies and long floaty tops, riding their bikes along Harbord Street, or drinking and laughing on the outdoor patios of Markham. While people were nice, they did not make eye contact or smile as we passed on the sidewalks, and though I told myself it wasn't personal, I felt suburban and rebuffed. I had never before lived in a pedestrian-friendly city, where every outing became a chance to compare myself (unfavorably) with the people around.

But as the weeks went by, the differences between Canada and the U.S. no longer seemed enormous. In new jeans and a new purse, with my old sunglasses and a big straw hat, I sweated my way through humidity and out to vintage shops and Portuguese/Italian bakeries. I bought fiddlehead ferns and ramps at the Dufferin Grove Farmers' Market; local yogurt at a natural grocery; thick injera from an Ethiopian and Eritrean deli; and custard buns (far too many) from the two Korean bakeries within half a mile of our apartment. Erik and I made some friends, and held yelled conversations over loud music and beef-cheek tacos at the Grand Electric.

Toronto was beginning to feel like home, and we talked of moving there after we finished our travels.

Then came Montreal. "It's different than here," our Toronto friends told us, a fact which became immediately apparent when we boarded an express bus at the airport, and at the other end were greeted by instructions and signs *en Français*.

At first in Montreal, I hardly dared open my mouth, unable to remember much past *bonjour* and *merci*, and as embarrassed by my ignorance of French as I had been by my clothes during our first weeks in Toronto.

Montreal seemed, if anything, even more crowded than Toronto; there were festivalgoers, food sellers, and sidewalk vendors all over Boulevard Saint-Laurent every evening and all weekend. After one look at the masses thronging the cobbled streets and picturesque buildings of the old town, Erik and I escaped to the relative quiet of the waterfront. Several hours and many miles later, in a dimly lit Peruvian restaurant, we were relieved to hear the proprietor greet us warmly in English. After a comforting and affordable three-course meal, I said, *"Gracias,"* and thus commenced a conversation in Spanish, switching to English when Erik joined in.

"¿Le gusta Montreal?" he asked me.

"Sí," I replied, *"pero...¡todo el francés!"*

"Ah, sí," he said sympathetically. *"Francés es un poco difícil."*

I thought about what it must be like as an immigrant, having to learn a new language to make my living in a foreign country. Like this man, or like my parents back home. As we left the restaurant, the waiter said, "If you have any questions about Montreal, come back and ask me."

Was it the foreignness I felt in Montreal that made me begin to feel sad? Or was it that we'd been traveling for almost two months? Or maybe, it was the recent passing of my dear grandfather (and last remaining grandparent), for whose funeral we'd returned home briefly just before our Montreal trip?

On our last full day in Montreal, I went into a vintage store and found a cat curled up on an old-fashioned sofa. As I petted her, she purred and looked up at me with green eyes full of love, just the way our own cat always did. But our cat was in San Jose with my parents, and we wouldn't see any of them again for months, maybe even a year. I scratched the cat's ears and blinked and blinked until the tears spilled over and I had to duck into a corner of the shop and wipe my eyes. If the shopkeeper noticed, she was tactful enough to pretend she didn't.

At first I had thought this a single moment of extreme vulnerability brought on by being in what felt like such a foreign city. But back in Toronto, on one of our last nights before leaving the city, Erik and I decided to go to a seafood restaurant in Chinatown.

"We might not have good Chinese food for a while," I said. As we sat at our little square table, waiting for our stir-fried vegetables and steamed fish, I noticed the families gathered at the big round tables, tucking into crab and lobster, talking and laughing, and I ached with remembrance of countless such dinners with my own family. Again I forced back tears.

A few days later we arrived in Glasgow, a city in which we knew no one but our Airbnb host, an artist who greeted our dazed, sleepy arrival with smiles, hugs, and a refusal to let me carry my own suitcase up the stairs. Jet-lagged, I slouched around her flat for days, drinking herbal tea and eating Heinz baked beans from cans I found in the cupboard. When the sun finally broke through the rain, I could see the ruins of a nineteenth-century church from her bay window, and I watched the neighbors as they walked their dogs or got into their cars. When Erik and I finally ventured out for a restaurant meal, we went no further than the little café around the corner. The kind waiter asked where we were from, assured us we could drink the tap water ("Not like in London—if you ever go there, you don't want to drink that!"), and, when he learned we hadn't yet tasted haggis, he brought us a little plate with dollops of haggis and black pudding.

"You have to at least try it," the waiter urged. "Just don't think about what it is." I put a speck of haggis on my tongue, but was unable to follow his second suggestion. I couldn't stop thinking, *This has lungs in it!*

The black pudding I left alone. Erik enjoyed both.

No one we talked to appreciated Glasgow, not even the café man, who said he preferred Edinburgh.

"It's full of history," he'd said.

One of my friends had grimaced, "Glasgow's kind of rough." I'd expected a Scottish version of working-class Oakland, but now when I remember our ten days in Glasgow, I think of the kindness of our host and the man at the café; the apartment's cozy textiles and artwork, the city's museums, the rain-washed green of Kelvingrove Park, and the many rivers and waters Erik and I crossed on our walks.

Strangely enough it was Edinburgh, which everyone had told us we'd love, where I felt lonely. Our flat was a converted Victorian villa on Merchiston Crescent, in a neighborhood where Alexander McCall Smith and J. K. Rowling are both said to have lived.

At this place, we had an even bigger bay window in the dining room, looking out on a quiet front garden. At night we concealed ourselves from view with wooden shutters that folded back into the window and changed it into a paneled alcove.

The first time I walked out of Waverley train station, uphill and past the narrow buildings of curving Cockburn Street and out onto the hidden stairways and passages of the Royal Mile, I was in a place that I'd understood to exist only in imagination and historical fiction. But the constant rain, the enclosing grayness of tall stone buildings and cobbled streets, and yet another population where passersby made no eye contact, did nothing to assure me that I could make it through several more months (or longer) of travel through unfamiliar lands. I asked myself if I wanted to go home, rather than to face being a foreigner yet again and again. What stopped me was the knowledge that if I did return, I would still be facing the same questions of self, of meaning, of my place in the world.

I continued to feel distant from Edinburgh for another week or so, but then, suddenly and surprisingly, the city became comfortable. I made a friend through one of the weekly life-drawing groups I'd been attending, and as we walked one evening through the grassy Meadows and down past Greyfriars to Cowgate, we talked about what we both missed from home. My family and friends in California. Hers in Poland. A sense of cultural community.

I also connected with a friend of a friend, and Erik and I spent a glorious day with her and her partner in their Mini Cooper, touring the countryside and old monuments. I saw my first castle, which was a ruined fortress on the very edge of the sea. And when we parked on a hilltop, I ran along the deserted road and took video of the sheep, grassy hillsides, and the great open sky of mingled gold and mist.

Late that afternoon, as our group of four sat in the town of Musselburgh eating ice cream sundaes, the woman told us about the years she'd spent working in London and then in the Bay Area. I was asked whether anything had surprised me about traveling.

"Yes," I said, thinking how to explain. "I thought, somehow, that traveling was going to make me more cool. Because 'traveling the world' sounds like something a cool person would do, and I guess I just thought that once we started, I would become cool too. But now I don't feel any different…I just feel like myself." I had thought the others might laugh, but they nodded.

About a week later Erik and I were in a black cab in Glasgow, bound for the airport and for Reykjavík. The driver lifted out our bags, then he grinned at me, clapped me on the shoulder, and said, "Enjoy the ice cubes in Iceland." I was nervous about visiting this island just below the Arctic Circle—surely a faraway place if there ever was one. I studied the language lessons printed on the airplane headrests and bits of cultural trivia on the in-flight entertainment system.

Once we arrived, Reykjavík looked colorful; there were corrugated-iron walls and peaked roofs, imaginative street art, beautifully dressed locals, and more tourists than we'd encountered anywhere else. We walked often along Sæbraut, the road that edges the bay near downtown Reykjavík; the bay was calmer than I ever imagined an ocean could be, and every morning, afternoon, and evening, looked a different kind of stunning. One evening, the sky and sea pooled before us in a shifting, rippling expanse of silvery pale blue, just like the color of moonlight in a fairytale.

The entire population of Iceland is less than that of Edinburgh, so every time we walked along the water it was as if we were alone on the tip of the world.

One evening in the city, when we did encounter a few other walkers along Sæbraut, it seemed as if each one stared at us. I told myself it was not hostility, they were just curious. I forced myself to match their eye contact, and even to smile; but my friendly expression was not returned, and I could feel it faltering on my face. That weekend, as we walked through Austurvöllur square, a trio of preteen girls came toward us and one of them called out, "Hello."

Surprised, Erik replied, "Hello."

Then the girl blurted out to us *"Ni hao!"* Her friends looked mildly shocked, but they burst into giggles and went on their way. I was momentarily consumed by anger.

She's just a silly kid, I told myself, but the schoolgirl in me shook with impotent rage at the recollection of every confident girl at school who'd ever mocked me or other Asians within my hearing. When I came across the *Grapevine* article about the "missing" woman, a week later, I remembered all of these interactions and wondered how much her being Asian contributed to the mix-up. Surely a blonde among blondes would have merited a fuller description than "Blonde, 160 centimeters, speaks English well." But maybe not.

As we settled into our seven weeks in Iceland, the stares seemed less frequent, and Icelanders more friendly. Was there really a change, or was the transformation in my perception? In downtown cafés I found it was my fellow Americans I shied away from, especially young ones, with their loudness and, often, an obnoxious air of entitlement. Although I sometimes yearned for conversation, it was connection I wanted, not small talk. But one afternoon, as I relaxed alone in one of the hot tubs at the popular Vesturbæjarlaug swimming pool, a middle-aged woman joined me and said in a definitely American accent, "Isn't this nice!" I was pleased to have someone to talk to.

We established we were both from the U.S. (New York City in her case), and agreed that Iceland is quite expensive.

"And the people are just not generous," she said, telling me about a hotel café that would not give her a refill on her cup of coffee. "America is a great country—a really great country. Don't you think so?"

I gave a hesitant yes, not wanting to be drawn into a patriotic discussion.

"And the American people are just so kind," she added.

I said I had found that people were quite nice everywhere.

She seemed a bit put out that I refused to agree effusively to her statements. After a moment she continued, apropos of nothing, "And Americans are *so* not materialistic!"

To this I could say nothing whatsoever.

After a brief silence, during which several middle-aged Icelandic men entered the hot tub, she asked if I could recommend any restaurants in the city. Discomfited at being asked when there were Icelanders in our midst, I hedged, saying it depended what she liked.

"Oh, seafood," she said, which describes about half the restaurants in Reykjavík.

In great embarrassment I suggested the restaurant Sjávargrillið, but couldn't bring myself to try pronouncing it in front of the Icelandic men, so I described its location to her instead. We briefly discussed the langoustines, which are on nearly every restaurant menu, though usually referred to as lobster.

"Of course," this woman declared, "nothing beats Maine lobster."

Another afternoon at the same swimming pool, I encountered a petite Asian woman with a cheery, girlish face, who asked, "Are you from China?" I said my parents are, but she asked again, "Chinese?" I gave in and said yes. "*Wo yeshi zhongguoren,*" she said, repeating in English, "I am also from China." The Mandarin that I could muster awkwardly on visits to Taiwan and Hong Kong had grown very rusty in the months since we'd been back in the States, and I was barely able to respond to her questions, but we managed a bit of conversation.

"*Ni zhu zai zheli?*" I asked her if she lived here, guessing that she was not a tourist. She nodded, and added that she worked in Iceland, "*Wode gongzuo zai zheli.*" I did not have the words to ask her what her line of work might be, and since she didn't specify, I didn't want to pry.

I saw her again later in the showers, and when I left the locker room, we nodded, smiled, and waved. Though I made several more visits to Vesturbæjarlaug, I didn't see her again.

Several weeks and many miles distant, in the mountains outside the hot-springs town of Hveragerði, I had another conversation with a different half-dressed Chinese woman. Erik and I had hiked the 2.2 miles uphill from a badly rutted road to find the "hot river," skipping across streams, skirting fumaroles, and ascending past a vast, breathtaking waterfall and countless fat Icelandic sheep. We finally stood on its bank. The woman was sitting in the water in her bra and a pair of white shorts, red-faced, steam rising all around her. She addressed us in Mandarin, exhorting us, "Get in, it's not too hot!" At her urging, I undressed and got into my swimsuit—right there on the riverbank, as others were doing too—and joined her. The river was shallow and rocky-bedded, but the water was clear and its temperature just this side of bearable. The woman had a little brown-haired boy with her, and eventually introduced him as her grandson; I hadn't thought she was old enough for a grandson, though she was clearly too old to be his mother. When I said my Mandarin wasn't very good, she laughed and agreed, and gesturing at her grandson, said, "His Chinese is not good either. But he speaks very good English." She turned and pointed to a mixed Asian and European group sitting in another bend in the river, and said, "This is my family." She lived in Reykjavík, it turned out, but "came to Sweden twenty years ago, and moved to Iceland last year." It was Swedish, then, that she spoke to her grandson when they weren't talking in English; I hadn't recognized it, but could tell it wasn't Icelandic.

"Do you speak Icelandic?" I asked, and she looked at me like it was a dumb question.

"Yes," she said, but then, reconsidering, said, "Not all of it. But mostly." I would have liked to know more about her, but bound by shyness, courtesy, and the language barrier—and lulled into peace by the heat of the water—I didn't ask.

By the time we left Iceland, I was thoroughly comfortable in Reykjavík, and had even gone so far as to check the immigration website and find out the requirements—just in case, and for my own edification. Friends saw my Iceland photos on my blog and said I looked so happy; was I pregnant? To tell the whole, strange truth, I had never wanted to be pregnant until we stayed in Iceland. "There's something in the water," Erik and I joked.

I have never felt so absolutely safe anywhere; by our last days there, I had even learned not to mind the occasional stares. I've tried not to idealize the place in my memory, but after we left, I read an article in which Jón Gnarr, actor-comedian and mayor of Reykjavík, referred to Iceland as the Shire (from *Lord of the Rings*). In Reykjavík we saw bikes left unlocked and MacBooks unattended in the library; at the pool I took communal showers with the women and girls of the neighborhood (and the occasional small boy); at Þingvellir, the national park, we hiked the continental rift and the silence was so profound we heard a crow's wings slice through the air above us. I think my body knew we were in a good place, where the air and water are clean, and babies cherished. It wasn't just my biological clock kicking in, because a couple of days after we left Iceland, the feeling vanished.

It is now the end of our second week in Istanbul. It is the sixth month of our travels, and in another two weeks we will be in Paris. Yesterday, as I was sitting waiting for the ferry at the Maiden's Tower on the Bosporus strait—an old, pretty, but hardly towering structure not 275 yards from the shore—a young, bleached-blonde woman and her daughter approached me, smiling apologetically. I stiffened slightly. The day before, as Erik and I sat in a neighborhood park in Aksaray, a woman in a black dress and headscarf had come up to us, saying, "Money, money." She remained before us for several minutes, glancing at me as I sketched the park, repeating over and over, "Money. Money." But this lady and her daughter were asking something different. The girl, a chubby child with two long pale-brown pigtails, peered at me curiously and asked, "Where you from?"

I spluttered a moment, then said, "California." I looked at the mother, who shook her head, still smiling deferentially. "America," I said, but she shook her head again. "United States?" I didn't know if they understood me.

Her smile deepened and she looked even more apologetic, as if she regretted coming up to me, but she said, "Turkish, Turkish." Not knowing if it was an explanation or a question, I shook my head, and she bobbed hers at me and made as if to walk away with her daughter. But then she looked at me again, smiled with even greater embarrassment—as if she'd been caught out in some great breach of courtesy—and said, with a heavy accent, "Velkom."

Dying Abroad

Budapest, Hungary

Rachael Levitt

THOSE FIRST FEW hours in Budapest started out brilliantly: a reunion with my good friend Alex, drinking lager beside the Danube River while watching the moon rise over the massive Hungarian parliament. We were content to go to bed early and excited to explore more of the city the following day. But then in the middle of the night, Alex woke up dying. At least that's what she told me.

"You are just hung over," I tried convincing her.

"No, definitely not," she replied, totally coherent but looking unwell. "I have to go to a hospital."

Whoa. This was big. Back home, we didn't even have health insurance, let alone go to hospitals. I knew in an instant that she might *actually* be dying.

The cab ride to the hospital was a panic. When we arrived, no one spoke English, not even pleasantries. The doctors fumbled over Alex like an alien, finally admitting her when she screamed in pain at their poking of her abdomen. Then they hooked her to an IV, ran a bunch of tests, and left us alone to wait.

The next day we met a male nurse who spoke a bit of English. He had printed out some pages to show us from Google Translate: appendicitis.

Alex's morale was deteriorating rapidly. We were unable to communicate with the staff, except for the heavily accented, "Not good, very not good," updates, and we were put off by the lack of sterility (the staff wore open-toe shoes, to our horror). Alex prepared to die.

Later that day, the doctor who had been assigned to Alex came into the room. He was a burly man who did not speak, presumably checking on medication or blood pressure. Without warning, he stuck his hairy, fat finger into her mouth—no glove, no tongue depressor—to look in her throat. Alex's eyes widened, catching mine. The doctor made some notes and left the room. I squeezed her hand.

"Don't let them cut me, Rachael. Promise you won't let them cut me," she begged me through her drugged fog.

Up to this point I hadn't been too worried about her medical care; I'd assumed that even without shared language, doctors are doctors. I had been busy notifying the American embassy, wiring in money, and trying to hire a translator. Suddenly I feared the possible treatment more than the appendicitis.

As it turns out, they never did operate. The gloveless doctor gave Alex medicine and prescribed rest. In a few days she felt normal and the hospital released her with a bill of USD $127.

When we returned home to the United States, Alex splurged on a checkup. There was no evidence of appendicitis, so back in Budapest there must have been some sort of language kerfuffle. After growing up in the sterilized, technologically reliant West, socialized medicine seemed so different; but those four nights in a Budapest hospital cost Alex far less than her brief U.S. check up—though she swears she's emotionally scarred by the memory of that hairy finger. Me, I've never been able to look at health care the same.

A New Tongue

Paris, France

Molly Headley-Benkaci

HE IS TALL enough to see over crowds and strong enough to lift me onto his shoulders, though my thighs shake and I clutch his neck. I am used to being a low-slung, ground-dwelling kind of girl. I was raised barefoot as a tribesman in Idaho, so that my toes could clutch at grass. Yet here I am in Paris, far from the ground, as planes hurl through the sky up above in perfect formation, blowing smoke of red, white, and blue. Tipping my head back, I watch them, enchanted.

"She's such a child," he says in French to his friends, who stand around looking bored. He thinks that I won't understand but I do. *Quelle enfant.*

I understand because it feels as if I am again next to my father's legs, when I stand near him. He carries a gun and works for the state. He wears a tasseled uniform and salutes with a sword. Mine is the cliché of what an American might be hoping to find when looking for a French lover. Yet still I am small of hands and full of questions. "How do you say this?" "Why do you say that?" "Are there ghosts in Paris?" "Do they float?" "Or do they walk dragging their chains like bathrobes?"

I ask because I want him to look me in the face and blink. I want him to say he doesn't understand. But instead he answers, *"Oui, mon coeur."*

His military certainty fazes me, though I know he's not really listening. It is too easy to ignore a language that is not one's own. I see the city filled with specters, the Seine belching up its own past. Sometimes in my mind I am one of them. Homeless ghost girl, a feather at odds with the sky.

"You are so lukewarm. Are all French men like you?" I ask after the parade, when we are back at home and he fails to lift me in his arms. When he is doing dishes rather than making love to me. When his back is like a mountain of reality.

"What is *lukewarm*?" He says finally, looking not at me but out the window. This time I am ready. I take his hand and hold it under the faucet. I change the water temperature from hot to cold until I have it just right. "This," I say, and after a moment he nods.

"I understand," he says. "I'm like the temperature of your skin." He smiles, and kisses me on the mouth, as if I could only give him compliments.

Like the temperature of skin or the temperature of blood, like the hot insides of things. These are the words I think of when I look at him. Outside there is the sound of marching. It is another military service and the gendarmes are lined in their sky blues and ceremonial swords. A single shot is fired into the sky and then the trumpets begin.

Maiko

Tbilisi, Georgia

Rhonda Gibson

A BLACK AMERICAN woman in an Eastern European country that didn't see much diversity: man, was I an easy target. Looking back, those first few months in Georgia were filled with so much hate. Maybe it was the men who followed me from the subway thinking I was a prostitute. Or the old woman who took to shouting at me in Georgian on the bus. Or the children screaming, "Fuck you! Fuck you, bitch!" as I walked to my apartment.

To them I was so different. I couldn't be myself, and I became depressed.

I lived in the capital city of Tbilisi in 2010 for nearly nine months. Initially, I was confused as to what brought me into Georgia's arms. Then I remembered, *Teach in Europe*. That's what the ad said.

It was probably the most deceptive wording since "Free iPhone, details apply."

From the day of my arrival, I felt harassed on every side—especially by the government.

Months before, Georgian President Mikheil Saakashvili had extended an invitation for English-language teachers. This invitation included food, lodging, and airfare. Against him stood the opposition party, who targeted us as foreign monsters stealing income from their people. They purchased television airtime to frequently broadcast their distaste of the Western arrival. An opposition leader was even quoted as saying, "No leader of any self-respecting country would bring 10,000 people over from America so that its children would speak with a pronounced New Jersey accent."

We were a media circus, and it was not uncommon to have a camera shoved into your face at any given part of the day. This continual attention led to some teachers being stalked and beaten, among the worst of things.

Somewhere along the way, I met Maiko. She was one of ten students in an intensive conversational English course. Determined as she was, Maiko spoke very little during our sessions. I would ask open-ended questions, yet her clever mind found ways to avoid answering. I did not understand why.

One day during a rainstorm, she offered to take me home. We rode, mostly in silence, until a river of English language flowed from her mouth so eloquently that it floored me. "Why don't you talk in class?" I asked. She told me that she was afraid to speak, afraid to make a mistake. "I don't care if you make a mistake as long as you are learning." She was silent. As I left, we exchanged numbers. "Call me," I said, "let's hang out."

This was the beginning of a friendship that blossomed despite the turmoil around me. Maiko would be the first person who helped me feel safe and showed me the meaning of local hospitality. *"Gogo,"* she would say, her voice that same beautiful river, "I would like to invite you..." Usually that meant experiencing something new and exciting about the Georgian culture. Given that I am a New Orleans native, it was befitting that she started with food. Food is the language I speak no matter the country. A good meal can cure the blues or cause them. With Maiko, it was always a cure.

On our first outing together, we ordered *khinkali*, a traditional Georgian dumpling stuffed with meat, or cheese, or potato. She showed me how to eat the piping hot knobs of dough, holding one by its stomach and then taking small nibbles of the flesh to suck out the juice before devouring the goodness inside. Next I tried *lobio*, beans cooked in a clay pot. We would eat them with pickled cucumbers, tomatoes, and peppers. "We have something like this in New Orleans, except we call them red beans," I once explained.

"Which do you prefer?"

"This one." I said with a smile.

From there it was the Georgian National Ballet, best seats in the house. I learned that each dance was a tribute to the region where it was born. There were men with swords, fighting athletically as they spun into the air. And women with gowns flowing white whose shoulders moved up and down in perfect unison. It was magical.

Sometimes we would go to the cinema and watch a Georgian film. We'd sit side by side in silence, engulfed in the world before our eyes, and then afterward have conversation over coffee about the characters and themes the filmmakers presented.

A month later, I met Maiko's family and they too welcomed me into their home. We would cook dinner and watch a Georgian talent competition and complain about the acts. This became my home away from home.

Sometimes I don't think I did enough to show how much I loved and appreciated my friend. She was sure that she needed my native tongue to improve her skills. But I was sure I needed her heart, her smile, and her constant patient understanding as I attempted to adjust to a new place.

Rugby World Cup

FRANCE AND NEW ZEALAND

AN INTERVIEW WITH
LOUIS STANFILL, AMERICAN RUGBY PLAYER

WHY HE LOVES THE GAME:

The best part about rugby, in my opinion, is that within the laws of the game you are allowed to hit someone as hard as you want. No pads, no cheap shots, just one man's will, strength, ability, and smarts against another's. Through this, there is a complete understanding that when you step between those lines, you will either win or lose. The code of honor and conduct rarely get lost. Does a player ever get punched in the face or receive a cheap shot? Sure, from time to time. But rugby is a thinking game. In high levels, the coach does not shout from the sideline or send plays in with substitutions. The coach is in a box in the stands, and the players are responsible for how to play. Every player is expected to hold a similar set of skills. While some may kick or scrum and others may not, everyone is expected to run with the ball, tackle, catch, pass, and more.

There is a famous saying about the sport of rugby. It goes, "Rugby is a hooligan's game, played by gentlemen." In rugby, there is an ethical code of honor where the game stays between the lines. After each game, all ill will is forgotten over a beer. I suppose what I can say about the culture of rugby is that it is true and honest. How sport should always be.

WHERE HE'S BEEN:

My first World Cup game was played in Lens, France, the United States versus England. It was the year 2007. Up to that point, I hadn't played in front of a large crowd, or against an opposition full of players I had only read about in the news or seen play on the television because they were so high profile. The Lens stadium had a capacity of about 41,000, maybe a tad more, and it was full of England fans. But this wasn't to deter our team from playing our hearts out. England was the World Cup 2003 winner, so needless to say, we were not expected to win.

WHAT IT LOOKED LIKE FROM THE INSIDE:

After we belted "The Star-Spangled Banner" as if it was the last time ever, England, along with the entire stadium, sang "God Save the Queen" in perfect unison. As soon as the song ended, another started. It was "Swing Low, Sweet Chariot," and one section of the stadium started to sing, then the next section to their left, then the other, and then the last. It was pretty breathtaking. Enough to temporarily take you away from mental preparation and focus on the opposition, and to stare wide-eyed at the moment you have found yourself in. As I looked around the packed stadium, I struggled to find any supporters. It was not intimidating or aggressive, but only sobering. White flags with red crosses drowned out any sign of anything else, but it was not to deter the pride within us. Soon after that, the starting whistle blew, and that primal game mentality kicked back in and on the first hit, you knew what you were there to do. We were expected to be blown out of the water. But we came out with intensity, passion, and accuracy. The final score was twenty-eight to ten, England. Our heads were high and proud.

BEFORE THE BIG GAME:

So I played in the 2007 Rugby World Cup in France and the 2011 Rugby World Cup in New Zealand. Opening ceremonies for the games typically do not incorporate all the players from each squad. A representative from each team is present. The ceremony is less extravagant than the Olympics, but still special. In the New Zealand games, however, our team was greeted by the local townspeople whenever we arrived at a new city. Sometimes this meant the local Maori people would set up a traditional welcome, which meant a *haka*, which is a challenge laid before the guest. It was a very intimidating scene, definitely worth looking up. In Paris we had a private tour to the top of the Eiffel Tower, and went to the Louvre and had an extravagant lunch at the American embassy.

I feel that being a rugby player from another country makes me a guest in these places, and as such I feel that it is important to open up to other countries' practices, and also learning the most important phrases: please and thank you. I feel like sometimes when tourists travel, there may be a sense of entitlement because of bringing in and spending money. While this may be true, I feel it is also true that we are all guests outside of our borders. The Golden Rule should apply wherever you are: treat others how you want to be treated.

NUMBER 6:

When I am back in the United States, outside of friends, family, and maybe the odd acquaintance, no one knows that I am a rugby player. But I have been so fortunate to represent my country abroad, allowing me to travel all around the world to play against many other countries' best rugby players. While travel and lodging has not been a cost to me, playing the game is not a highly lucrative business. Like many people who have chosen passions over other jobs—passions that may take them away from what they love most, their family and friends—it often means living a little bit more frugally. But back in my second World Cup games, in New Zealand, I truly felt appreciated. Everywhere we went we were greeted and asked for photos and autographs. That is a feeling that does not come along too often as an American rugby player and really made the experience more memorable.

There was one night when I met up with my parents and our friends at a local pub. I was dressed in normal street clothes, nothing with the U.S.A. Rugby logo. An Argentinean man approached me and asked if I was player number 6 for the U.S.A. team. After I responded yes, he began to praise me in a mix of languages. Then he shook each of my family members' hands and asked if he and his friends could get a picture. I obliged as six of his buddies gathered around. Then they all greeted me and my family members, kindly thanked me for my time and left. That was one of the most memorable and special moments away from the field I have had during the World Cup games.

FAVORITE GAME MOMENT OF ALL TIME:

It would have to have been against Samoa, in the 2007 World Cup. In the closing minutes, I scored a very unlikely try against one of their higher profile players. He played a position of a typically smaller, faster guy, but he was as fast as the competition in his position. He was bigger than me (I am 6'4", 250 lb.). At the last possession of the game, there were five meters between him and me and he was on the try line. Obviously, there was a collision. And I won.

TOUGHEST OPPONENTS:

The toughest team I have ever played against would have to be South Africa, also in the 2007 World Cup. Our teams were each others' last pool-play game, and then after, South Africa went on to beat England for the championship and the trophy, a William Webb Ellis Cup. That team had it all: speed, strength, power, skills, and the type of play that slaps you on the back after a hard tackle.

WHAT'S NEXT:

As for countries I have played rugby in, that list travels all over the United States, many countries in Europe and the United Kingdom, as far south as Uruguay and New Zealand, and all the way to Japan. And I am still going strong. My goal is to continue playing until 2015, when the games will be held in England.

Russian Face

St. Petersburg, Russia

E. B. Bartels

JUST AS ATHLETES make mix CDs to pump themselves up for games, I created a playlist on my iPod called "Riding the Metro in St. Petersburg." American friends from home browsing my music library, expecting fun, happy, Russian pop, are taken aback by forty minutes of '90s rap and hard beats. But a girl has to do what a girl has to do to get psyched up for her commute. Every morning, after being stuffed full of *blini* pancakes or sweet, cheesy, chocolate-covered *sirok* bars from Olga, my Russian host mother, I exit the apartment using a six-inch skeleton key, put on my headphones, and start this playlist. I leave the sweet, friendly, overly polite and thankful exchange student in the apartment with Olga, and put on my game face. Better yet, fuck you guys, I am putting on my Russian face.

As The Notorious B.I.G. deafens my eardrums, I walk down the gritty stairs in the unlit cave of a stairwell and press the unlock button by the door, issuing a mechanical melody as I exit into the grungy courtyard. With each step and beat, my face muscles harden. I walk past the three drunk homeless men playing cards, the waitress smoking a cigarette in the back of the corner restaurant, and onto the street, making a left, a right, and entering the Vladimirskaya metro station as The Coup and NWA yell in my ear to *"Fuck the police!"* By the time I check the balance on my blue commuter card, with one swift tap on the machine as I walk past, my face is already tense and ready. I swipe myself through the turnstile, avoiding eye contact with the *militsioner* in his intimidating police uniform as he watches my every move, and I step onto the escalator as the playlist shifts to M.I.A. My Russian face is on and ready for the descent to the train platform. No one is going to fuck with me today.

A Russian face is not actively angry, but more aggressively disgusted and apathetic. Not openly hostile, but annoyed, world-weary, bored as hell, tired, judgmental, over it. More than just an attitude, a Russian face is crucial for survival in crowded, cold St. Petersburg and especially on the metro. Your face is your most powerful weapon. The St. Petersburg metro is nothing to be taken lightly. One of the busiest and most crowded rapid transit systems in the world, it opened in November 1955 designed for a city with a population of just over 3 million; this same system now functions for a city of over 4.5 million, with an average of 3.43 million passengers riding the metro every day. Since its opening, the Petersburg metro has expanded from one to five lines, the most recent—the Frunzensko-Primorskaya line—opened in the fall of 2008, during my year of Petersburgian commuting. But despite the new lines, more new stations are opening in the outskirts, while main stations in the city's center have remained the same size and become overcrowded.

At rush hour, all four sides of my person are touched by at least four other individuals. The sweat of other passengers mingles with your own and you leave the metro smelling, at best, of some else's perfume. The man to your right smells like cigarettes and stale beer, the woman in front smells of garlic. Russians already value personal space significantly less than what I've grown up used to and people have no qualms over physically pushing you out of the way if you are too lethargic. The sweet older woman who teaches grammar at 11 a.m, claws people out of her way like a rabid cat at 9 a.m. to get into a metro car. I was shoved daily by various four-foot-eight *babushkas*, elderly Russian grandmother-types with elbows of steel. My daily commute from my host family's apartment to the university is four stops in total, passing smack through the center of the metro system and transferring at one of the busiest stations during the morning rush. I was thrown right into the middle of things from the beginning. During my first week in St. Petersburg, there was a very quick evolution of my Russian face as I was subject to sexual harassment, a sort of metro hazing. Along with advice to never go without slippers in front of your host mother, my worrywart program director taught us during orientation that approximately 98 percent of Russian women have been sexually harassed on the metro. But I asked myself, why would any Russian man bother with me when I could not compare to the supermodel Russian *devushki*—the young women in flawless makeup, heels, styled hair, at 8:30 in the morning? Easy: they all mastered the Russian face long ago, and at the time I had not.

The first incident occurred as people crammed into a metro car during my transfer at Mayakovskaya. I felt my skirt flutter, and the hand of the man behind me on the back of my bare upper thigh. The hand made contact and then almost immediately disappeared, as if a mistake perhaps. But the next day, there was something else that was definitely not a mistake. I felt what I hoped was somebody's umbrella handle on my backside. The metro car was packed far beyond capacity, and fellow passengers and their belongings were pressed up against every surface of my body. I was having trouble moving my diaphragm to breathe let alone move away from the invading force. I shifted away as much as I could, which wasn't very much at all, but the pressure returned, striving toward that very personal space between my legs. I shifted again, but when the pressure returned a third time I struggled to reach my own hand behind me to investigate. My hand met another hand. The rough skin of the anonymous fingers immediately repulsed me, but I pushed the hand away fiercely and severely, as that was all I could do in that crowded space. I could not move. I could not turn around to stare at the offender. I was not even sure if it was the individual directly behind me—it could be someone a person or two away, the space was that packed. The hand, it grabbed mine and twisted it, as if with the goal of breaking my wrist. Even while gripping my hand, the offender kept pushing between my legs. I should have yelled, but I was face-to-face with—practically kissing—a Russian grandmother. If I had been facing him, I could have glared, I could have channeled my outrage, but front and back were different worlds. It made it impossible to believe what was actually going on. The train stopped, people drained out, and with a final *Fuck you* kind of shove the "umbrella" made one more assault and disappeared. It could have been anyone. A young man, an old man, a babushka, who knows? The anonymity made it feel like the entire St. Petersburg metro had harassed me.

I suddenly understood why Russian women stand with their backs to the train wall whenever possible. Their glaring eyes were preemptive armor: *Stay the hell away. Do not touch. I can't stop you from looking, but I am going to look the fuck right back.* Men have their own version of the Russian face, to fight through crowds, to preserve personal space, and to prevent personal assault (I met foreign men who had been creepily rubbed up on during rush hour); but the male Russian face is generally more apathetic and bored, while the female version is tougher and spikier.

A Russian face is not limited to the tensing of jaw muscles, slacking of eyes, sucking of teeth, turning down of mouth. Once, I accidentally backed into a woman in the middle aisle of a car. The moment our backs touched, she all but threw me off with her spine. She arched it so it spiked, muscles tensing, bristles out. Everyone with a Russian face is a porcupine with quills ready. *Don't touch, or I'll bite. Get it? Good.* I perfected my Russian face through observation on the long escalator rides during my thirteen months of commuting. The Petersburg metro is one of the deepest in the world due to the city's swampy geography, so I took advantage of the three- to five-minute escalator rides to analyze the Russian faces of the passengers on the escalator moving in the opposite direction. *Devushki* my age or younger dressed to kill in leopard-print miniskirts, black leather and furs, and poisonous red lipstick pouts that say simply, *No.* Burly, young tough guys, big on top, poured into tight acid-washed, pre-distressed jeans; they were all shoulders in shiny black vinyl, creating a physical wall of separation. Mothers fiercely clutched the hands of pink bundled little girls, innocent but already glaring at every potential enemy. And babushki, of course, solid, squat and hunched, ready to beat anyone out of their way with blue-and-red plaid plastic grocery bags, the lines of their Russian faces deep from years of practice. What seemed paradoxical to me was that the more I emulated these Russian faces and the more unapproachable I appeared, the more Russians approached me for directions. Every time a Russian would ask me which line to ride, or where they should get off for so-and-so, I would fight not to smile at successful emulation. A Russian face may not look friendly, but it implies you know what the hell you are doing.

In America, I would never ask directions from someone with even half a Russian face. Steer clear, someone's having a very bad, bad, bad day. At home for a brief visit during my year abroad, I wondered why everyone on the Boston T gave me such horrified looks until I realized my Russian face had accompanied me to Massachusetts. Frequently American tourists in Petersburg think Russians are rude. Coming from the U.S., they expect smiles all the time. Customer service with a welcoming grin. Too bad for Americans, but in Russia, smiling at strangers is a waste of energy. It is thought to be insincere and unnecessary to smile at people you are never going to see again. If a stranger catches you smiling, he will assume you are mentally unstable. But not smiling is also about self-preservation. In a country with more than one major economic crisis in recent history, food shortages, inflation, and more, the mindset is to take care of yourself, take care of your parents, take care of your kids. Get yourself on the train, get yourself home.

I discovered that a Russian face can be slipped on and off. Coming home at night, the moment I step out of the train at Vladimirskaya, I stop listening to my metro playlist. I ride the escalator listening to the Cure. Avoiding eyes, I walk through the turnstile to the folky drones of the Magnetic Fields. I exit, making a left, a right, back into the courtyard, the waitress still smoking, the alcoholics still gambling, as New Order's synth harmonizes about romantic troubles. Unlocking the door, I climb the gritty stairs, and as Modest Mouse fades away, I remove my headphones and enter my host family's warm orange apartment where I am greeted by the Russian face's polar opposite: the smiles for the few wonderful people accepted into the tightest radius of one's life. In that circle, Russian smiles are the friendliest, most sincere smiles you will ever see. Perhaps I appreciate them more since I know how genuine they are. After a day of Russian faces, with my cheek, mouth, and forehead muscles sore from holding such a tense pose for grueling hours, I loved to be greeted by my Russian family, to sink with exhausted relief into the kitchen sofa. My face would finally relax. As Olga prepared mushroom soup and pierogi for dinner, asking about my day, my face would crack into the most sincere Russian smile. And I was ready to do it all over again the next day.

"I Was in College, and By the Time I Went to Study in Italy We Were in This All-Out War"

FLORENCE, ITALY

An interview with
Joey Cavise, law student

THE MADONNA OF COLLATERAL DAMAGE:

Italy is covered with Catholic symbols, images of the Madonna and Jesus. In Florence, when I was there to study abroad as an undergrad, there was a street artist who had drawn in chalk—it was really incredible actually—he had drawn *The Madonna of Collateral Damage*. His was a Mary holding a baby Jesus, and Mary had a crater in her face and bandages wrapped all around her. Jesus was missing limbs and bleeding. The artist had a message written below, all in Italian, asking why people let the United States continue its war of aggression and illegal acts, dragging the whole world into another conflict and propagating stereotypes about world cultures and people. The message had to do specifically with bombing campaigns. It was about bombing campaigns killing civilians. So I engaged with this guy. I spoke to him in Italian and English. As soon as he asked if I was American, and I said yes, he just started yelling, "Fuck you, please! Fuck you, please!" He yelled it over and over again. A conversation was obviously not going to happen.

WHEN THE U.S. WENT INTO IRAQ:

I was in college, and by the time I went to study in Italy we were in this all-out war. I always felt this weird sense of responsibility while I was there. I don't know if that has to do with how I was raised politically. I was there at a very strange time in the world. I actually ended up at a lot of political demonstrations. I did some traveling too. I don't remember what year it was, but at one point George W. Bush was doing a tour of Western Europe and it was like he followed me everywhere. One day I got off a plane in London and there were all these protests and American flags with swastikas on them instead of the stars and stripes, because of Bush's tour. I'm telling you, he followed me everywhere. Another time, I went to Rome to see a friend and I ended up walking around a corner and getting tear-gassed. Actually, I got tear-gassed multiple times. I once got spit on. I went to many other protests by choice, because I didn't agree with Bush's policies and was against the wars as well. I went with my Italian friends, who were all very lefty.

I once went out to a house party with one of the kids I lived with. His parents hosted the party, and they were talking about an alcoholic drink that I'd never heard of in the States called Tequila Boom Boom. I hadn't met the father yet. The kid tapped the father on the shoulder and said, "Dad, did you know that in the States, the Americans don't know what Tequila Boom Boom is?" The father, before meeting me, he said, *"Americani sono animali."* Americans are animals. Then I just shook his hand and said, "Hi. I'm Joe from Chicago."

GOVERNMENTS AND PEOPLE:

Anyway, the idea is generalization. The artist with the chalk decided I sucked because I'm American. The dad of my friend dissed all Americans because the government was indiscriminately bombing people. Clearly it's not difficult for me to empathize with the sentiment. But it's also very true that no matter where you go, everybody can be guilty of making broad generalizations. It has to do with how we view the world and how national governments affect the way people think about entire populations. What's especially interesting here is that Florence is a city flooded with tourism. It has thousands of American students every year. Not every place is like that. If you go to Berlin, which is a massive city, or Rome, which is a massive city, visitors tend to blend in. Of course you know where to go to find the tourists, but otherwise they blend. So in a lot of ways, Florence is like a small college town. I hung out with a lot of Italian kids there who were incredibly accepting right away. A lot of that had to do with their own politics, but certainly they had to feel me out. You have a responsibility, I think, to not fit stereotypes. I also think it takes time. People have to trust you.

ITALY AND FLORENCE:

I actually fell in love with Italy and Florence that year. It was my junior year of college. My first semester I was pretty typical, doing the typical study-abroad stuff. Then I had the opportunity to stay for the second semester and decided that I wanted to do it totally different. That second semester, I can safely say, is up there in terms of the best six months of my life. Being in Italy that year, and then again after I graduated college, was the time when I felt like

I became a person. I don't mean for that to sound too dramatic, but Italy allowed me to realize who I was and what was important to me. I feel like being there was the first thing that I really did on my own. It was my first taste of complete independence and my first exposure to what it means to be young in an ever globalizing world. I was hanging out with young Italians, realizing what I have in common with them and realizing where our differences lie. And not just politics, but relationships with the world around you. The culture of transportation there is so different. Of food, of drink, music, history, art, the land.

Up until somewhat recently, I could think about Florence and I longed to be there badly. To be drinking good wine, to be sitting in a piazza, to be doing a *passeggiata*, where you just stroll down the streets with your arms behind your back on a Sunday evening. I miss speaking Italian. I really love speaking Italian. By the time I left, I considered myself completely fluent. I had Italians telling me that I sounded like I was from a specific region in Tuscany. It makes me laugh now, because I remember the very first time I went to Florence. It was actually for two weeks during my sophomore year. I didn't even know what the city was called in Italian. I took a train down to Florence from Genoa to stay with an Italian exchange student that I knew from high school. I remember that I sat on the train and checked my ticket and I thought, "Wow, I should be there by now." I saw that my ticket said I was going to *Firenze*, and I thought, "Whoa, I don't even know what this is." Turned out, *Firenze* is a way to say Florence in Italian. That's how little I knew about what was going on. I didn't know a word of Italian. So when I went back to school, I ended up taking Italian 101. I did two semesters of Italian and then I went for the year. After I graduated, I went back for two years.

AFTER GRADUATION:

While I was living there, I went to visit a group of immigrant workers from Senegal. The Italians who took me there were my friends Andrea and Riccardo. They're brothers. Andrea is the longtime boyfriend of Jen, an American expat who also lives in Florence. When I was younger there, Jen was like a fairy godmother to me. She's still a close friend and I stayed with them all for two weeks this past June—with Jen, Andrea, and their new baby. That particular day, I didn't know Andrea well yet, but I was staying in their house. So he and Riccardo, one day they said, "Do you want to come with us?" We went for a drive to a town called Greve in Chianti. It's a big Chianti-producing area in Tuscany. We got out of the car and we went into a regular building like any other. There was an apartment inside and there were these three guys from Senegal. I think everyone had met while playing a pickup game of soccer in a park and just started talking.

So we were out there at the apartment, and these guys were factory workers but they weren't getting paid much. I'm sure they were charged an outrageous rent. I can't for the life of me remember what the factory produced, but I actually do think it might have been a shoe factory. At the time my Italian was bad enough that I didn't catch every part of the conversation. But amongst the five other people in the room, we all spoke enough of everything to fill me in whenever it was clear that I couldn't understand. So Andrea and Riccardo brought clothes and shoes. And obviously, there's the irony in delivering shoes to people who work at a shoe factory. But that's not even necessarily uncommon here in the United States. So we handed them the bags of clothes. The guys from Senegal went through the bags to see what fit.

By happenstance, the guys from Senegal had prepared a meal and they were just about to eat. So they added three extra plates and split the portions they had already made for themselves. They asked if we wanted forks. At first, Andrea and Riccardo said, "Yeah, of course. We'll have forks." Then the guys from Senegal said, "We're going to eat with our hands. This is a traditional Senegalese dish." So Andrea and Riccardo said, "Don't give us forks if you guys are going to eat with your hands. We're eating your food. We're going to eat with our hands too." Now, this was a dish of rice and different sorts of grains. There were big pieces of meat. The meal was delicious. It was the first time I ever got to eat with my hands. I don't think I've eaten with my hands since.

During the meal we talked. The Senegalese guys talked about how they want to find other work and how it's really difficult because they can't do anything else without getting different papers and different visas. But there were also a lot of moments of laughter, because there's only so much heavy conversation that you can have with someone you don't know well. It was a great night. Also, Andrea and Riccardo really trusted me, which was a great feeling too. At that point, I spoke enough Italian and I understood enough. But throughout the beginning months of my time in Italy, anyone who spent time with me was really generous. Imagine you're in Chicago, and some German kid walks up and doesn't speak much English, but you invite him everywhere anyway, and take him out with you anyway. That's how these guys were to me.

How to be a Russian
Sleeper for U.S.

Classified

Laura Madeline Wiseman

1) Develop a cover story

Welcome to Hotel In Time. Here is your mattress with white duvet, your floor to ceiling curtains patterned with black squares inside larger black squares inside the larger black square that is your building. Here are your two chairs and two water glasses, your luggage rack, your series of metal hooks. We offer individually wrapped bars of soap, packets of shampoo, and packets of something in our tongue, not yours, and finally two pairs of disposable paper slippers at no additional cost. Return the room key to the front desk each time you leave.

You remember this conversation, you do. You left U.S. Tuesday at noon, flew to Chicago, then Poland, then Russia, and finally arrived Wednesday at midnight in Moscow. There was the matter of customs, of the baggage claim, of stray dogs that hovered at the exit, low tails between a long queue of taxis. There was the bus and the sense that your role on this trip was different than in previous trips abroad. You weren't girlfriend or wife. This wasn't going to be handholding, long kisses in the umbra of cottonwoods, sex under foreign skies. And you weren't in charge, the leader, the one to explain the rules and implement them, though clearly your group of twenty-plus were the types you tended to organize, assign tasks, and evaluate. And finally you weren't a colleague, because these were not your smoky suits and scarlet ties, smart phones and laptops, the constant flicker of screens in their eyes.

No, this time you are a watcher, a taker of notes, a newly born keeper of secrets, a spy, in a word, undercover, a sleeper, ready to be activated whenever. If anyone asks why you're here in Russia, you'll say, *Oh, I'm a just a poet*, because in U.S. poets seem harmless, superfluous, or at the very least, underpaid. We'd never shoot a poet because they wrote a poem, right?

So you climbed the steps of the bus, sat in your small, dirty blue seat, and observed the empty Russian streets, airport to hotel—a place where glowing billboards rotated to offer vehicles three sides of ads and neon signs sported some wordage and logos that looked like McDonalds, Pizza Hut, Baskin Robbins, and Starbucks—and then the concrete jungle closed around you. Here, places were tucked inside other places, behind black gates, barbed wire, and guards. You received your key, your rules, and settled into your room, number three at the Hotel In Time. You certainly were *in time*, but you wondered which one.

2) Remember, someone is always listening

At the Hotel In Time you must whisper, cull your tongue to a series of shushes and rasps, pull in all the sounds from lungs to diaphragm, to talk about the weather, the long walk from hotel to faculty to city walls, to simply say, *I love you*. You roll up one of the two stained towels and press it to the wedge between floor and door to muffle what would be words, but are today breaths stretched out over the downy comforter as the breeze stirs the curtains and lets in the fairy fluff of cottonwood to hover in the air, the brown blur of a teeny moth at the light above the bed, the burnt electric smell of diesel from whatever place is near the hotel, around a corner where you cannot see. When you lean from your window and see the trees lift up from where they've risen between buildings, there you recognize the rise and fall evident in the air, the sounds and words that would be spoken, but aren't, as heads bend together to say the necessary and that is all, for this city is an ocean of cars on pavement, the occasional alarm that leaps from quiet for a few bleats, the sparrows that whisper in the park, and the musical hush and pull of pillow talk and secrets, of words uttered just barely in the dark, when all the world around you is silenced and large.

3) Gadgets are essential

Sleep, like a lover who pulls off all your clothes to suck on your nipples at just the right time, is always the thing you want, whether or not you get it. So you bring your gadgets to bed, pink earplugs in a slim white plastic case, a satin eye pillow scented in lavender, an MP3 player with two hours of guided sleep meditations where the sleep lady tells you to breathe and to *forget about sleep* and to *focus on the body* while birds chirp, wind rustles leaves, and bells tinkle. If she doesn't do it for you, you play sleepy ocean, an hour of surf over a rhythmic pulse of beta waves, the length of which is supposedly your brain when it dreams, though your brain isn't right now. The eye pillow, cast in silver moons and stars, seals away the yellow din of the city where cars rush and tumble down streets. The squishy earplugs silence the white flash of a colicky baby two rooms down, the bright splash of a door's slam, and the glitter of snow thoughts make of dry eyes, tired of hearing the pitch and intonation of how to be when in Moscow, with the Muscovites *who never know,* but who *walk a lot,* and who likely find sleep without effort, without gadgets, and thus, never see the blue belly of dusk at four or hear the tide of cars approach as they pull in morning like a lover who normally would suck on your nipples, but right now isn't a good time.

4) Let others do the talking

All the Russians you meet have dark hair, dark eyes, pale skin, and speak broken English, like the conservative one who, at twenty-five, has only left her hometown of two hundred thousand once, a beach of low waves stalked by pigeons and stray cats festooned with flees, or like the slim one with a silver charm of a man at her neck who rides the chain below her clavicle like a swing. She says to you she's *an atheist*, but doesn't know what she'll do when she has *kids*. You pause, think *OK?* Your eyes slide over the granite buildings and glass windows of tee-shirts and tourist stuff to buy, buy, buy. You study the six-foot gates and locked doors, the spear-pointed fences and security men in black who flank metal detectors. How have you missed the segue? You thought you were talking about the Soviet Union or was it the KGB? What was the turn of words that brought you to religion and children and what one might do about all of that? You ask, *Are you expecting anytime soon?* as you point to her slim, hard, twenty-year-old stomach. *No,* she says simply as you stroll along the asphalt toward the bus, but must pause yet again for another group photo. Flash. Flash. Smile. In slow sentences, three or four words at a time, she explains about a father she's never met, but who works in a massage parlor, about her mother who works two jobs— one as a nurse and the other, at the same parlor, cleaning—about the government incentive program that gives women who have additional children money they can spend on a flat or their child's education. How did you get to this topic? There must have been another segue somewhere. You can't seem to follow the Russian turns, the alleys and bypasses, the corridors that bring you to the sector you want to be in, even when those turns are spoken in a language you understand. You do, then, what any normal person would do, you change the subject to what you can point at. You ask about the man on her necklace and its meaning, its significance, if it's particularly Russian. She tilts her head back and laughs, one hand caressing the silver man at her neck and says, *It has no meaning, whatsoever, at all.*

5) Bloodshed is always a possibility

Once a resort in a resort town, once a hospital during the Second World War, once built by Stalin, once impressive with new red paint, but now merely a two star hotel, this Hotel Primoskaya, where you reside in sector four, room 117. You have a suite with private shower and toilet, a porch with two drooping laundry lines to string your shirts and slacks to drip dry as best they can in the humid sea air and two twin beds with a pillow a piece, each likely dating from the 1940s. Perhaps you and the husband are not to touch, body to body, in this beautiful hotel, so confined you are to your slim, low to the floor beds. You like that the sink drips, that tiny wall lice-bugs crawl from cracks below the mirror toward the individually wrapped soap, that the shower shudders and leaks on the floor, that the electricity isn't up to the U.S. code with its thumb switches dangling on cords for the lights above the twin beds. You like the swooping black hairs on your 1940s pillow that are not yours. You like the blood stains—quarter-sized drops—on your sheets. You like the woman around your age who comes in each day to leave fresh towels, to take out your trash bag heaping with empty bottles of *still* water, and to add a new roll of gray, streamer like toilet paper to the hook. You like that next door to the hotel, behind a six-foot fence and a billboard that extends the fence another five feet, a gash has been dug into the ground, and there, workmen drive diesel engines every other day. You like that one night, at ten past ten, fireworks explode twenty feet from your porch, and it sounds, *swear to gawd*, like a car bomb, like a terrorist cell, like the last sound you get to hear before you too are a few quarter-sized splatters of blood, a few stray hairs on a hotel bed in a country far, far away.

After the fireworks cease their flashing colors and noise and once the smoke drifts up and away, you stretch out on your twin because here in Sochi your voice can be a little louder, here you know you will sleep, here you will begin to gather your intelligence.

6) *Gather intelligence*

McCarthy didn't like the communist and you didn't like McCarthy turning everyone into a communist in his witch-hunt. In a red puff of smoke, *poof*, he's a communist. From a list of red names, *poof*, she's a communist. Here's the red proof, *poof*, everyone's a communist. You get a red communist. And you get a red communist. Everybody gets a red communist.

Your favorite color is red, though you've never met a communist and all the while you were in grade school in the '80s with one mindless president or another, no teacher spoke of the communists, no fear was passed out after recess in saddle-stitched booklets, no one hid under desks or crouched in the hallways with arms crisscrossed over their necks, no one thought they would be buried, no one was a spy, the only cold wars were the ones passed runny nose to sore throat to cough to headache, kid to kid. And now, today, your head aches as you sit at a table with U.S., who are all drinking glasses of Standard Russian Vodka, except you, and sharing communist stories, except you, because you're invisible. *Repression in the Soviet Union*, one says. *A bitter cold and gray winter*, says another. *Cuban missile crisis*, a third. *We will bury you*, another and around it goes as they dig up more and more communist stories.

The Russian intelligence you have gathered thus far, pre-arrival mind you, is this: some Russian movies (*12, The Return, The Prisoners of the Mountains, Moscow Does Not Believe in Tears*), some Russian books turned into movies (*Dr. Zhivago, Anna Karenina*), some translated Russian poetry (*Against Forgetting*), some theory (Marx), some travel tips (Lonely Planet's *Russia*), and some random advice from a flotsam of people who want to know why you're going to Russia, to which you reply, *I'm a poet*. What you don't know, or rather what you and your generation missed, is a lot of the anti-communist, xenophobic propaganda. Or maybe it's like the axiom: the more you know, the less you're sure of. Or like this: you're skeptical. Why do you know what you

know? Why do the people you talk to say Russia is _____
and communism is _____? Everyone, everywhere
seems to have an opinion about Russia, but you and you're OK with
this because you like to think awhile before you decide.

Later when you return to U.S., Russia will suddenly be everywhere,
like a new word just learned and that now appears in every publication,
every mouth. You read Lisa See's *Dreams of Joy*, a novel set in communist
China, and a collection of poetry on Tina Modotti, who joined the
communist party in Mexico. Given the rise of flood waters around two
nuclear power plants in Nebraska, Soviet Russia's delay in announcing
the Chernobyl disaster is rehashed in the news. *Is our current president
more or less forthcoming than the communist regime?* Some want to know.
Russia, Moscow, communists, Soviets, and socialism are everywhere.
At work a colleague, The Annoying Colleague, asks, *What jobs do they
do in Russia?* You reply, *What do you mean 'what jobs?' They do the
same jobs as we do here. They're just like us.* And they are. However, you
tell the colleague about all the security guards. You're sure this only
feeds his paranoia, because you notice him later at a meeting, deep in
thought with one red eyebrow raised, chewing on his hangnails and
swallowing what he manages to bite off.

Perhaps you really are a secret agent, a Russian bent on espionage,
a communist, a U.S. spy. You keep secrets. You watch, investigate, and
listen to what is said as closely as you listen to what is not said. Of
course, you have no spy ring, no messages that self-destruct, no salary
paid by the government, no drop-off point, but you are a sleeper. You
lie in wait. What you know is this: 1) there are no good guys, no bad
guys; 2) there's never one story, one truth. Instead what you have is
perspective, a view of the scalloped, bright curves of Basil's Cathedral,
the red brick of the Kremlin walls with its bright red stone stars on the
watchtowers, and the squat, granite block of Lenin's mausoleum. Here,
people walk the cobbles for snapshots and then walk some more. At
night they trade in their boots and trousers for pajamas bottoms and

paper slippers. They climb between sheets and hope for sweat dreams, just like us, just like we do in U.S.

7) Be attentive to language differences

In Russia, all the colleges are called the faculty, as in the building, the physical place where deans do their work. Here, all the deans are called rectors or vice rectors and are announced by title without irony, perhaps because all the toilets are Turkish style and squatting is part of the daily ritual. You, of course, do not squat often. Your yoga friend said Americans don't squat enough. You laughed and then squatted in sage pose, having had enough of crow. In Russia, all the crows are hooded, all the buildings are faculty, and all the deans are rectors, so then what is a Russia, exactly? Is it a continent of nesting dolls and fur hats? Does it come with hooded crows, white wag tails, and albino pigeons? Does everyone there drink white Russians and are they confused by this as they tip back their heads? Have they seen *The Big Lebowski* or read *1984*?

If Russia isn't a place, but a spirit, an essence, or a soul, do you get one at the airport or on the airplane after you reach cruising altitude? Does it come with your *coffee white*? Are you the only one they pat down, arms outstretched, legs, hips, thighs, and breasts palpitated by blue latex hands? Are they looking for the Russia? You'll give it back. Just ask. Why does everyone need to see your passport, your invitation letter, your hotel registration card, your visa, your list of declarations, the whites of your eyes? Aren't you technically a Russia now, even if it only lasts as long as the visa does? There are cameras in every room, every doorway. At the breakfast buffet, sleep yellow and crunchy in the corners of your eyes, feet heavy and lurching toward the silver coffee urn and then to your table for black bread and honey, and there's a camera capturing you fork up each oozing mouthful. What exactly are they capturing? Is it possible to quantify every photograph and digital recording of you as a Russia? Why must you be counted? You never count at home. Who does U.S. count, exactly? Now that you're to return, are you still part of U.S.? What must one do to become U.S. again?

8) Know where you are at all times

Omaha to Chicago. Chicago to Warsaw. Warsaw to Moscow. Moscow to Sochi. In three weeks, reverse. The way there isn't so bad. Sure, there's a six hour layover in Chicago and another in Poland. Sure, you sit by a co-ed who coughs and sneezes for nine hours. Sure, all the babies cannot pop their ears, so moms, dads, and grandmas pace the aisle with red faced squalls pressed to their armpits. You do sleep, in that drowsy in and out doze of planes, cars, and trains, your head snuggled in a black neck pillow, pink earplugs swallow all the noise, and your moon and stars eye mask blots the light. Plus, there's the adventure of lunch, or dinner is it? Maybe breakfast? Food wrapped in cellophane to open, tiny paper cups of *coffee white* to sip, and refreshing towelettes to wipe hands and release the odor of rubbing alcohol and laundry detergent. How the hours pass as you watch the flight attendants in orange, with the hammer and sickle threaded in gold at cuff, make their way to your row when you can say, *Water. Спасибо. Thank you.*

You leave Sochi mid-afternoon Wednesday to sleep at some shady airport hotel behind corrugated walls Wednesday night, to board a plane midmorning Thursday and thus begin the longest Thursday of your life. You leave Russia for Poland at ten to arrive in Poland at ten. You leave Poland at noon, fly some nine plus hours to arrive in Chicago at two where you must stay until eight, catch another flight to arrive in Omaha at eleven, to drive another hour, getting you home a few minutes before midnight Thursday. After this thirty-six hour Thursday, you sleep or try to sleep and try some more over the next two weeks, but the elusive sleep lady arrives whenever, after dinner while you read a novel or on the couch while you balance a glass of ice water on your navel, a cat splayed between the crooks of your crisscrossed thighs. A precarious position, this glass, below the hum of the ceiling fan, inside the chatter of robins and sparrows, as it rises and falls with your breath, tipping further toward the brown tabby until the husband says, *You awake, little sleeper?* And you suddenly are, awake enough to down the water, set the glass on the coffee table and resume your position with cat, under fan, awaiting the sleep lady to pull you toward and into a blackness made bright only by Russia.

9) Never lose your soul

A week back in U.S. and still you shut your eyes and see Russia. As you doze in a chair in that in-between place of dreams and wakefulness, reality and elsewhere, you're sure you can step from your front door to the long curved walk above the Black Sea, the feral cats skulking the bush as they await the cat lady with her sack of kibble, calling *Ks-ks-ks.* You do not dream in Russian, in Cyrillic, but you do dream you're in Russia. You reach to stretch in some yoga pose and Russia flitters before your eyes, a resort of grand staircases and palm trees, grassy parks festooned with the white, round heads of dandelions, crowded subways flickering with florescent lights, and tunnels of venders who want to sell you scarves patterned with red flowers and golden knots. Someone wrote that jetlag is the consequence of your soul trying to catch up with your body because you were never meant to travel so fast. Perhaps, you think, but what you know is your disorientation is real, the visions, the memories, like thoughts are trapped in your body. Whatever it is, you're only partially here in U.S. and partially still in Russia.

10) Learn how not to get caught

When you returned to U.S., you talked at length to your Chili's server, said, *Keep the tap water coming.* At the first U.S. Starbucks you said you've just been to Russia, *as a poet,* and then ordered the drink with the most shots of espresso, skim milk, lots of ice. You were so happy to talk. All your words made sense. At the O'Hare airport, you read with slowness all the signs and banners because you understand. You felt a little jilted when the customs woman didn't stare you down and only said a monotone, automatic, *Welcome back*, after glancing at your passport stamped in black by Polish and Russian guards. And when you wanted to stand by a random window and gaze sleepily at planes tended to by men in thin florescent green vests that lifted and tilted as they gestured with glowing orange batons, you did. When you wanted to lie down on the airport floor, stretching out in the small shadows beneath the benched seats of your terminal, you did, drooling a little in a sleep that snatches you immediately as if you were a child. When you decided to ask someone at an airport help desk a question on which queue is your queue, no one yelled with a hard mouth and sharp blue eyes phrases and orders you didn't understand, to finally say in perfect English, *This is not your class*. At which point, you backed away saying, *Thank you*, and, *спасибо*, eyes averted. You wonder now, what was that all about? In Poland, you suppose you were economy class or of the American class or, generally speaking, of the literate class, or lower middle-class or perhaps classless, gauche, and vulgar, the last term the one a random Russian used to describe a woman with long red varnished fingernails his friend returned to again and again for sex. Perhaps he meant sex-worker? Or simply odd and strange? Perhaps some essential flaw in her character was lost in translation. No matter. But now that you are here in U.S., you are left wondering what class you were anyway.

It is true that in the seventh grade you had a teacher with the poster of an orange and blue butterfly net that said, *aim at nothing and you will catch it*, that Language Arts was not your best class. You failed Handwriting in grade school. Typing earned you a D freshman year high school. Every once in a while in college and grad school, you ran across some PhD who awarded you a C+ or B or made you haggle for a better grade, say, in Shakespeare to get him to overlook a few measly typos and comma splices on the meaning of the word "hand" in *Measure for Measure*. When you were there, in post-Soviet Russia, a country that challenged a class system and set up a new one, you were ecstatic that you could count to ten in Russian, though it never helped much give that twenty-eight rubbles equaled one American dollar, and nothing was priced at nine or seven or five, the numbers you could speak with verve. Your biggest linguistic triumph was *thank you* and you said that phrase fifteen to twenty times a day, not wanting to be caught as a rude American. And just as you approached the end of your stay, you'd begun to catch, or rather, to recognize *good morning, you're welcome*, and *good day*. If only, you think, if only you could've stayed a little while longer you could've learned the alphabet and gathered more intelligence. You could've spoken, maybe with effort, broken Russian, you could've passed as a *rusky* or the feminine version of one, and then whenever the venders called to you under the swaying palms in Park Rivera or from below the fluttering awnings above stalls that lined the Black Sea or from inside a striped smock at the head of the queue at the grocery till, you would've known how to say, *goodbye*.

CAREFREE

USEDOM, GERMANY AND POLAND

CHANEY KWAK

WE ARE WAITING for a train in Mokrzyca Wielka, a Polish village of less than two hundred residents. In this sleepy hamlet, the only sound we hear is from a father teaching his teenage son to ride a motorcycle—right on the station's battered platform.

Sophie and I have just finished cycling sixty miles from Usedom to Wolin, two Baltic islands that kiss each other at the border between Germany and Poland. Together we biked across young wheat and barley fields. When we tired of staggering pine forests and poppy-sprinkled meadows, we sunbathed in Ahlbeck, a graying resort town lifted from Thomas Mann's Venetian fantasies.

For Sophie, the Baltic Sea awakened salt-tinged childhood memories. In the regimented East Germany of her childhood, she said, Usedom had been one of the few places where her family could feel free. There, they'd shed their clothing and stand against the lung-clearing gusts, gazing toward the invisible landmass across the sea that was far beyond their reach.

Her stories must have touched something in me.

Bicycling on a beach is a tricky balancing act. On dry sand, your bike skids and wags before turning stationary; too close to water, you'll sink or topple. But like in any type of journey, if you find that sliver of just-right territory between inertia and chaos, you'll glide effortlessly.

From Usedom, the sand dunes rose and fell to our right as we cycled on the beach. The sun soothed the Baltic gusts' sharp edges; an azure horizon stretched like a promise. We pedaled, swam, pedaled. This was the stuff I wish my own teenage years had been made of, instead of suburban boredom and bookish endeavors. But why mourn for a past I never lived, when now at last I had a chance to live it.

That's how we arrived in Mokrzyca Wielka, legs shaking and hearts unburdened. We wait, but the train never materializes to take us back to Germany. But I'm not fretting. In that lull between movements, as sun-soaked breezes tickle my back, I am happy to simply be.

BRAVERY IN THE FACE OF CHANGE

CORK, IRELAND

JESSICA REFF

THIS IS A story for people like the old me, the shy and the unadventurous. I was never one of those people who could handle change well. I always wanted a schedule and liked the stability of being a student. My sophomore year in college I had to have surgery and missed a bit of school. After returning, things felt odd. I didn't like it or feel comfortable there anymore.

I started thinking about how I'd only ever traveled via the pages in my books, and until then that had been enough adventure. I decided I wanted to study abroad and ended up choosing Cork, Ireland—after all, there was some new culture to have and I'd be able to get by in terms of language. I decided that going for one year instead of a semester, and with a program, would give the stability and consistency I needed.

At first, life abroad was hard. I did not fit in with the other people in my program, and despite the United States and Ireland sharing English, there did turn out to be a bit of a language barrier. Trying to make the most of my experience, I joined a few school clubs. That's when I finally felt at home in Cork with the help of the LGBT society.

Everyone I was introduced to was warm, and everyone instantly liked me. Even the strange bits of my personality that my friends at home joked about, were wonderful and perfect to my Irish friends. I tried new activities and even went dancing—something I had always been too shy for in the States. I joined choral groups, where no one cared if my voice was good or bad.

Cork was a magical town. It had lakes and rivers and beautiful greenery. I lived across from a beautiful church. This trip and studying abroad opened up a world for me that I'd never dreamed possible. After my year in Ireland, I'd become stronger and I decided to travel more. I bought a backpack and spent five months backpacking Europe by myself. This experience helped get me through my final year in school and gave me the courage to apply for my current job, teaching English in China. I know it sounds corny, but living and studying abroad opened my eyes to a world of possibilities and pushed that shy awkward girl out the door.

CONTRIBUTORS

ADAM KARLIN was born in Washington, D.C., raised on the Chesapeake Bay, and has been traveling for about a decade. He seeks things odd, interesting, intoxicating, alluring, enlightening, and "home"—amidst the roam. He writes for *Lonely Planet*, *Worldhum*, and other travel publications, and has contributed news writing for the *Christian Science Monitor*, *Chicago Tribune*, *USA Today*, and analysis for *Jane's Intelligence Digest*.

ALISON MEDINA wasn't about to stick it out in the U.S.'s disappointing 2010 job market. After college at the University of Colorado at Boulder, she stuck her diploma in a cardboard box, sold her car, packed up two bags, and decided Brazil would be a good travel challenge. Alison landed in Rocinha, the largest favela in Brazil. For five months she taught English, Spanish, and Recycled Art, while catching motorcycle taxis and zipping around the neighborhood. Living for almost three years in Rio, Alison has discovered a rich and troubling cultural environment where the extreme, festive highs of Carnaval clash with the daily realities of a quarter of the city's residents who live in favelas.

ANDREW BISHARAT is one of the most recognizable voices in climbing writing, best known for his irreverent and popular column "Tuesday Night Bouldering," which appears monthly in *Rock and Ice* magazine, where Bisharat is the editor-at-large. He is also the author of the how-to climb book *Sport Climbing: From Top Rope to Redpoint, Techniques for Climbing Success*, which won the 2010 National Outdoor Book Award for best instructional. In the course of Bisharat's decade-plus tenure as a climber, he has climbed 5.14, El Cap aid routes in a day, and has worn through enough ropes, carabiners, harnesses, and sticky rubber climbing shoes to rival the national inventory of REI. He most enjoys testing climbing shoes because, "It's the only piece of gear that actually helps you climb better right away."

BRENNA FITZGERALD is a thirty-year-old MFA candidate in creative nonfiction at the University of Arizona in Tucson. She was born in Wisconsin, started kindergarten in Prague, and grew up in New Orleans and Ithaca, New York. At the age of eighteen, Brenna ventured abroad again to live in India as an exchange student and spent most of her twenties traveling. She has lived and/or traveled in twelve different countries on three different continents.

CARYS CRAGG—an instructor, counselor, writer, and perpetual wonderer—likes to travel to learn, to be challenged, and to be transformed into someone new. Distance doesn't seem to be a factor. "Preparing for a Lesser-Known Journey" is the first chapter of her in-progress memoir, tentatively titled *A Necessary Part: A Journey of Peace in Response to Injustice*. Her writing has appeared in *Perspectives, Cognica, Guru, Insights into Clinical Counseling*, the *International Journal of Children's Spirituality*, and *Canadian School Counselor*. She can be reached at Tangerine Ideas: Life Coach Counselling.

CECILIA HAYNES is an American Third Culture Kid who has lived in twelve international cities and traveled to countless more over the course of her twenty-four years. A State Department brat, she grew up as a nomad encased in embassy compounds in China, India, and the Philippines. After graduating from the University of Virginia, she headed over to Hong Kong and taught English at an education center for a year. Continuing the spirit of globetrotting, she currently lives in Alanya, Turkey, and occupies her time with blogging, writing, and eating everything in sight.

CHANEY KWAK is a correspondent for *Condé Nast Daily Traveler* and has written for *The New York Times, Washington Post,* and other publications.

CHRISTIAN LEWIS is a songwriter in the Brooklyn-based musical collective Nomadic Attic (nomadicattic.bandcamp.com). He also edits short fiction and reviews for *The Strand Magazine* and works as a staff editor for *Law360*. His writing has appeared in *Narrative Magazine, The Rambler, Hersam Acorn Newspapers, Ridgefield Magazine,* and *Multichannel News.*

COLIN SOUNESS was born in Argyll and Bute, Scotland, and grew up to love the highlands and all their empty wildness. This love never left him, and he's spent his years so far seeking out challenge and adventure in wild places. Colin found himself fulfilling a dream by sailing to Antarctica—an experience that changed his life and gave him a new confidence in the ability to make adventure for himself. With a stint in the military and a PhD in glaciology now under his belt, he's had the privilege of getting to some truly unforgettable places, yet says that "Few however come close to beating Antarctica in terms of sheer grandeur. I fully intend to go back, maybe sooner rather than later!"

CRAIG SMITH, a native of Corvallis, Oregon, attended Vanderbilt University where he earned a B.S. in secondary education and Spanish. Smith has taught high school Spanish in Charlotte, North Carolina, and middle school Spanish in Oakland, California. He was a founding member of Manna Project International – Ecuador, where he volunteered as the educational program director and directed an assets-based community assessment. Craig has also served as a Peace Corps Volunteer.

DANIEL KETCHUM, during his career at Marvel Comics, has had the opportunity to contribute to the very titles he loved while growing up, including UNCANNY X-MEN, AMAZING SPIDER-MAN, WOLVERINE, and RUNAWAYS. He lives and works in New York City, and fights crime on the side.

DEREK HELWIG is a television producer who has made shows for CBS, Discovery, Travel Channel, and NBC. He produced 12 seasons of The Amazing Race, producing in more than 30 countries. He graduated from Chapman University with a bachelor's degree in film, and completed his master's degree at King's College in London. Derek is now married to his girlfriend from the Rwanda trip, Deanna. The couple has sponsored education costs for two of the children they met in Virunga.

DOC HALLIDAY GOLDEN is from Woodstock, New York, and is the oldest of four siblings. She has been involved in humanitarian efforts throughout the world and is an active volunteer in her local community through youth and sports outreaches. Doc currently works in marketing and communications at Times Square Church in New York City. She received a bachelor's degree in music education from New York University and has visited thirty-five countries to date.

E.B. BARTELS is a native of the Boston area, currently pursuing an MFA in nonfiction writing at Columbia University's School of the Arts. She regularly uses her "Russian face" on the NYC subway.

EDWARD C. DAVIS IV is from the South Side of Chicago. A well-versed linguist, he speaks fluent English, French, Portuguese, and Lingala, and is conversant in Spanish and Swahili. Presently, Edward is a full-time faculty member at Malcolm X College – City Colleges of Chicago, where he teaches African American Studies and Anthropology. He earned a master of philosophy degree in Anthropology from the University of Cambridge and a master of arts degree from University of California, Berkeley in African Diaspora Studies. He has been awarded the Gates-Cambridge Scholarship, the University of California Graduate Fellowship, and the Foreign Language and Area Studies Fellowship. Over the past decade, Edward has lived in New York, Paris, the Brazilian Amazon Rain Forest, the Democratic Republic of Congo, California, and England.

FRANK IZAGUIRRE is a writer and ecocritic whose passions for literature and exploration have taken him across Latin America. He teaches creative nonfiction and journalism at Pittsburgh School for the Creative and Performing Arts (CAPA). He's had his travel and nature writing published in *ISLE*, *Terrain*, and *Flashquake*, and has an essay forthcoming in *Fourth Genre*. When not reading, writing, or teaching, he makes sure to get outside and search for the birds that travel farther than he ever could.

HAROON MOGHUL is the author of *The Order of Light* (Penguin 2006). He is a graduate student at Columbia University, and speaks and writes on religion, identity, and Islamic thought. He is an expert guide to the Muslim history and culture of Bosnia, Spain, and Turkey, and works with the Multicultural Audience Development Initiative at New York's Metropolitan Museum of Art.

IAN BARDENSTEIN grew up in Cleveland, Ohio, and currently lives in San Francisco. He writes his capital 'N's from right to left and would like to thank John, Anneke, and Mia.

JESSICA REFF grew up in Los Angeles, California, and currently teaches English in Shenzhen, China. Jessica is passionate about education, and hopes to one day teach preschool in Cork, Ireland. She believes that everyone should have a chance to travel and experience a different culture.

JOEY CAVISE, recently admitted to the Illinois Bar, is now a public interest attorney.

JUSTIN "NORDIC THUNDER" HOWARD is a life loving, people admiring, fun-seeking man who believes air guitar can change the world. He began his professional air guitar career in 2006. Since then he's suffered two air guitar related surgeries, has won four Chicago regional competitions, won the U.S. title in 2011, and on August 24, 2012, he became YOUR 2012 Air Guitar World Champion.

KAITLIN SOLIMINE, raised in New England, has considered China a second home for almost two decades. While majoring in East Asian Studies at Harvard University, she was a Harvard-Yenching scholar and wrote and edited *Let's Go: China* (St. Martin's Press). She was a U.S. Department of State Fulbright Creative Arts Fellow in China and the Donald E. Axinn Scholar in Fiction at the Bread Loaf Writers' Conference. Excerpts from her forthcoming novel, *Empire of Glass*, have won the Dzanc Books/Disquiet International Literary Program award and appeared in *Guernica Magazine* and *Kartika Review*. Kaitlin writes the "Saving China" column for *The World of Chinese* magazine. Another essay on her life in China can be found in the anthology *Unsavory Elements: Stories of Foreigners on the Loose in China* (Earnshaw Books). She is co-founder of HIPPO Reads, a literary-based media start-up that curates and delivers high quality, previously published long reads with an academic bent.

KIM COLEMAN FOOTE was a 2002/2003 Fulbright Fellow in Ghana, where she conducted research for a novel. She has published fiction and several essays about Ghana in *The Literary Review, Obsidian, Crab*

Orchard Review, Black Renaissance Noire, and elsewhere. Her writing honors include a Rona Jaffe Foundation/Vermont Studio Center Fellowship, Pan-African Literary Forum creative nonfiction award, Illinois Arts Council Fellowship for creative nonfiction, and fellowship writing residencies at Hedgebrook and VCCA. She received an MFA from Chicago State University and has written a novel about the slave trade in Ghana. Originally from New Jersey, Kim now lives in Brooklyn.

LAINE STRUTTON is an interdisciplinary PhD candidate in law and society at New York University. She is currently writing her dissertation on the role of women in oil protests in Niger Delta, Nigeria. Her primary research interest is the role of gender in natural resource conflicts and her work also explores issues of geography, governmentality, and economic power. Prior to and during her MA in human rights at Columbia University, Laine pieced together every form of alternative travel she could on a student's budget. This included teaching English in Korea, working as conflict resolution consultant in Kyrgyzstan, doing medical interpretation in Honduras and Bolivia, and serving in the Peace Corps in Mozambique. Although she has spent much of the last decade traversing five continents, it doesn't feel like it has been nearly enough yet.

LAURA DRUDI will be entering a vascular surgery residency training at McGill University in Montreal and pursues aerospace medicine research.

LAURA MADELINE WISEMAN has a doctorate from the University of Nebraska-Lincoln where she teaches English. She is the author of several chapbooks including, *Branding Girls* (Finishing Line Press, 2011) and *She who Loves Her Father* (Dancing Girl Press, 2012). She is also the editor of the forthcoming anthology *Women Write Resistance: Poets Resist Gender Violence* (Blue Light Press, 2013). Her poetry has appeared in *Margie, Feminist Studies, Poet Lore, Cream City Review, Pebble Lake Review, The Sow's Ear Poetry Review,* and elsewhere. Her prose has appeared in *Arts & Letters, Spittoon, Blackbird, American Short Fiction, 13th Moon,* and elsewhere. Her reviews have appeared in *Prairie Schooner, Valparaiso Poetry Review, 42Opus,* and elsewhere.

LINDSEY LAVEAUX is a Returned Peace Corps Volunteer (2006-2008) and in 2013, received her Juris Doctor from the University of Pennsylvania Law School and her Master of Arts in International Studies from the Joseph H. Lauder Institute at the Wharton School and School of Arts & Sciences of the University of Pennsylvania.

LISA DAZOLS is a licensed clinical social worker who has worked in HIV services the past ten years in San Francisco. In 2011-2012, she traveled around the world for a year with her partner to make the documentary *Out & Around* about LGBT world leaders. She was named among the Top 25 Most Significant Queer Women in 2012 by Velvet Park.

LISA HSIA is an independent writer and artist. She and her husband, Erik Lee, have been traveling without an itinerary since late April 2012. She blogs her experience, her photos, and her sketches at satsumabug.com—which is ever in danger, especially since Istanbul, of becoming a food blog.

LIZ QUINN is a family physician and writer living north of Boston. She has witnessed births in Mexico, Guatemala, the Dominican Republic, Brazil, Zambia, and the United States. She has returned to Guatemala five times since first living there and is joyfully toiling away on a history of the country's midwives. Liz attended Harvard College and UMass Medical School and now works at the Greater Lawrence Family Health Center where she cares for many Guatemalan immigrants.

LOUIS STANFILL, after making his international debut in 2005 at age 19, played important roles for the U.S. at the 2007 and 2011 Rugby World Cups, starting three matches in 2011 and leading the team in tackles in two of those matches. Stanfill competed collegiately at the University of California, Berkeley, winning several national championships. As a member of New York Athletic Club, he earned MVP honors at the 2012 Super League Final. Stanfill signed with the Vicenza Rangers rugby club in Italy for the Serie A 2012-13 season.

MARI AMEND is a senior at Stanford University, majoring in Comparative Literature. Her passions include oral histories, radio shows, poetry, ukuleles, and nostalgia.

MARK BESSEN is a student at Stanford University studying English and environmental science. He enjoys hiking in the mountains, verbal mixology (i.e., writing), and watching raindrops slide down leaves.

MIKE MADEJ served as a Peace Corps Volunteer from 2006-2008 in Msambweni, Kenya. Mike greatly enjoyed his time traveling throughout East Africa and hopes to return soon. While in Kenya Mike met his wife, Libby, and currently resides in New Orleans with their new baby boy, Eli.

MOLLY HEADLEY-BENKACI is originally from Boise, Idaho, and Los Angeles, California, but has been living in France for the past five years. She received a bachelor's degree from California Institute of the Arts in 2000 and a master's degree in creative writing from the University of Oxford in November 2011. In 2006 her poem, "Remains of Water," was published in a literary journal entitled *Beginnings*. "Remains of Water" won third place in their annual poetry competition. In 2011 her poem, "Flood," was included in an online anthology called *Swamp*. She is currently working on a novel and collection of poetry.

NATHAN MYERS grew up in the avocado capitol of the world and is the author of the world's definitive guide to guacamole combat, *Guac Off*. He is also Global Editor of *Surfing Magazine* and has worked on surf-travel films such as *The Drifter* (writer), *Castles in the Sky* (writer/producer) and *Innersection* (director/producer). His 2012 film *Here & Now* (director) was awarded "Best Picture" at several of the world's leading surf film festivals. He lives in Bali and writes everything by hand.

NICK DALL is a South African writer. He has lived, fished, and taught in Europe, South America, Asia, and Africa. His work can be seen here: www.nickdall.co.za.

PRIA ANAND is a third-year medical student living in California.

RACHAEL LEVITT is an MFA in creative writing student at Chatham University in Pittsburgh, Pennsylvania. She writes short stories and children's literature. She has had work published in *Vagina: The Zine* and *Forty Ounce Bachelors Literary Magazine*. She loves tacos and travel.

RHONDA GIBSON is a NOLA native who enjoys life, food that sticks to her ribs, and her boyfriend, Alex. She is an MFA creative writing student at Minnesota State University, Mankato, and has yet to lose her mind. The story "Maiko" is her brief thank you to a woman who helped change her outlook on The Republic of Georgia.

S. IMRAN ALI is a water and sanitation specialist with Médecins Sans Frontières (MSF) in the Jamam refugee camp, South Sudan. He previously worked with MSF in Pakistan during the Indus River floods of 2010; in India running a research collaboration between Canadian and Indian universities; in Sri Lanka on a post-tsunami livelihoods project; and in Bolivia doing agriculture and environment research in the Andean foothills. Originally from Toronto, Canada, Imran recently completed a PhD in environmental engineering, looking at safe water and public health in low-income urban communities in the Indian subcontinent.

SARA COOPER is an award-winning Off-Broadway theatre writer, and educator.

SARAH KHAN was an editor at *Travel + Leisure* magazine in New York for almost five years, before she recently moved to Cape Town, South Africa, where she is now a freelance travel writer. Her articles and essays have appeared in the *New York Times, Wall Street Journal, Atlantic, Vogue India*, and other publications. You can read more of her work at www.bysarahkhan.com or follow her on Twitter @BySarahKhan.

SIERRA ROSS GLADFELTER has been in love with mountains from the age of three, when she rode a llama 3,100 miles across the backbone of the North American continent on the Continental Divide Trail. Born into a family of long-distance adventurers, Sierra grew up traversing the world with her mother's work as a travel writer. As a student at Temple University, Sierra spent a summer conducting a study on the sustainability of Peru's trekking routes to Machu Picchu. Recognizing that travelers cannot turn their backs on their place of origin, Sierra designed a college course at Temple to engage students with watershed issues by canoeing the length of the Schuylkill River. In 2011, as a student with the School for International Training, she investigated the effectiveness of tourism policy in Nepal and Bhutan at alleviating poverty in rural, Himalayan communities. After graduation, Sierra spent six months living in China teaching English at a primary school in Sichuan Province. Circling home to the headwaters of the Schuylkill

River, Sierra now works for a watershed NGO organizing communities and coordinating conservation projects.

SOPHIE CHAMAS is a freelance writer and editor based in the UAE. Her work has been featured in *Al Jazeera* English, *TheState*, *The Outpost*, and *Jadaliyya*, among others. She is co-editor of *Mashallah News*. Never quite capable of settling down, she continues to think of herself as "in between" countries.

THEOPI SKARLATOS is a freelance reporter and documentary filmmaker, working for the BBC, ITV, and independent production companies. She has reported from destinations as varied as Rwanda, Iraqi Kurdistan, and Jamaica, covering subjects ranging from the tourism industry to post-war traumatic stress. Her work for BBC *Newsnight* on the economic crisis in Greece contributed to the show winning the Royalty Television Society's Programme of the Year Award for 2012, and she has continued to produce the show's ongoing coverage of the crisis in both Greece and Cyprus. Theopi also regularly contributes to the BBC's renowned *From Our Own Correspondent*. She studied at the University of Leeds and her passions are writing, traveling, and people. She is inspired by her family and those who fight for their dreams in a difficult world but refuse to give up.

VANESSA MDEE is an MTV VJ, Choice FM DJ, HIV/AIDS activist, model, speaker, lover of audible art, and lover of peace. Vanessa recently spoke at the World Economic Forum on Africa, in support of women's health. She is based in Dar es Salaam, Tanzania.

YUKI AIZAWA was born and raised in rural central New York but periodically lived in Japan throughout her childhood. Her father, a Professor of Japanese and East Asian Philosophy, took the family along with a student study group to Tokyo and Kyoto. Yuki attended Japanese schools and tagged along with her father's students to numerous shrines, temples, pachinko parlors, and noodle stands. Yuki received her MFA in nonfiction from the New School. Upon graduating she joined the nonprofit organization StoryCorps and spent a year traveling the U.S. recording the life experiences of everyday Americans out of an AirStream Trailer. She is currently pursuing a master's in film editing at the American Film Institute Conservatory in Los Angeles.

ACKNOWLEDGEMENTS

There are so many very cool individuals who generously gave of their time, stories, brilliance, enthusiasm, good looks, discernment, and other support to help make this project happen. I want to thank all of the wonderful friends and strangers who backed the Kickstarter campaign in 2012 and helped to spread the word. Your generosity and awesomeness cannot be stated enough. As promised, here's an extra-special shout to those of you who've requested to see your name in lights. The—

Digital (Not So) Underground: Angela Rothschild, Cecelia Lacayo, Cynthia Williams, David Crowley, Isabelle Bouthillier, Jean-François Chiasson and Kim Chénier, Kari Lucas, Katie Riegel, Lauren O'Rourke, Meng-han Chi, Paul Swaney, Scott Rossow Jr., Stephanie Soussamian, Tatiana Rodriguez, Tausha Cowan, Thai-Binh Bui, Tiffani Willis, and Vance Erese.

Planetary: Alex Richmond and Dominique Brisebois, Christine Sever, Francois Messier, Gail Agas, Isabel Fernandez-Maillard, Klaudia Ziemba, Ludwig Defrenne, Nina Westphal, Stephanie Vicuña, Sylvain Pottras, and Yvonne York.

Tribe Called Artist: Daniel Brisebois and Emily Board, James and Doris Curry, Jason Ortiz, KuSandra Davis Veal, Martin and LaCheryal Veal, Ronald and Maureen Brisebois, and Thomas Gagné.

Thank you again to the eight passionate individuals who sat for interviews, sharing their stories and ideas in this book.

Big thanks and respect to the very talented and clutch Ravenn Moore, Libby Sentz, Jana Vukovic, Jason Wong, and Brian McGovern.

Special thanks to Abbie Patterson, Aimee Ortiz, Allison Prouty, Antonio Thompson, Azim Mangee, Cary Barnette, Cemere James, Daniel Ketchum, Derek Helwig, Evan Patterson, Fahmina Rahman, Jasmine Faustino, Jason Choi, Jenn Zahrt, Jill Dearman, Joanne Jacobson, Juan Hayem, Lillian Kass, Lindsey Laveaux, Maggie Pakula, Molly Brisebois, Nakeena Covington, Nicole Nitsche, Pauline Nguyen, Rebecca Krause, Shani Leitch, Stephany Oliveros, and Tanya Garrett.

Thanks and hugs Mom, Dad, Grandma and Grandpa, Ms. Delois Reed, Ms. Arletha Threatt, Mr. James Phillips, Brenda Williams, Antoinette Threatt; Carl and Wendy McBride, Carol Bell, Travis and Velma Parker, Ms. Sal Naidoo, Ms. Doris Davis, Dr. Lee Kao, Margot Tiff, and Wanda Lee Evans.

And you, Joseph Brisebois, are a pretty stellar human being to be able to observe everyday of life. Love you.

CPSIA information can be obtained at www.ICGtesting.com
Printed in the USA
LVOW06s0358180814

399611LV00003B/25/P